# More praise for *Strategies for the Green Economy*

"Few on the 'greenscape' possess Joel Makower's potent mix of expertise and ability to translate it succinctly into business-defining action; a must-read for any business leader striving to succeed in the green marketplace."

—Jeff Swartz, president and CEO, The Timberland Company

*"Strategies for the Green Economy* offers a hopeful vision of companies transforming challenges into opportunities, re-imagining not just their products and processes, but themselves. Makower's engaging stories and sharp insights show that companies need to comply not just with the laws of government and the marketplace, but also the laws of nature. This is an indispensable guide for any company seeking to not just survive, but thrive in years ahead.

—William McDonough, architect and coauthor, *Cradle to Cradle: Remaking the Way We Make Things*

"For twenty years, Joel Makower has been a clear, credible, and sensible voice on the greening of mainstream business and a resource that I return to again and again. In *Strategies for the Green Economy*, he brings together the best of his great breadth in thinking and experience, untangling the complexities and cynicism of the green marketplace to show how companies can tap its growing opportunities. Any company on the path to creating long-lasting and meaningful changes toward sustainability should be reading this book."

—Shelley Billik, VP, Environmental Initiatives, Warner Bros. Entertainment

"Joel Makower's essential new book will strengthen every company's ability to develop a winning sustainability strategy."

—Aron Cramer, president and CEO, Business for Social Responsibility

"Joel Makower makes a provocative case that going green offers rich rewards to forward-thinking companies, but it's not for the feint of heart. *Strategies for the Green Economy* shows how to minimize the risks and maximize the opportunities—the perfect combination of sobering insights and empowering advice."

—Bill Morrissey, VP of Environmental Sustainability,
The Clorox Company

"A growing number of companies are finding pathways to a more sustainable future. No one tells this story better than Joel Makower, whose *Strategies for the Green Economy* charts the course for a new era of business, one in which forward-looking companies are creating products and services that aren't just greener, but serve their customers better. This is critical reading for anyone who seeks to understand where tomorrow's economic winners are going."

—William K. Reilly, founding partner, Aqua International Partners, and former administrator, U.S. Environmental Protection Agency

"When it comes to analyzing the greening of business, no one is more clear, insightful, or level-headed than Joel Makower. *Strategies for the Green Economy* is a masterpiece of wit, wisdom, and strategic thinking."

—Andrew Beebe, president, EI Solutions

"Today's global economy has been shaped by economic forces, not ecological ones, but smart companies are learning that the two go hand in hand. As Joel Makower makes clear in *Strategies for the Green Economy*, there are rich rewards awaiting companies that seize the opportunities of the emerging green economy, creating new sources of business value in tandem with a healthier, more prosperous, and more secure world."

—Lester R. Brown, cofounder, Earth Policy Institute, and author, *Plan B 3.0: Mobilizing to Save Civilization*

# STRATEGIES
## FOR THE
# GREEN
## ECONOMY

## OPPORTUNITIES AND CHALLENGES
## IN THE NEW WORLD OF BUSINESS

## JOEL MAKOWER

### EXECUTIVE EDITOR,
### GREENBIZ.COM®

### WITH EXCLUSIVE MARKET RESEARCH BY
### CARA PIKE

New York   Chicago   San Francisco   Lisbon   London
Madrid   Mexico City   Milan   New Delhi   San Juan
Seoul   Singapore   Sydney   Toronto

1  2  3  4  5  6  7  8  9  0    DOC/DOC    0  1  0  9  8

ISBN     978–0–07–160030–9
MHID     0–07–160030–2

McGraw-Hill books are available at special quantity discounts to use as premiums and sales promotions, or for use in corporate training programs. To contact a representative, please visit the Contact Us pages at www.mhprofessional.com.

GreenBiz.com is a registered trademark of Greener World Media, Inc.

---

### ENVIRONMENTAL BENEFITS STATEMENT

The pages within this book are printed on Rolland Enviro 100 paper manufactured by Cascades Fine Paper Group. It is made from 100 percent postconsumer, de-inked fiber, without chlorine. According to the manufacturer, this product saved the following resources by using Rolland Enviro 100:

| Trees | Solid Waste | Water | Air Emissions | Natural Gas |
|-------|-------------|-------|---------------|-------------|
| 77 | 4,861 lb | 45,882 gal | 10,675 lb | 11,124 ft$^3$ |

# Contents

# Acknowledgments

I have had the great fortune of working with and learning from some remarkable people over the past two decades or so, and the fruits of those relationships and experiences are reflected in these pages. I couldn't possibly name all of them here, but several deserve special recognition and thanks.

They include my terrific and talented team at Greener World Media, notably my partner, Pete May, along with our other valued colleagues, sponsors, and partners; Neil Black, Nicholas Eisenberger, and Andrew Shapiro and their colleagues at GreenOrder; Ron Pernick and team at Clean Edge; and Stephan Dolezalek, Bill Green, and colleagues at VantagePoint Venture Partners.

I am also grateful to an extraordinary corps of individuals whose support, encouragement, and inspiration have been influential in my work and this book, including Brad Allenby, Rory Bakke, Andrew Beebe, Janine Benyus, Suzanne Biegel, Nicole-Anne Boyer, Michael S. Brown, Richard Brownlee, Majora Carter, Martin Charter, Aimee Christensen, Kevin Coyle, Aron Cramer, John Davies, Joyce Deep, John Elkington, Christine Ervin, Steve French, Gil Friend, Andrew Friendly, Lisa Gansky, John Garn, Mark Goldstein, Alisa Gravitz, Marc Gunther, Julia Hailes, Denise Hamler, Paul Hawken, Denis Hayes, Graham Hill, Gary Hirshberg, Nancy Hirshberg, Jeffrey Hollender, Yukiko Imanaka, John Javna, Fisk Johnson, David Johnston, Van Jones, Ronen Kalmanson, Dan Kammen, Kazunori Kobayashi, Justin Lehrer, Bob Langert, Peter Liu, Amory Lovins, Hunter Lovins, Beth Lowery, Frances Makower,

Alice Markowitz, Michael Martin, Liz Maw, John May, Josh McClellan, Bill McDonough, Jeff Mendelsohn, David Monsma, Eric Olson, Jason Pearson, Gifford and Libba Pinchot, Dan Reicher, Norman and Lorraine Rosenberg, Will Rosenzweig, Auden Schendler, Maki Sato, John Stauber, Rob Shelton, Deborah Sliter, Alex Steffen, Coro Strandberg, Terry Swack, Wood Turner, Sanjay Wagle, Diana and Beni Warshawsky, Adam Werbach, David Wigder, Clint Wilder, Andrew Winston, Lisa Witter, Diane Wood, Josh Yoburn, and David Zucker.

Deep thanks to my friend and colleague Cara Pike for her thoughtful and significant contribution.

Grateful appreciation to Donya Dickerson and her team at McGraw-Hill, including Herb Schaffner, Seth Morris, and Ann Pryor, who have been a pleasure to work with; to Joy Tutela at David Black Literary Agency for her unfailing support and enthusiasm; and to Jonathan Bardelline and Gwen Mariano for their research assistance.

Last of all and most of all, to Randy Rosenberg, whose love and laughter are the best part of each day.

# Introduction

Wat's your green strategy?

This isn't merely a marketing or public relations question related to your company's environmental image. It's about the fundamental nature of your business: how it operates, what it does and sells, and how it interacts with a wide range of people both inside and outside the company walls. It's a question that companies increasingly find themselves asking, whether they are large or small, offer products or services, or sell to consumers, other businesses, or anyone else. In many cases, companies don't fully understand what it means to have a green strategy. They just know they need one.

Why bother? In the first decade of the twenty-first century, a growing green economy is emerging that addresses the world's environmental and social challenges while creating new opportunities—and challenges—for companies of all sizes and sectors. In the green economy, wasteful and polluting products and business processes are giving way to more efficient ones that harness cleaner technologies. Pressing environmental problems such as climate change are being seen increasingly as opportunities for innovation, spurring new products, processes, markets, and business models. Driven by a variety of factors—competition, fear of government intervention, activist pressures, customer demands, rising energy prices, shareholder concerns, changing public expectations, the need to attract and retain talent—companies are seizing these opportunities to create business value while improving their operations and reputation.

The greening of mainstream business is not a new phenomenon. It has been growing for many years, despite its absence from the mainstream media. Since the 1980s, and even earlier in some cases, companies have found that they can reduce costs, risks, and liabilities by cleaning up their acts well beyond what is required by law. They did these things not necessarily because they hoped to "save the earth" but because these activities—cutting waste and pollution and improving efficiencies—simply were good business practices. Many companies have been reluctant to boast about their environmental initiatives and achievements, finding that doing so can bring unwanted scrutiny, perhaps exposing company environmental challenges about which the public wasn't previously aware. Contrary to conventional wisdom, environmental responsibility is an arena in which companies have been walking more than talking—that is, doing more than they've been saying.

Those days are drawing to a close. With increased societal demands for accountability and transparency, and the desire for consumers and businesses to buy from "good" companies, business leaders are finding that being humble is no longer an asset. Companies, including both those selling goods and services to consumers as well as to other companies, are being asked to be more forthcoming about their environmental and social impacts—both the things they're doing right and the things they aren't. This means that companies need to have good stories to tell, stories with substance and significance.

This is no mean feat. At the same time that customers are demanding greener products and services, many are skeptical about company claims and pronouncements on these issues. That skepticism is aided and abetted by the media and environmental activists, many of which are quick to criticize companies' imperfections and slow to applaud their progress. As some companies have found, no green deed goes unpunished.

These skeptics' concerns are not unfounded. As you'll see in the pages of this book, the industrial sector's contribution to environmental problems is often greater than most people recognize. One example: The amount of solid waste produced in the manufacture of goods, including the extraction and production of raw materials, overshadows by 65 times the municipal solid waste that most people refer to when expressing concern about "the landfill crisis." That waste is largely hidden, not typically captured in publicly reported statistics, although this may change.

Given all this history and skepticism, companies that seek to be green leaders and that derive business value from the new green economy confront a number of questions and challenges:

- What does it take to be seen as an environmental leader and to garner the business benefits therein?
- How good must your company be to be seen as "good"?
- What are the standards, implicit or explicit, that you must meet?
- How do you talk about what you are doing right—and what you're not?
- How do you circumvent the distrust and skepticism?
- How can you be heard amid all the "green noise" in the media and online?

*In short:* How do you succeed in a world gone green?

## MY ROAD TO HERE

I began looking at the greening of business in 1989, when researching my book, *The Green Consumer*. The book was published during the media frenzy of Earth Day 1990, when the world (or at least some of it) awakened to the significant environmental challenges we faced. We learned that the climate was changing, that the ozone layer was thinning, and that we were running out of water, energy, natural resources, and landfill space. At the same time, we were told by best-selling authors and other self-appointed mavens that there were "simple things" we could do to save the earth, and we felt empowered.

At the time, it seemed like a floodgate of greener products was about to open. Large consumer product companies such as Procter & Gamble and Unilever were dipping their corporate toes into the green waters, with the expectation that they would eventually dive in. Big retailers such as Home Depot and Wal-Mart conducted in-store promos highlighting greener products. We could smell change coming.

It didn't come. A number of companies' public commitments to be environmentally responsible citizens turned out to be fleeting, if not fraudulent. Many of their early products were outright failures: biodegradable trash bags that didn't degrade (or degraded a little too quickly), clunky fluorescent bulbs that emitted horrible hues, recycled tissue with the softness of sandpaper, and greener cleaners that couldn't cut the mustard, literally. Many of these products were expensive and hard to find. The Federal Trade Commission (FTC) weighed in during the early 1990s, eventually slapping a few marketers on their corporate wrists.

By 1992, after spreading my green consumer mantra far and wide ("Every time you open your wallet, you cast a vote—for or against the environment!") in more books, a weekly syndicated newspaper column, countless media interviews, and speeches around North America and beyond, I peered over my shoulder and realized that I was more or less standing alone. The vast green consumer movement never materialized.

There are several good reasons for this. Marketers largely failed to excite and motivate consumers. Consumers were skeptical and conflicted about making changes in their purchasing habits. Environmentalists weren't supportive of the fledgling green marketplace, especially of big companies that were starting to turn over a new leaf. It turned out that there weren't many "simple things" most of us could do that actually had an impact on the planet's problems. Instead, the growing environmental problems demanded a relatively small number of more challenging actions.

As discouraged as I was with consumers, I was impressed by how a growing corps of companies were seeking to address their own environmental impacts, some voluntarily, born of operational and reputational benefits, and others dragged kicking and screaming into the conversation by activists. Unlike consumers, who had little personal motivation for making changes and who received few tangible rewards when they did, companies had significant incentives to change. Because companies can use huge volumes of resources and create vast amounts of waste and emissions, it became apparent that they stood to reap financial rewards by being more efficient. Even "simple things" could have a big impact when done on the scale of a multinational corporation. And companies found they could benefit in other ways from being cleaner and less polluting, such as in being attractive to the growing generation of college students seeking to work for companies that shared their values.

And so I shifted my focus to the greening of business—writing, speaking, and advising companies that were seeking to profit from environmental responsibility.

Over the years, I've had the great good fortune of working directly with dozens of companies and speaking to thousands of businesspeople about shaping and implementing their environmental strategy toward the goal of reducing their impacts and garnering business value from their efforts. I've helped companies to understand the challenges and opportunities associated with talking openly about their green strategies and progress with their employees, suppliers, customers, the media, activist groups, and others.

Some of this work has been done through Greener World Media, the media company I cofounded that produces GreenBiz.com and other Web sites, events, and research reports on the greening of mainstream business, and prior to that, *The Green Business Letter,* the monthly newsletter I published from 1991–2005. Some of it has been through my affiliation with GreenOrder, an environmental strategy and management consulting firm that works with some of the world's largest companies, and with Clean Edge, a research and publishing firm focusing on clean technologies, which I cofounded. I've also advised more than a dozen leading public relations, advertising, and marketing firms on shaping clients' green strategies, products, and messages. Many of the examples and case studies in this book come from those experiences, as well as from the rich conversations I have had with readers through my blog, "Two Steps Forward" (*www.readjoel.com*), which examines issues related to the greening of business strategy and marketing.

## CARA PIKE AND THE AMERICAN VALUES SURVEY

This book also benefits from the research and analysis of my colleague Cara Pike, one of world's top social change marketers. At the end of this book is an appendix with insights from the landmark Ecological Roadmap, a research project she directed based on the American

Values Survey (AVS) in 2005 and 2007. It will provide insight into the consumer mindset that can be helpful in crafting and executing a green economy strategy.

Until 2007, Pike served as vice president of communications for Earthjustice, the nation's leading nonprofit environmental law firm. While there, she commissioned the Ecological Roadmap that is based on the data gathered in the American Values Survey, which examines more than one hundred social values through one of the largest in-home studies ever conducted in the United States—1,900 respondents. Based on responses to 900 psychographic questions, the AVS goes beyond what can be understood through traditional polling techniques by uncovering the underlying values and worldviews that influence behaviors and opinions. This is an extremely valuable approach as consumers become more difficult to segment and target based on demographic information alone.

Pike found that when it comes to the environment, the buying public can be divided into 10 distinct groups reflecting a wide range of values, opinions, and behaviors. The good news is that more than 93 million Americans have strong concerns about the environment. The challenge is that what *green* means to one segment of the public and how ecological concerns are put into practice are often in sharp contrast to those of other segments. This has significant implications for companies—as well as for activist groups, government agencies, and others—seeking to motivate the public to respond to environmental messages and marketing.

In her appendix, Pike will show how a great deal of green strategy and messaging misses the mark by failing to understand and address the subtle but vital distinctions among various audiences, opting instead for a one-size-fits-all approach.

## FIND YOUR STRATEGY

This book's nearly 40 short chapters are organized in five main sections:

Part One takes a look at the history of green business and the green economy—the winding path that got us where we are today.

Part Two looks at the marketplace—what consumers are saying, what they're actually doing, and the challenges of reconciling the two.

Part Three examines the question, "How good is 'good enough'?"—from both product and company points of view.

Part Four follows the paths of several companies, big and small, as they've pursued green-economy strategies.

Finally, Part Five examines a bigger and more challenging question, "How good is sufficient?"—that is, whether and how the sum total of company actions is addressing our society's and planet's environmental challenges.

In the pages that follow, you'll tour the landscape of green-minded consumers, companies, activists, media, and others and understand the challenges companies have faced in traversing the green marketplace. You'll learn about some pathways forward, including the lessons learned from a wide range of firms that have succeeded (and some who have not) in the growing green economy. And you'll find research data that undergird this story line.

This book is designed to be read in short sittings or in one long one, front to back or in a more random order. Its short chapters build on one another but are also intended to be self-contained, stand-alone readings. Both veterans and novices will find insights and inspiration.

# PART 1

# HOW DID WE GET HERE?

In August 1989, a London- and New York–based consulting firm called the Michael Peters Group issued a research report about U.S. consumers' interest in buying products and services with fewer negative environmental impacts. It was nothing short of a revelation. The study, based on a telephone poll of 1,000 consumers, found that a whopping 89 percent of shoppers said that they were concerned about the environmental impact of the products they purchased. And nearly as many—78 percent—said that they were willing to pay as much as 5 percent more for a product packaged with recyclable or biodegradable materials compared with its conventional counterpart.

In marketing circles, those were eye-popping numbers. No one had ever gauged consumers' attitudes toward making environmental choices when they shopped, let alone come up with such a stunningly high level of interest. The results suggested a vast, untapped opportunity for companies selling everything from cleaners to cars to cosmetics. The message was clear and compelling: Build a greener mousetrap, and the world will beat a path to your door.

The timing of the Peters report was fortuitous, and not coincidental. Earth Day 1990 was eight months away, the twentieth anniversary of the original event, and it promised to be a media extravaganza. Indeed, the event's organizers were conscripting some of Madison Avenue's finest to ensure that Earth Day, this time around, would miss no one's attention. The event's advertising work was done by Pacy Markman, the agency veteran who crafted Miller Lite's indelible slogan, "Everything you always wanted in a beer, and less." Earth Day's organizers sought major corporate sponsors and hired a Los Angeles company that handled merchandise licensing for such movies as *Platoon* and *Robocop* to generate revenue from Earth Day–branded clothing, gear, and souvenirs. Perhaps ironically, given that the original Earth Day in 1970 was a protest against corporate environmental misdeeds, Earth Day 1990 may have been the world's first major green marketing campaign.

A good part of the messages surrounding Earth Day that year focused on green products and the companies that made them. Environmental groups urged citizens to switch to products that were recycled or recyclable, made with fewer toxic ingredients, packaged in biodegradable materials, or were otherwise kinder and gentler to the planet. They advocated boycotting big companies seen to be polluters and to support a new breed of smaller, values-based businesses such as Aveda, Ben & Jerry's, The Body Shop, Patagonia, and Seventh Generation. Several guides to green living and shopping made bestseller lists (including my book, *The Green Consumer*), and one of them—*50 Simple Things You Can Do to Save the Earth,* a small, self-published tome by a Berkeley-based pop-culture writer—sold five million copies and spawned a rash of imitators. (The author, John Javna, eventually became cynical and discouraged that his book might be lulling the citizenry into complacency by encouraging incremental actions, although he reemerged in 2008 with a new edition of the book that tried to address green issues more substantively.)

None of this was lost on the business sector: the market research, the media attention, the merchandising, the shopping advice, the boycotts, the best-sellers, and more. As the *New York Times* reported in November 1989, "Earth Day organizers expect virtually everyone in environmentally related businesses, from health food stores to publishers of environmental books, to jump on the bandwagon with publicity, sales, and events to stimulate participation." It seemed that many companies were ready and willing to jump.

We'd already seen this happen in Europe, particularly the United Kingdom, where my book's predecessor, *The Green Consumer Guide,* written by John Elkington and Julia Hailes, had been a number-one best-seller and helped foment a green shopping ethic among Brits. London department stores such as Marks & Spencer were showcasing recycled and other products, and many were selling well, aided by London's upscale High Street shops, which helped to make green living fashionable.

By the time Earth Day 1990 rolled around, on April 22, green products were proliferating on the American side of the pond, too. Fully 26 percent of all household products introduced that year boasted that they were ozone-friendly, recyclable, biodegradable, or compostable, or made some other green claim, according to Marketing Intelligence Service, which tracks product launches. Even firms that didn't sell directly to consumers wanted to join in. Everyone from the chemical industry to the nuclear power industry took out full-page ads in magazines and newspapers proclaiming their environmental commitment.

The greening of business and the marketplace was in full swing. Or so it seemed.

# Chapter 1

# The Oat Branning of Green

It turned out not to be so simple. Many of the products didn't live up to their hype. Some labeling claims were found by investigators to be inaccurate, unverifiable, or simply meaningless. Many of the terms being used—*safe, earth-friendly, nontoxic, organic,* and *natural,* among others—had no legal or generally accepted definitions. Still others were technically true but functionally false. A polystyrene foam egg carton was, as some packages suggested, "recyclable." Indeed, the technology existed to reclaim polystyrene, but since almost no one had access to that technology, the claim was, well, barren.

It was a reversal of fortune for the fledgling green business movement. Environmentalists who had weeks earlier been egging consumers to "shop green" were now lambasting companies for false and misleading claims—"greenwashing," as it came to be known. Competitors started criticizing one another for deceptive practices. Procter & Gamble, for one, publicly railed against competitors that claimed their products would degrade in landfills. The U.S. Federal Trade

Commission launched hearings, as did a task force of state attorneys general, led by Minnesota's Hubert Humphrey III. They publicly spanked companies like Mobil Corporation, which promoted its Hefty plastic trash bags as "photodegradable," meaning they would deteriorate over time after exposure to sunlight and oxygen. (Again, technically true but functionally false because trash bags end up buried in landfills, hidden from sun and air.) Some activist groups that had been urging consumers to choose green products from good companies began boycotting products bearing environmental claims. It wasn't all a sham, of course. Some companies truly were making improvements in their products and processes. But it wasn't a simple story to tell.

And it all started to resemble oat bran.

For those too young to remember, or who have conveniently forgotten, eating oat bran became the rage in the late 1980s, seen as a way to reduce serum cholesterol, a major risk factor in heart disease. Oat bran quickly found its way into countless processed foods—products that up to that point had contained neither oat nor bran: bagels, potato chips, tortillas, even beer. For several months in 1988, Quaker Oats couldn't produce enough oats and bran to meet market demand, resorting to posting apologetic "Dear Customer" letters in cereal aisles when supplies needed to be rationed.

All that came to a screeching halt at the end of the decade, when a review of several studies examining the link between oats and heart health said, in effect, "Well, maybe not." They concluded that at best, oat bran may modestly reduce blood cholesterol, although gaining even that benefit might require one to ingest ungodly quantities of the stuff.

It was a defining moment in marketing: A nutrition movement born of scientific research suddenly was seen as yet another cynical ploy to separate shoppers from their wallets.

And so it went with green products, which followed the "oat bran era" by not many months. A social movement that started off as a clamor quickly became a calamity: Conflicted consumers, angry activists, inquiring regulators, finger-pointing companies—and reporters—all too eager to tell the unfolding story, along the way creating corporate heroes and then knocking them off their pedestals when they were found to be flawed. As a result, companies that had once boasted of their commitments and progress toward "saving the earth" clammed up, recognizing that the benefits of being a cleaner, more efficient, and more responsible company were outweighed by the reputational risks associated with talking about it publicly. Many companies, viewing the complex and challenging landscape, abandoned their green strategies altogether, although most continued their efforts, albeit quietly.

It was the right thing to do. Companies found that they could get much more done, environmentally speaking, away from the spotlight. Not because this was some nefarious endeavor that needed to be hidden from public scrutiny. Quite the opposite: Much of what companies have undertaken since the early 1990s has been substantive and admirable, wringing out the waste and inefficiency and the energy, resource, toxic, and carbon intensities of their products and processes. Much of this activity didn't show up in products, at least not directly, but it helped companies to reduce their environmental impacts significantly, cutting costs and risks along the way. It was simply smart business, regardless of whether or not activists and customers ever acknowledged or appreciated it.

Things are changing once again, however. Today, with the renewed focus on climate change, water issues, toxic products, and other environmental and public health issues—not to mention the broader interest in corporate citizenship and social responsibility—companies increasingly are finding that they must operate within the spotlight of environmental concern. Business leaders are learning that they are expected to be engaged in cleaner, more efficient practices and otherwise pay close attention to the environmental impacts of everything they do. And they are expected to talk about it—not necessarily to shout it from the rooftops, but to be open and transparent about what they're doing right and what they're still working on. The school kids of Earth Day 1990 are now in the job market, seeking not just to make a living, but to make a life worth living—in part by working for companies they believe in. Behind them is another generation of budding consumers and future job seekers, for whom thinking about nature is, well, second nature.

Meanwhile, shoppers are becoming more sophisticated. While the jury is out about how much people are willing to bend in order to buy green (much more on this later), there's little question that their awareness of environmental issues is growing, helped along by the advertising power of major consumer product companies. We haven't yet reached the point where average consumers are as well versed on their carbon footprints as on their weight and cholesterol numbers, but some are, and that's a sea change.

Being an environmentally responsible citizen is becoming less of a fad for many and more of a way of life, born of genuine concern for the future. Small habits such as recycling, bringing your own bag, and turning off computers are helping to ingrain a new greener ethic among an ever-broadening segment of the public. Green products are improving in quality and availability, with fewer tradeoffs that turned off consumers earlier. Technologies are bringing forth a wealth of innovative products, harnessing renewable energy, biobased or organic materials, fewer toxic ingredients, more recyclable components—or made with just plain less stuff.

Amid all these competing and compelling forces, how do you develop and communicate your company's environmental strategy and progress, even if, like most companies, you're far from perfect? And how do you derive tangible business value from your company's good, green efforts along the way?

As you'll see, it's not always easy, but it can be done.

# Chapter 2

# From a Movement to a Market

Most people—in business, the media, politics, and activism, as well as individual consumers—view green business as a recent phenomenon, something that's suddenly sprung up, perhaps thanks to Al Gore's movie or other influencers. In fact, this is an "overnight sensation" that's been several decades in the making. To fully understand the greening of mainstream business, it's important to understand this trajectory. Following is a four-minute history of green business.

In the beginning—let's say the 1960s—there was pollution. It was dirty and unhealthy and threatened our very way of life. So began the notion of *pollution control*—stopping illegal activities as well as the spewing smokestacks and drainpipes that were legal but seen as egregious. In 1970 came the U.S. Environmental Protection Agency, followed by a series of laws in the United States and other countries that for the first time regulated pollution of air and water. Enter the scrubbers-and-filters crowd, the engineers who learned how to capture and control emissions sufficiently to comply with those mandates.

By the 1980s, a few smart companies figured out that if you didn't pollute in the first place, you didn't have to worry about controlling it or cleaning it up. So began the idea of *pollution prevention* and its cousins, *waste reduction* and *energy efficiency,* in which companies began rethinking their processes and management systems to reduce waste and costs. One of the pioneers, 3M, maker of everything from Post-it Notes to Scotchgard, created a pollution-prevention program in the 1970s that continues to this day, having saved the company billions of dollars.

By the 1990s management stepped in and declared, "We need systems!" and "What gets measured, gets managed!" and other management bromides. And so environmental management systems and something called ISO 14001 were created, the latter promulgated by the International Organization for Standardization, which established a baseline set of rules for how companies should organize themselves environmentally. And somewhere in the 1980s, while the work of W. Edwards Deming was in vogue, the notion of *total quality environmental management* had 15 minutes of fame.

While more companies began to understand the many environmental impacts of how things were manufactured, a few companies realized that they needed to look at the "things" themselves—the full environmental impacts of their products. And so began the notion of *cradle-to-grave thinking,* along with an entire toolkit. Suddenly, environmental managers were tossing around such terms as *life-cycle assessments, design for the environment, end-of-life management, dematerialization, demanufacturing, remanufacturing, reverse logistics, product takeback,* and *extended producer responsibility.* Companies began to better measure, and manage, their materials throughput—how many units of product emerged from every unit of raw material used. Eventually, a well-known green designer and architect, William McDonough, and a Swiss chemist, Michael Braungart, came together to tell us that cradle-to-grave thinking shouldn't be the goal, that we needed to set our compass to achieve *closed-loop, cradle-to-cradle* products and processes. They developed a methodology for doing this and, eventually, a certification scheme for such products.

As companies scrutinized their products and operations, they began to understand how much of their environmental impacts were affected by those outside their organizations—their suppliers, contractors, and business partners. And so, *supply-chain environmental management* became the watchword, with companies striving to push the clean-and-green mantra ever further upstream. In some cases, they partnered with their suppliers to identify and procure nontoxic alternatives or alternative materials derived from plants instead of oil or trees or to use other techniques that could reduce or eliminate problematic ingredients. A science writer named Janine Benyus taught companies about "biomimicry," design inspired by nature, that married biology with engineering and industrial design to create innovative new products and processes that borrowed knowledge from a myriad of insects, fungi, animals, and other critters. It asked the question, "How would nature design this?" and identified a toolkit born of Mother Nature's more than three billion years of research and development activity. (Biomimicry eventually would become implemented in such companies as DuPont, General Electric, Hewlett-Packard, Nike, Steelcase, and a host of smaller firms.) A group of chemists put forward the seemingly oxymoronic notion of *green chemistry,* a breed of more environmentally friendly chemistry that reduces waste and yields fewer hazardous substances, all while creating safer products.

While all these activities gained popularity, some leading-edge business models emerged—for example, *industrial ecology,* in which business systems behaved like forests or other natural systems, with waste products from one process becoming the feedstock for another. Some companies pursued the vision of *zero waste,* closed-loop factories with no smokestacks, drainpipes, or dumpsters. Others strived for products, facilities, or events in which the associated climate emissions would be offset to the extent that these things could be declared *carbon-neutral.* And companies learned that by embracing the principles of *natural capitalism,* they could be not merely benign, but actually restorative.

And companies ultimately came to learn the S-word—*sustainability*—the three-legged stool consisting of people, profit, and planet.

For more and more companies, this intergenerational Golden Rule has become the new goal post, albeit an aspirational one, because true sustainability—the ability to continue one's business operations indefinitely in a way that doesn't create limits for future generations—is out of reach for most companies. For better or worse, sustainability has become a term of art, even though it is frequently used, inappropriately, as an interchangeable term for *environment* or *green.*

The past few decades of green business evolution can be represented by three waves of change. It began with a sort of eco-Hippocratic oath—"First, do no harm"—in which companies aimed to get the worst environmental abuses under control.

Next came "Doing well by doing good," in which companies found that they could reduce costs—and enhance their reputations—by taking a few proactive steps.

And then came "Green is green" (as coined by General Electric Chairman Jeffrey Immelt), the recognition that environmental thinking can do more than improve the bottom line. It can help to grow the top line through innovation, new markets, and new business opportunities.

This is the point at which *sustainability* becomes, well, sustainable.

It's important to note that this entire spectrum of change still exists—from pollution control to the most cutting-edge thinking—sometimes within a single company. Indeed, it is this wide range of green actions and behaviors, across a single company or an entire economy, that is confusing and confounding to the public. It makes identifying the real leaders an extraordinarily difficult task for everyone involved. And it creates both challenges and opportunities for companies seeking to differentiate themselves as true green leaders.

# Chapter 3

# Twenty-First Century Green

The course of the modern environmental movement has been more or less linear, with various organizations and causes building on one another since the 1960s. With the exception of a relative handful of headline-grabbing events—nuclear and industrial accidents, hurricanes and other natural disasters, oil and chemical spills, and the like—the movement has grown, and sometimes stagnated, in fairly orderly fashion. The same cannot be said for environmental problems. Even a cursory look at the size and nature of our planetary challenges shows a step change.

Consider two disparate images:

One is the burning Cuyahoga River of Ohio, where fires erupted along a small stretch in June 1969. The notion that water could become so toxic as to ignite was a wake-up call to U.S. industry and captured the imagination of writers and activists. (It also inspired songwriter Randy Newman to pen "Burn On" in 1972.)

Consider now an image from Al Gore's movie, *An Inconvenient Truth*. Nearly any image will do—perhaps one of those graphs showing rising concentrations of greenhouse gases in the atmosphere or one explaining the rising surface temperatures on Earth.

Hold onto those two images—the Cuyahoga and climate change—simultaneously for a moment. Now consider how different they are.

The burning Cuyahoga represented an environmental challenge that was local, immediate, visible, relatively singular in cause (i.e., factories dumping waste into the river), short-lived (i.e., the river was cleaned up within a decade), and thus solvable.

Now consider climate change. It is global, largely invisible, resulting from millions of sources over a century or so. Its magnitude and persistence make it debatable whether it can ever be controlled, let alone solved.

These are not your parents' environmental problems. It's no longer just about the "landfill crisis," or smoggy urban air, or the extinction of cute, cuddly critters. These are not problems that can be solved by doing a few "simple things." That ship has sailed. Today's environmental challenges are far beyond anything we've faced before, affecting not just the birds and the trees but also, potentially, the economics, public health, and well-being of all humans, too.

Things have changed, though not everything. Politicians and regulators still try to command and control problems away; it works sometimes, but not always as well as market incentives and other nonregulatory signals that reward companies for acting in more environmentally responsible ways. Activists still put their stock in protests and boycotts, although some have gotten a tad smarter about the potential of partnering with the business sector. And many companies still maintain a defensive posture, doing only what they must to fend off whoever is barking loudest at the time.

Environmental problems are different now, more complex, harder to ignore and dismiss. Times have changed, too. Company strategies need to reflect these changes and complexity, going beyond simple slogans or random acts of greenness to reflect some fundamental changes in how business is done.

# Chapter 4

# A Dysfunctional Conversation

Whether you have a green strategy in place or are just starting out, you will inevitably bump up against a basic reality of the green economy: It is largely dysfunctional, at least from the perspective of mainstream companies doing business with the mainstream consumers and also, to a lesser degree, with other companies. It is dysfunctional because the parties involved don't communicate well with one another. When they express themselves, their messages frequently are misunderstood, or simply missed, by the intended recipients.

Whose fault is this? There's plenty of blame to go around:

• For nearly two decades, research studies have shown consistently that a high percentage of consumers and a growing percentage of companies in the United States and other developed countries are interested in buying products that help them to reduce their environmental impacts, but the day-to-day reality is that most people (and many companies) aren't willing to change their buying habits just because something is green, and they often don't trust companies making such claims.

- Companies, especially major corporations, have been gradually integrating environmental thinking into their operations, often because being greener means being more efficient and more profitable. But the benefits of such efforts often can't be seen directly in their products, at least for labeling and marketing purposes. And because there are no standards defining a green or environmentally responsible business, it's up to every company and consumer to create their own definitions. Because of this lack of standards, many companies are reluctant to promote their environmental progress for fear that it may not be good enough or that it may unwittingly illuminate problems the public didn't know the company had, setting the company up for criticism instead of praise.

- Environmental activists, long conditioned to seeing business, especially big business, as "the enemy," are much better at being the "bad cop" than the "good cop." They are adept at confronting and challenging companies for their shortcomings and misdeeds but relatively inept at praising them when they change. They rarely say, in effect, "Thanks. Now do more." It's more likely, "No. Not good enough." (Or even, "How dare you talk about that achievement when you have all these other problems!") Moreover, these idealists aren't very good at accepting incremental improvements, which is the way most companies operate. Rather, activists seek bold, even radical changes in the behavior of companies; anything less may be deemed unacceptable.

There's more. Most regulators and politicians—both local and national—don't seem to know whether they should lead, follow, or get out of the way of companies that are voluntarily addressing their environmental challenges beyond what the law requires. Wall Street doesn't, as a rule, value companies' proactive environmental actions, even if they can be shown to reduce risks, improve operating efficiencies, or otherwise create business value. And the mainstream media pay fleeting attention to all this, usually viewing the greening of business as a novel but marginal notion and missing many of the important stories on the topic. And they can be fickle, even cynical, alternately helping to build corporate heroes and then knocking them down when they prove to be less than perfect.

The result of all this—motivated but distrustful consumers, proactive but humble companies, aggressive but often misguided activists, the media's mixed messages, and the lack of norms and standards of what is "good enough"—is that it is almost impossible to create a workable green strategy that meets the expectations of a confused and cynical marketplace. Customers—both businesses and individual consumers—don't know who or what to believe, sometimes throwing up their hands in exasperation. "Green business is just another marketing scam," they say, in the process dismissing both leadership companies and poseurs alike.

Did I mention that this is a dysfunctional conversation?

This needn't be a show-stopper. Successful companies are finding their way through this thicket, crafting policies, processes, messages—and, of course, products, services, and strategies—that address both individual and institutional customers' needs. Later on in this book we'll look at how companies are managing, and largely succeeding, to navigate these challenges in the green economy.

# Chapter 5

# What's a Green Business?

One of the big problems companies confront when they set out to devise, implement, and communicate their green strategy is that there is little agreement about what it means for a company to be seen as green. It's funny when you think about it. For all the newspaper articles, magazine cover stories, television specials, Web sites, blogs, consultants, conferences, speakers, and other efforts that promote the notion of environmentally responsible business, the definition remains in the eye of the beholder.

We know what it means to be a *green building*. There's a voluntary industry standard for that, called the Leadership in Energy and Environmental Design (LEED) Green Building Rating System, in the United States and Canada, and it has counterparts in many other countries. We know what it means to be a certified *organic tomato*—there's a law defining that and other organic products, at least in the United States.

But we don't know what it means to be a *green business*.

This is a big problem. Nearly every emerging product, idea, trend, or market requires norms and standards to achieve public acceptance and scale. Think about the standards we use every day: your computer's USB connection (which allows it to connect seamlessly with most printers, mice, and other devices), the unique International Standard Book Number on the back cover of this book (which allows it to be ordered from nearly any computer or bookstore), the rules governing who can call themselves a certified public accountant (enabling them to be licensed and able to provide to the public attestation opinions on financial statements), or even a company's membership in the Better Business Bureau (which attests that the company is in good ethical standing and is committed to resolving disputes with customers). All these provide some level of assurance to customers, business partners, employees, and others, and that, in turn, allows markets to grow and prosper more efficiently.

So what's the standard for determining whether a business can be called *green*? What set of environmental commitments should it make? How should it operate? Is there some minimum standard for waste, energy use, transportation, toxic ingredients, and so forth? How open should the company be about its impacts? How does it know that it is meeting society's expectations? In short, how does it know that its environmental policies, programs, and progress will be viewed as "good enough"?

It's a daunting challenge. Is it even possible to create a single standard, or even a series of standards, that defines an environmentally responsible business—a standard that can be applied to a large or small company in any type of business? Is there a uniform standard that can be applied to a local restaurant, nail salon, or bank, as well as to a multinational chemical company or a major retail chain?

The answer, so far, has been no. Each company is different, even two companies in the same city doing essentially the same thing. Sure, most companies have commonalities, such as maintaining offices that use computers and paper or having employees who need to get to and from their jobs. However, the environmental impacts of such activities may be significant for one company and trivial for another.

There are green business certification programs, mostly for smaller firms operating at the local level. Several cities and counties have programs in which local businesses that meet a set of criteria can receive a certification attesting to their environmental commitment and performance. But few larger firms apply for these, and certification rarely carries over from one jurisdiction to the next, meaning that a company doing business in several cities, counties, or states may be required to apply to several independent programs, each with its own standards. A program called Green Business Network, operated by the nonprofit Co-op America, has a membership of about 4,000 companies that must meet social and environmental criteria to join. Most of its members are small, even tiny operations, a miniscule fraction of the more than 25 million small companies operating in the United States, according to Census Bureau data. One reason is that membership is limited to companies that pass its screening process, which determines a company's "familiarity with and commitment to social and environmental responsibility" as well as "significant action" it has taken in this regard.

There also are standards governing specific aspects of green business. For example, the Global Reporting Initiative (GRI) has been adopted by dozens of large companies as the de facto standard on how to report a company's environmental and social performance, although it doesn't dictate what that performance should be. A company could, theoretically, be out of regulatory compliance and doing little or nothing to reduce its major environmental impacts and still hew to the standard by issuing a GRI-compliant sustainability report detailing its inaction. There is an international standard for environmental management systems, known as ISO 14001, that defines the way a company should establish an organized approach to systematically reduce the impact of the environmental aspects that the company can control. But it applies to specific facilities, not to a company as a whole. And it only certifies that there's a system in place, not that the system is effective. A company could be out of compliance, sued by major environmental groups, and make toxic toys for kids—and still pass ISO's muster.

And there are dozens of standards for individual product categories, such things as sustainably harvested wood, shade-grown coffee, chlorine-free paper, dolphin-safe tuna, free-range beef, cruelty-free cosmetics, biodegradable packaging, and on and on. (Consumers Union maintains a respectable list at *www.eco-label.org.*) Some of these standards are highly credible, vetted by respected scientists, environmental activists, business leaders, and others. Others are less so, having been promulgated by a single organization with relatively little involvement from interested parties. But few, if any, of these apply to a company, only to specific products.

The lack of a uniform standard, or set of standards, defining environmentally responsible companies means that anyone can make green claims, regardless of whether their actions are substantive, comprehensive, or even true. Want to put solar panels on the roof of your toxics-spewing chemical company? You can be a green business! You can encourage your employees to take mass transit, print on both sides of the paper, and toil amid furnishings manufactured from certified sustainable materials in your offices, from which your company imports cheap, radioactive metal trinkets from across the ocean—and deem yourself green! You can do almost anything you want.

I'm being a little facetious here—but only a little.

The ability of any company to call itself green means a high potential for stretching the truth, however well intentioned, and for customers to become frustrated and cynical, unable to separate hype from reality. And it means that companies that truly *are* leaders— those that have integrated environmental thinking deep into their operations in a substantive and strategic way—can't easily distinguish themselves to those they most want to influence: customers, employees, job seekers, the media, investors, and others.

Since the 1990s, government, industry, and nonprofit entities have created dozens of voluntary environmental and social standards that focus on products, facilities, and company operations. These cover a wide spectrum of policies, practices, and performance on such issues as marine and forest stewardship, energy efficiency and climate change reduction, sweatshop labor and worker rights, business ethics, minority purchasing, community investment, board diversity, and many others. But there remains no easy way to assess the full measure of a company's environmental, let alone social, performance.

It's hardly surprising that no such standard exists. Creating a comprehensive standard for green business is a complex and challenging proposition, but it is not impossible. A number of groups have been working on such a scheme, although few have been launched, and none has yet achieved widespread adoption.

In 2004, a small group of green business leaders in the San Francisco Bay Area was approached by a staffer from a state legislator in Sacramento, California's capital, and was asked to support a bill that would give state procurement preference to "sustainable businesses." I was a member of that group, and we declined to offer support because the bill lacked definitions of that term, but the episode started a conversation among a number of us. Thus began a focus on the question of how to develop a "level playing field" ratings system that would lead to ratings, benchmarking, and learning opportunities to help companies improve their environmental and social performance.

The product of that exercise was the Sustainable Business Achievement Rating system (SBAR), a means for comprehensively assessing a company's environmental, economic, and social performance. Modeled in part on the LEED green building standard, which offers good-better-best ratings across a wide spectrum of issues related to the built environment—SBAR covers five dimensions of sustainability: environment, workplace, marketplace, community, and governance. With funding from a progressive Alameda County, California, public agency, our small SBAR team spent three years developing the rating system and built portions of it. Lack of funding, as of this writing, has limited progress.

The emergence and success of LEED is telling. Prior to LEED, just about anyone could declare that a building was green and get away with it. "We've got energy-efficient windows, low-flow toilets, and recycled carpeting—we're a green building!" All good, of course, but barely scratching the surface of what building professionals believe is adequate to invoke the green moniker.

LEED answered the question, "How good is good enough?"—at least for buildings. It established a comprehensive set of standards and has been credited with the sharply increased demand for green buildings in recent years. By creating a unified standard, it has enabled product manufacturers, architects, developers, city planners, landlords, and tenants alike to speak the same language and operate on the same playing field. And the green building marketplace has skyrocketed and will continue to do so. According to the U.S. Green Building Council (USGBC), there were roughly 1,000 buildings in the United States that had been certified under the LEED standard at the end of 2007. Within three years—by the end of 2010—the USGBC anticipates that this number will grow by two orders of magnitude, to about 100,000 U.S. buildings.

SBAR was propagated on the notion that creating comprehensive standards similarly could boost the market for green businesses, a foundation on which to build a robust and competitive marketplace. Such a standard may yet find its way into the marketplace, but none, including SBAR, is in the offing. For now, companies will have to learn how to operate in a world without standards, defining for themselves what they believe is "good enough" for their customers, employees, communities, and the natural environment.

# Chapter 6

# Do Consumers Really Care?

Remember the 1989 Michael Peters Group study, the one that said nearly nine in ten U.S. consumers were concerned about the environmental impacts of their purchases? It was the first of a lengthy and continuing parade of market research studies of consumers' attitudes about shopping and the environment. Each study has its own biases, methodologies, and sometimes, agendas, but all of them are relatively consistent in their findings.

And most of them are wrong.

This may be an overstatement, but not by much. As I've watched the steady stream of studies unveiled since 1989, they all pretty much say the same thing, and that "thing" never seems to jibe with reality. Indeed, the numbers haven't changed much despite 18 annual Earth Days, five presidential administrations, and the birth, death, and rebirth of the electric car.

Consider a sampling of the findings that crossed my desk during 2007 and through Earth Day 2008:

- Seventy-nine percent of U.S. consumers say that a company's environmental practices influence the products and services they recommend to others, according to GfK Roper Consulting. Four in ten Americans say that they are willing to pay extra for a product that is perceived to be better for the environment.

- Sixty-four percent of consumers worldwide say that they are willing to pay a higher price—a premium of 11 percent on average—for products and services that produce lower greenhouse gas emissions, according to a study by Accenture.

- A survey of consumers in 17 countries across 5 continents by market research firm TNX found that 94 percent of Thai respondents and 83 percent of Brazilians were willing to pay more for environmental friendliness, although "only" 45 percent of British and 53 percent of American respondents were willing to dig deeper to help the environment.

- Sixty-nine percent of European consumers claim to do a lot to reduce their energy consumption at home, whereas 75 percent make a direct link between climate change and their individual action to save energy, according to a survey by LogicaCMG. Eighty percent of European consumers are concerned about climate change, and seventy-five percent feel that their personal actions help to reduce its impacts.

- Consumer recall of advertising with green messaging is very high, with more than a third (37 percent) of consumers saying that they frequently recall green messaging and an additional third (33 percent) recalling it occasionally, according to Burst Media.

- Fifty-three percent of global consumers—representing just over a billion people—prefer to purchase products and services from a company with a strong environmental reputation, according to a global survey by videoconferencing company Tandberg. A company's environmental reputation is a clear preference not only for its customers but also for its employees, according to the survey. Eight in ten workers surveyed say that they prefer to work for an environmentally ethical organization.

- Consumers expect to double their spending on green products and services within one year, totaling an estimated $500 billion annually, or $43 billion per month, according to the ImagePower Green Brands Survey. The survey found that consumers perceive green as "a direct and positive reflection of their social status, in addition to recognizing its broader value to society and the world."
- Approximately 50 percent of U.S. consumers consider at least one sustainability factor in selecting consumer packaged-goods items and choosing where to shop for those products, according to a survey by Information Resources, Inc. Approximately 30 percent look for eco-friendly products and packaging in their brand selection, and up to 25 percent of those surveyed consider fair-trade practices along with eco-friendly or organic designations in determining where they shop.
- Most Americans say that they are making efforts in their personal lives to intentionally reduce their environmental impact, according to Cone's 2007 Consumer Environmental Survey. Specifically, Americans say that they are conserving energy (93 percent), recycling (89 percent), conserving water (86 percent), and "telling family/ friends about environmental issues" (70 percent). "Americans are calling on companies to be proactive in their day-to-day operations when it comes to the environment," concluded Cone, adding that "solid majorities support meaningful company actions."
- Around 40 percent of consumers said that they were willing to "do what it takes" to protect and improve the environment, and more than half always recycle at home, according to the Shopper Environmental Sentiment Survey from corporate real estate giant Jones Lang LaSalle. The survey was taken across 34 Jones Lang LaSalle–managed shopping malls.
- Nearly nine in ten Americans say that the words *conscious consumer* describe them well and are more likely to buy from companies that manufacture energy-efficient products, promote health and safety benefits, support fair-labor and fair-trade practices, and commit to environmentally friendly practices, according to the BBMG Conscious Consumer Report. While price (cited by 58 percent as

"very important") and quality (66 percent) remain paramount in purchase decisions, convenience (34 percent) has been edged out by more socially relevant attributes: Where a product is made (44 percent), how energy efficient it is (41 percent), and its health benefits (36 percent) are all integral to consumers' purchasing decisions.

I don't profess to have studies that refute these, but you don't need to be a social scientist to know that few of the preceding conclusions are on the money. Half of consumers likely do not consider sustainability when buying packaged goods—everything from cosmetics to cleaners, Rice-a-Roni to razor blades. (Do half your friends and family members shop this way?) Four of ten mall shoppers are not likely to "do what it takes" to improve the environment. And to think that 90 percent of us are "conscious consumers" when it comes to the planet? C'mon. Most of us aren't even conscious *eaters.*

Can market researchers be accused of "greenwash"?

If you sell to consumers, it's pretty compelling research, perhaps enough so to make you want to "green up" not just your products and services but your whole company in order to cash in on this bounty of interest among consumers, employees, and others. Before you do so, though, you might want to consider this *other* batch of stories that came my way during the same period:

- Seven in ten Americans and 64 percent of Canadians say that when companies call a product green or better for the environment, "it is usually just a marketing tactic," according to an Ipsos Reid study.
- Only 10 percent of U.S. and U.K. consumers trust what companies and government tell them about global warming, according to a study by AccountAbility and Consumers International. Seventy-five percent of consumers, although concerned about how their consumption affects climate change, feel paralyzed to act beyond small changes around the home.
- Sixty-four percent of U.S. consumers can't name a single "green" brand, including 51 percent of those who consider themselves environmentally conscious, according to a study by Landor Associates.

- While 63 percent of U.S. consumers say that they are "very concerned" about the effects of climate change or global warming,
  two-thirds do not know how most electricity is produced, according to the Shelton Group Energy Pulse study. Fewer than 4 percent
  could correctly name coal-fired electricity production as the biggest
  human-made contributor to climate change.
- Thirty-seven percent of consumers feel "highly concerned" about
  the environment, but only one in four feels highly knowledgeable
  about such issues, according to Yankelovich's "Going Green" study.
  And only 22 percent feel that they can make a difference when it
  comes to the environment.

So which is it? Are citizens engaged and interested, ready to
reward environmental leaders with their purchases, investments, and
job applications? Are they sufficiently knowledgeable and concerned
about environmental issues to understand and appreciate the
marketing claims and messages emanating from your company and
others? Are these issues sufficiently important to them that they are
able to break through the clutter in a time- and attention-con-
strained world filled with myriad other concerns and needs? Or are
they dazed and confused, beset by a lack of understanding of environment problems and solutions, ready to throw up their hands at
the vast number of green messages they hear from companies, many
of which seem believable, but a few of which just don't seem right,
thereby tainting the rest? The truth is, we don't really know. And
that's a problem.

So what do all these surveys tell us? In essence, two things:

First, consumers are looking for ways to be more responsible in
their lives, and they look to companies (as well as government) for
solutions about what to do. They are willing to do things that are relatively easy and that don't require (m)any changes in habits or levy
additional costs. And they want companies' help, in the form of products and value propositions that better enable them to understand not
only why something is really, truly better for the planet but also the
difference consumers will make if they buy the greener product

instead of the others. They want this in simple terms that can be communicated in a few seconds.

Second, being greener is not enough. Sad to say, but for many consumers, greener goods start with a reputational deficit: They may be perceived as inferior until proven otherwise. This means that a product or service must promise additional benefits beyond its superior environmental attributes—it must be cheaper, faster, whiter, brighter, easier to use, more effective, or simply cooler.

In other words: Products and services need to be more than merely greener—they need to be better!

None of this is to say that being seen as green is a waste of time. Far from it. There are many stories of both large and small companies that have successfully positioned themselves as green leaders or that have marketed everything from cars to cosmetics using environmental friendliness as a selling point. There are many other companies that have prospered more quietly, reaping the financial savings of new-found efficiencies and boasting only internally.

Despite many market researchers' and activists' long-held predictions that a wave of green consumers would align their purchases with their environmental concerns and values, the green economy has remained challenging and elusive for most companies. This is a lost opportunity for companies and consumers alike. The pipeline of green products and services is growing and will soon approach critical mass in some categories as new materials and technologies become viable and as entrepreneurs and large companies alike harness environmental thinking as a platform for innovative products, services, and business models. Green business is rapidly shifting from a movement to a market and from the margins to the mainstream.

The market potential for this burgeoning green economy is enormous, sufficiently so that it is drawing the attention of some very big players: retailers such as Wal-Mart and Home Depot, consumer product companies such as Clorox and Procter & Gamble, the major automobile makers, energy companies, homebuilders, banks, computer companies, and more. And thousands of smaller firms are positioning themselves and their products and services to address what they perceive as a growing market interest. Hollywood, music moguls, and politicians are helping to fan the flames. And the power of online social networking is poised to help bring this gumbo of voices and interests to a heady boil.

So, do consumers really care? They do! But there's a gulf between green *concern* and green *consumerism*. Bridging that gulf requires a deeper understanding of consumers' interests and motivations and the barriers that keep them from "shopping their talk."

# Chapter 7

# Green in Spite of Ourselves

One irony of the green economy is that over the past two decades, while consumers have expressed both an ambivalence toward changing their shopping habits and cynicism about companies' sincerity in being more environmentally responsible, the products we've been buying have gotten greener, often unbeknownst to the public. In many cases these environmentally improved products make no green claims at all.

The reason: Companies in nearly every sector are continually improving their efficiency, engineering waste, inefficiency, and toxicity out of their manufacturing and distribution processes. Many companies have learned how to deliver products and their functionality using far fewer resources; a few have upended their business models in the name of resource efficiency and enhanced productivity. They do these things partly because of the reduced environmental impact but largely because they make good business sense.

Companies that pollute are inefficient. Simply put, waste and emissions represent things that a company bought but which had no direct value to the customer and for which a company may have had to pay to get rid of. In other words, it's lost profit. Thus it's not surprising that in an age of globalization, in which companies are competing to be the hyperefficient, low-cost provider of goods and services, one by-product would be a reduction in their emissions and waste.

Consider five somewhat random of examples of what companies have done:

- Anheuser-Busch developed an aluminum can that is 33 percent lighter. This reduced use of aluminum, combined with an overall recycling plan, saves the company $200 million a year.
- Thanks to a smaller box used for about half the phones sold by Nokia during 2006–2007, the company saved $150 million in packaging and transportation costs related to packaging. The packaging is also made of 100 percent recycled paper.
- Over the past decade, Procter & Gamble, the giant consumer products company, has reduced the weight of its Pampers disposable diapers by about 40 percent and their packaging by 80 percent while improving their performance (measured in terms of their ability to retain moisture and reducing diaper rash) along the way. Meanwhile, Pampers has become P&G's largest brand with more than $7 billion a year in sales.
- General Motors has made a concerted effort to eliminate manufacturing waste in its assembly plants. In the mid–1990s, it set out to reduce or eliminate the 86 pounds of packaging waste that resulted from building the average car, managing to reduce it to a pound or less in some facilities. Eight of its North American assembly plants and 14 plants globally send no waste to landfills.
- McDonald's eliminated the embossed golden arches on its napkins, making them 24 percent thinner. That freed up shipping space by the equivalent of roughly 100 tractor-trailers a year.

What's spurring these efficiency efforts? The motivations invariably include cost savings, reduced liabilities, improved community relations, and enhanced corporate image—all valuable commodities for companies. Yet none of these efforts can be found on a product label, brochure, hang tag, or advertisement. Which makes good sense. Should Anheuser-Busch's profitable aluminum-saving effort result in an eco-label on cans of Busch and Bud? Does GM's zero-waste factories yield a greener Yukon SUV? Should Big Macs be included on a list of environmentally preferable products because of less-wasteful napkins?

In all cases, of course, the answer is "probably not." And yet most of these companies' efforts—which represent only a tiny fraction of similar waste-reduction and efficiency-enhancing measures I've heard about over the past 20 years—arguably yield significant environmental benefits, possibly far more than some of the green-labeled trash bags, cleaning products, and recycled paper goods hyped as being better for the planet.

Here are a few more interesting facts about big companies, current as of early 2008:

- Wal-Mart and Nike are the world's largest buyers of organic cotton.
- General Motors is the world's largest user of landfill gas to generate electricity.
- Intel and Pepsico are the two largest corporate buyers of renewable energy.
- Starbucks is one of the world's largest buyers of fair-trade coffee.
- Home Depot is the largest buyer in the United States of wood certified by the Forest Stewardship Council to be sustainably harvested.
- McDonald's is one of the largest buyers of recycled products, committing to spending at least $100 million a year on recycled products and materials.

Again, none of these facts is meant to suggest that the companies named are "green" or even "good." In most cases, the achievement in question represents a token percentage—of, say, GM's energy use or Starbuck's overall coffee purchases. But it is an achievement nonetheless—one that no doubt each of these companies would love to trumpet, if only it believed it could do so without risking a backlash from consumers or activists complaining that it isn't good enough. And it probably isn't, as impressive and surprising as some of these achievements may be.

All this adds complexity for consumers. Should an eco-conscious shopper consider individual products, or can he or she have more impact by seeking out companies with exemplary environmental records, even though not all these companies' products may be seen as green? Is there even any way to determine the greenest companies? Who should decide, and on what basis?

Companies aren't necessarily waiting for consumers or activists to figure this out. They're forging ahead, regardless of whether their efforts receive the attention they're due.

Before you forge ahead, though, it's helpful to have a consumer's-eye view of the green economy—the diversity of definitions, world views, and perspectives on the environment—and the opportunities and challenges for companies looking to be seen as green leaders.

# PART 2

# WHAT DOES IT MEAN TO BE GREEN?

If you've spent any time tracking the green marketplace, there's a reasonable chance that you've emerged with your head spinning. I can't promise that what follows won't have the same impact.

The confusion stems from more than just the dozens of polls and surveys each year that show some significant portion of consumers interested in, if not eager to buy, greener products and services. It's also the segmentations—the various ways marketers divvy up the populace into distinct groups that behave in the same way or have similar attributes or attitudes. And then there's the spin—the way marketers seize on these data as a way to promote their products or to justify their marketing strategies.

Suffice to say that these studies' data are better suited for posing questions than for answering them.

One problem with much of the green marketing research is that its real value comes from drilling down into the data. The top-level findings portrayed in press releases and marketing brochures are titillating to a point but aren't very helpful. Many companies don't bother to take the deeper look that will help them to understand the nuances of the green marketplace. And many of the surveys don't even have much depth—they're produced primarily to generate headlines and thus favorable publicity for the company or cause promoting it. ("Seven of Ten Americans Favor Nuclear Energy," according to a 2006 poll conducted by . . . the Nuclear Energy Institute. I'm not making this up.)

But there's a bigger problem that most of these surveys don't bring to light: *Under what conditions are consumers willing to make a greener purchase?* Few marketers ask this, yet the answers they'd likely get would be significant. "Yes," consumers would respond, "I'd happily pick the greener product—*if* it comes from a brand I know and trust, *if* I can buy it where I currently shop, *if* it is at least as good as the product I'm currently buying, *if* it doesn't require me to change habits, *if* it doesn't cost more, and ideally, *if* it has some other additional benefit beyond being green—that it lasts longer, looks better, saves money, or will be perceived by others as cool."

That's a lot of *ifs.* Simply put, consumers want green without compromise or sacrifice, but with tangible benefits for themselves and the world.

This is a high bar—so high, in fact, that not many products can clear it. Contrast these criteria with the assertions of many of the self-proclaimed green products, especially in the early 1990s, the early years of the green marketplace. For example, some of the early household cleaning products positioned as green came from small companies with unknown brands and poor distribution; in many cases, you had to send away to such places as Burlington, Vermont (Seventh Generation), or Ukiah, California (Real Goods), to buy them. The products often required new and awkward habits—for example, pouring a small vial of concentrate into a used cleaning bottle and then adding water to reconstitute it—and sometimes required you to apply them in different ways, perhaps applying a bit more elbow grease. The products cost more and smelled funny. Oh, right—and many of them didn't work well.

Things are changing. There is a growing number of green products from larger, more mainstream companies—products that have been field-tested by consumers, focus-grouped by marketers, analyzed by scientists, scrutinized by environmentalists, and widely distributed through national chains. In some cases, not only are they comparable to the category brand leaders, but they *are* also the brand leaders.

Ultimately, the question of green market research comes down to some fundamental questions: Do any of these surveys reflect consumers' actual shopping aspirations and habits? Or do they reflect how consumers like to think of themselves—as caring, compassionate, and conscientious shoppers—regardless of whether those attitudes are reflected in actual purchases?

The answer is likely a little of each. And therein lies the challenge for companies: How do you make sense of a world in which green hopes far outweigh green habits? Should your strategy focus on what consumers say they are willing to do, in the hopes that you can help them to realize that potential, or should you focus on what they've proven they can do?

And what of the other players—employees, customers, suppliers, the media, shareholders, activists, and all the rest? How much should you cater to their disparate definitions of *green* and their expectations of your company's environmental performance? Do you focus on what looks good to outsiders or on what really matters in terms of your company's impacts and potential to create value? Do you cater to short-term expectations or dig in for the long term, even if you take some financial hits along the way?

In short, should you lead the market or follow it?

# Chapter 8

# The Many Shades of Green Consumers

I t's one thing to conduct a poll of consumers about their environmental attitudes and actions. It's another to categorize them into meaningful groupings that describe and predict their behavior and predilections when shopping for anything from televisions to tomatoes. Toward this end, something called *market segmentation* has become the go-to tool for a wide range of companies.

Market segmentation was devised more than 40 years ago by Daniel Yankelovich, the pioneering public opinion analyst and social scientist. In 1964, he introduced in the pages of *Harvard Business Review* the idea that classifying consumers according to criteria other than age, residence, income, and other conventional demographic factors could help companies to determine which products to develop and how best to market them. At the time, Yankelovich asserted that "nondemographic traits such as values, tastes, and preferences were more likely to influence consumers' purchases than their demographic traits were."

In 1978, a group at Stanford Research Institute took this notion to the next level, introducing Values and Lifestyles (VALS), a commercial marketing tool that classified individuals according to nine psychological types as a means for predicting their behavior. It looked at purchasing history, product loyalty, and a propensity to trade up, among other things, all of which are informed by attitudes and values that lead consumers to view particular offerings differently. On the heels of the popularity of VALS, other companies chimed in with their own offerings, such as Claritas (now owned by the Nielsen Company, of TV ratings fame), whose Prizm marketing tool divides consumers into no fewer than 66 segments reflecting urbanization and socioeconomic rank as well as lifestyle stage—young families with kids, affluent singles, financially constrained families, empty nesters, retired couples, singles, and so forth. Today, an online search easily turns up dozens of firms offering some kind of segmentation service or tools.

Market segmentation collided with the green world in 1990 when Roper Starch, now GfK Roper Consulting, introduced Green Gauge, a five-part segmentation of the environmental marketplace based on in-home interviews with 2,000 or so Americans. At the time, the dawn of the green consumer movement, it was a welcomed and much-needed tool, opening marketers' eyes to the now commonsense notion that there are many shades of green consumers. How much Green Gauge truly helped companies to shape and assess their environmental strategies is unknown because those early days of green marketing were largely ineffective. At minimum, it underscored that Americans had different interests and motivations when it came to viewing their purchases and their lifestyles through a green lens.

In Roper's parlance, the five segments of the U.S. population are:

- *True-Blue Greens*—the most environmentally active segment of society and the true environmental activists and leaders
- *Greenback Greens*—those most willing to express their commitment by a willingness to pay higher prices for green products
- *Sprouts*—fence-sitters who have embraced environmentalism more slowly

- *Grousers*—those uninvolved or disinterested in environmental issues, who feel the issues are too big for them to solve
- *Basic Browns*—the least engaged group, those who believe that environmental indifference is mainstream

In 2005, Roper rechristened the last group as *Apathetics*, although the basic definition of the segment didn't change.

Green Gauge's findings didn't change much over the years—a comparison of the data between 1990 and 2005 shows that there was relatively little change in the percentages ascribed to each of the five segments. That is, until 2007. That was the year Roper changed its methodology, switching from face-to-face to online interviews. A funny thing happened: Consumers got greener. A lot greener. Figure 8–1 illustrates the changes that happened in the two years between 2005 and 2007.

Why did the number of the greenest consumers—the True-Blue Greens and the Greenback Greens—double in just two years, from

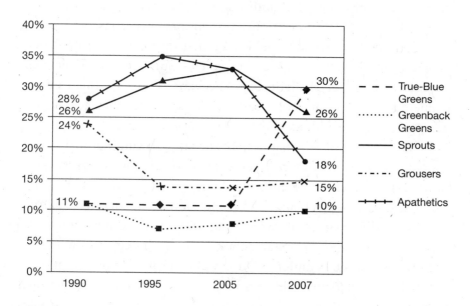

**Figure 8-1** Roper's Green Gauge since 1990. Note the dramatic change in 2007 when Roper changed from phone to online "interviews."

about 20 percent to 40 percent? Was it due to a jump in green consciousness, perhaps born of increased government and media attention to climate change, not to mention the popularity of the Oscar-winning documentary *An Inconvenient Truth*? Or were respondents, free of the constraints of confronting an in-person interviewer, suddenly more honest—or bigger liars?

It's hard to tell. Even Kathy Sheehan, senior vice president with Roper, who oversaw the 2007 research, isn't sure. She points out that the differences between in-person and online interviews are minimal for some types of questions and more dramatic for others. The biggest difference, she says, shows up with certain behavioral questions. For example, asking someone about his or her alcohol consumption might yield a more honest answer online, where one needn't face the scrutiny of another human being. But the anonymity cuts both ways, allowing some respondents to try on the persona that fits their aspirations or self-image. Researchers call it the *halo effect,* in which survey respondents shade their answers to reflect how they'd like to be perceived—by both themselves and others. In most cases, this means that they appear more conscientious, responsible, generous, and caring than their actual behavior would suggest. In the case of environmentally responsible habits, logic and experience suggest that people paint themselves in a greener light. Says Sheehan: "We know there's a disconnect between what people say they do and what they actually do. They give what they think is the right response."

What's the point? It's that despite the fast-growing number of surveys and research about the mind-sets and lifestyles of green consumers, there remain far more questions than answers. For all the clever segmentation schemes and names, few companies have a good portrait of the environmental attitudes of their customers or a sensible roadmap of how to create a market-facing strategy that works.

Roper is just the beginning. During 2007–2008, a number of companies have put forth their own research studies, each with its own market segmentations. This doesn't include countless other studies done specifically for major companies, such as Wal-Mart, Procter &

Gamble, Clorox, and others that have commissioned, and closely guard, segmentation research on their customers and markets.

One of the veteran market research firms is the Seattle-based Hartman Group, which has been tracking consumer attitudes, mostly related to food and organics, since the 1980s. In 2007, Hartman published, "The Hartman Report on Sustainability: Understanding the Consumer Perspective," which looked at "how consumers feel about a world struggling to live in balance today for the benefit of future generations." It parsed the consumer landscape this way, offering sample quotes that epitomize each group's mind-set:

- *Radical engagement*—"If people do not band together and employ radical means to overcome major problems, our future is bleak" (36 percent).
- *Sustained optimism*—"If we rely on rational intelligence and science, we can overcome major problems and secure a hopeful future" (27 percent).
- *Divine faith*—"If we leave things in God's hands, everything will turn out as it should" (20 percent).
- *Cynical pessimism*—"Save the planet? Who are we kidding? We can't even take care of ourselves" (9 percent).
- *Pragmatic acceptance*—"I don't worry about the major problems facing the world because they are beyond my control" (8 percent).

Another market segmenter is the branding firm Landor & Associates. In 2006, it released a study showing that 58 percent of the U.S. population considered themselves "Not Green Interested" (they don't care about environmentally friendly practices, including recycling, corporate social responsibility, or natural and/or organic ingredients), 25 percent were "Green Interested" (concerned about the environment but not active in its defense), and the remaining 17 percent were "Green Motivated" (feel it's very important for a company to be green and base purchase decisions on whether or not a brand reflects "green behavior" in its packaging, ingredients, and corporate actions).

In 2007, Landor released another segmentation, the ImagePower Green Brands 2.0 survey, conducted with the market research and consulting firm Penn, Schoen & Berland Associates and the public relations firm Cohn & Wolfe. It divvied the green landscape into "Bright Greens" (the most engaged but also the most skeptical, likely to demand environmental action on the part of companies—34 percent), "Green Motivated" (likely to accept corporate green programs at face value and as a step in the right direction—10 percent), "Green Hypocrites" (like to talk about green but don't want to go even slightly out of their way for it—26 percent), and finally, the unengaged "Green Ignorants" (19 percent) and "Dull Greens" (11 percent).

And then there's the segmentation from Yankelovich, the firm founded by the man who started it all. Its 2007 study, entitled, "Going Green," offered its own segmentation, including "Greenthusiasts" (13 percent of the U.S. population, or more than 30 million consumers), "Green speaks" (15 percent), "Greensteps" (25 percent), "Greenbits" (19 percent)—and the largest group, "Greenless" (29 percent). As with the other segmentation models, there is a rich lode of data and psychographics about each.

Yankelovich's segmentations are based both on attitudes and actual behaviors, which sets them apart from most others, which are based only on attitudes. This is where things get interesting. According to the research, green behaviors and attitudes often take divergent paths, so green attitudes don't always predict green behavior, and green behaviors often occur without accompanying attitudes. Example: Greenbits consumers say that they are more inclined to pay more than Greenspeaks consumers for green products, but their behavior doesn't sync up—they buy these products less frequently than the Greenspeaks.

Making all of this even more challenging is something Yankelovich calls the "Mushiness Index," a device developed by Daniel Yankelovich himself more than a quarter century ago. It measures the firmness of opinion on a topic—the degree to which consumers are comfortable and sure about how they think.

When it comes to the environment, opinions are pretty mushy, Yankelovich found. "The vast majority of people don't have very well-articulated views of the environment," Walker Smith, president of Yankelovich, told me. "They can answer an overnight public opinion poll. But that's not an answer they can necessarily talk about in-depth or understand the costs and consequences about those things. Even something like global warming, where there's been a lot of talk, the distribution of opinion is not very firm."

The problem, explains Smith, is that green marketing realities fly in the face of conventional marketing wisdom. He quotes Ted Levitt: "People don't buy products. They buy solutions to problems," Levitt, a marketing guru at Harvard Business School, famously put it in the mid–1970s. However, since most consumers don't see the environment as a problem, green marketers must take an extra step, helping them not just to understand the problem but also to actually care about it. For example, Smith points out that if you're trying to change the behaviors of Greenless or Greenbits consumers, increasing their knowledge has nothing to do with it. "It is strictly a matter of making it personally relevant," he says. "These are the groups that are most likely to think that the media are making things seem worse than they really are."

Some of Yankelovich's findings are sobering. For example, 37 percent of consumers feel "highly concerned" about environmental issues, but only 25 percent feel highly knowledgeable about environmental issues. And only about one in five feels that he or she can make a difference when it comes to the environment.

Perhaps the mother lode of market research comes from the market space called LOHAS, an acronym for Lifestyles of Health and Sustainability, which covers a broad swath of commerce, including alternative health care, wellness, fitness, meditation, renewable energy, alternative-fueled vehicles, green household products, natural fiber clothing, eco-tourism, green building, socially responsible investing, organic and natural foods, vitamins and supplements, and more. According to the lohas.com Web site: "The consumers attracted to this market have been collectively referred to as Cultural Creatives and represent a sizable group in this country. Approximately 16 percent of the adults in the United States, or 35 million people, are currently considered LOHAS consumers." The site goes on to explain that research by the Natural Marketing Institute conservatively estimated the LOHAS market in the United States at $209 billion "and growing."

Cultural Creatives, says sociologist Paul Ray, who coined the term, are described as individuals on the cutting edge of social change. As Ray explains: "They have a different set of values than the subcultures that have dominated America's past. They are interested in new kinds of products and services, and often respond to marketing and advertising in unexpected ways. They represent valuable new market opportunities if their needs can be met and addressed."

Cultural Creatives "are the careful, well-informed shoppers who don't buy on impulse," Ray counsels marketers. "They'll begin word-of-mouth campaigns, both positive and negative, about your products. . . . Their values and lifestyles are crucially important to them when making buying decisions on big-ticket items, such as cars, houses, and home furnishings."

"In essence," he concludes, "for the Cultural Creative, it's not about he or she who dies with the most toys wins—it's about living a meaningful life."

The term *LOHAS* dates to the mid–1990s, emerging from the natural products industry, which was looking at the connections among consumers interested in these various products and services. What were the commonalities? How could each of these markets address the larger market more efficiently? In LOHAS, marketers of a disparate group of products and services targeting a similar audience could pool knowledge and resources. Today, there's a LOHAS magazine and an annual conference that is equal parts entertaining and enlightening. Buff and nubile wellness gurus mix with three-piece-suited marketing managers from Ford or Dell, attending seminars with dashiki-clad and tee-shirted entrepreneurs proffering everything from energy bars to renewable energy.

The Natural Marketing Institute (NMI), the leading LOHAS research firm, segments the marketplace like this:

- *LOHAS* (16 percent of the U.S. marketplace) are very progressive on environment and society, looking for ways to do more. They expect companies to act responsibly and are less concerned about price. The reputations of companies affect their brand choices; these people are likely to help spread the word about companies they consider good or bad.

- *Naturalites* (25 percent) are concerned primarily about their personal health and wellness and therefore use many natural products. They are less sure about what they can do to protect the environment, although they believe that companies should be environmental stewards; these consumers are likely to be loyal to companies they believe are doing the right thing.

- *Conventionals* (23 percent) are practical and like to see the results of what they do, so they are likely to recycle and conserve energy. They understand that it may make sense sometimes to pay more for things that are energy- and water-efficient because they can reduce their utility bills in the long run. They want companies to be good environmental stewards but aren't generally willing to change brands to reward or punish good or bad companies.

- *Drifters* (23 percent) aren't highly concerned about the environment, believing that problems will somehow be fixed in time. When they do care about the environment, it's when things affect them directly. And while they don't necessarily buy a lot of green products, they understand that environmental concern is trendy, so they may like to be "seen" in Whole Foods Market or other places associated with environmental consciousness.

- *Unconcerned* (23 percent) have other priorities. They're not sure what green products are available and aren't interested in finding out. They buy products on price, value, quality, and convenience and pay little regard to what companies do.

The first of these segments, the LOHAS consumers, says NMI, are where the action is. They are forward-thinkers and major influencers in trends. These are the early adopters, the ones most likely to cotton to healthful or environmentally conscious foods, fashions, cars, cosmetics, and other products. But they're not necessarily a stereotypically affluent, Anglo group, says Steve French, NMI's president. Moreover, he says, they're not necessarily even that materialistic. "For a true LOHAS consumer, the notion of buying a hybrid car wouldn't automatically make sense," he says. "A true LOHAS consumer would say, 'I will live in the city because it reduces my footprint, and I will take public transportation, end of discussion.'"

Despite their countercultural tendencies, this is hardly a radical segment of the citizenry. The 2006 LOHAS Consumer Trends Database asked U.S. consumers to rank 50 companies according to their sustainability efforts and environmental impact. The top 10 companies named were Microsoft, Whole Foods, Kellogg's, McDonald's, Home Depot, Disney, United Parcel Service, Coca-Cola, Starbucks, and PepsiCo. Not exactly your basic Woodstock reunion.

Still, the LOHAS lens of the marketplace makes sense. Says French: "I can tell you from experience that it works out from a strategy perspective, which is what we're helping clients do. I can tell you that it works in small start-up companies and it works in Fortune Ten companies. I can tell you it works across a range of industries, from green buildings to transportation to consumer package goods to renewables." French's confidence is bolstered by the growing number of companies using LOHAS data and the growing awareness of LOHAS around the world, especially in Asia. In Japan, for example, there are LOHAS stores. A 2005 study found that 22 percent of the Japanese population over the age of 15 recognized the word. There's a LOHAS Business Alliance in Japan and several books on the topic. Suffice to say, LOHAS is trendy in Japan. It's also finding currency in Taiwan, Singapore, and South Korea, as well as in Australia and New Zealand. In Australia, LOHAS is a $12 billion-a-year market, according to the Mobium Group's 2007 "Living LOHAS" report. Singapore's tourism board markets the country to its Asian visitors as the LOHAS city, a reference to its spas, eateries, and recreation attractions. LOHAS may have lost something in the translation, referring more to the good life than to the green one.

So what should we make of all this segmentation name-calling? Is it really helping brand managers fine-tune their products, packaging, marketing messages, and all the other complexities of bringing products to market? Hard to say. What these studies do make clear is that there's a desperate need to smarten up the marketplace. Beyond a relatively small segment of LOHAS and other citizens who are more apt to be tuned into current affairs and environmental information—consider that roughly 82 percent of the U.S. population has neither read Al Gore's book nor seen his movie—most consumers are all but clueless about how to live a green lifestyle.

And this lack of awareness affects companies. Consider these two conclusions of the 2006 Landor study:

- "Consumers may be interested in green, but can't identify it. Sixty-six percent of the American population cannot identify the steps a company can take to make itself more green."
- "While two out of three consumers cannot name a brand they consider to be green, there are differences between perception and reality on what companies are green."

Confused? I promised you would be. With all we seem to know about consumers' environmental attitudes, you'd think that we'd be doing a better job of engaging, educating, and inspiring them to make good, green choices in their lives. As it is, companies fall short in educating the marketplace into which they are trying to sell. Thanks in large part to the sweeping and overly enthusiastic conclusions of the survey data cited earlier, they wrongly assume that the market is primed and ready for their company and its green offerings. In reality, both anecdotal and empirical research shows that this isn't the case. Consumers need more than inspiration: They need information and, more important, context to fully understand and appreciate how choosing a greener product will benefit them and their larger world.

The bottom line is that there is no one-size-fits-all marketing strategy when it comes to green. This may seem like common sense, but such wisdom seems to elude most marketers, who still insist on pushing out marketing efforts that are variously too vague, too technical, or way too—as Yankelovich puts it—mushy.

For the record, here's my own unscientific market segmentation, based on nothing but intuition, common sense, and 20 years of observing the green marketplace. Like the other segmenters, I divide the world into five kinds of green consumers:

- *Committed*—knows what to do and does it often
- *Conflicted*—knows what to do but often doesn't bother
- *Concerned*—wants to know what to do but doesn't yet
- *Confused*—doesn't know what to do or how to make a difference
- *Cynical*—doesn't know and doesn't care

Of course, any one of us, depending on the day, our mood, and what we're buying, can be any one of these five consumers or even a little bit of each.

# Chapter 9

# "I'm Concerned About the Environment"

Some of the communications challenges companies face in the environmental arena are simultaneously simple and complex. For example, most surveys gauging consumers' attitudes on the environment reveal a high level of interest—typically eight in ten people state that they are concerned about the health of the planet. But what, exactly, does this mean?

A lot of different things, it turns out.

In the mid–1990s, Robert D. Shelton, a leading consultant on corporate strategy and innovation, attempted to parse the seemingly simple sentiment, "I'm concerned about the environment." At the time, Shelton was researching the disconnect inside most companies between the environmental staff and the business staff—the fact that the former tended to have more in common, culturally speaking, with the regulatory crowd than with their business brethren, and the missed business opportunities that resulted from the lack of a common language and culture inside companies on environmental issues. This resulted in companies' inability to effectively communicate on environmental matters to their employees, customers, and stakeholders.

As part of this research, Shelton led a survey of about 900 Californians to gauge the level and nature of their environmental concern. The survey was conducted in seven counties that covered a variety of geographies and economies in English, Spanish, and Chinese. He found, much as other surveys had, that people overwhelmingly were concerned about the environment—upwards of 90 percent. But what that actually meant differed widely, depending on where and how people lived.

For one group of people, saying "I'm concerned about the environment" referred to big global issues: climate change, species loss, the hole in the ozone layer, the loss of tropical rainforests, and the like.

For a second group, the sentiment referred to more local, quality-of-life issues: air and water quality, suburban sprawl, and the loss of green space surrounding their neighborhoods.

For a third group, environmental concern focused on the loss of open space and wilderness, threatening their ability to hunt, fish, swim, hike, and canoe.

And for a fourth group, living in the inner city, concern about "the environment" referred primarily to crime, litter, noise, graffiti, and asthma.

"Where you stand on the environment depends on where you sit," Shelton told me. "Geographic and cultural aspects have a significant effect on what people consider important environmental issues. Assuming that environment protection and environmental management issues are the same for everybody can lead to problems in defining priorities for action, allocating resources, and having a meaningful discussion."

Of course, these four worldviews are not mutually exclusive. A well-heeled suburbanite and a less-well-off urbanite are equally likely to have concerns about global, regional, outdoor, or inner-city environmental issues. Moreover, Shelton's four dimensions of environmental concern probably apply only to those in relatively well-off countries. Those living in developing economies, as well as indigenous populations in developed countries, likely have still other definitions of what it means to be concerned about the environment.

Talking about "the environment" turns out to be anything but simple. Focused, more nuanced messages and communication styles are needed to ensure that your company's environmental strategy and messages aren't a one-size-fits-all affair and that your concern about the environment matches that of your employees, customers, and other interested parties.

# Chapter 10

# WITTs, YOYOs, and Why Consumers Don't Go Green

It's hard to understand why environmental groups remain powerful. After nearly 40 years since the birth of the modern environmental movement, the major environmental nonprofits cumulatively engage only a relatively small slice of the population—roughly 1 percent of Americans, for example, belong to environmental groups. Given the potential impact of environmental challenges—on our bodies, our families, our communities, our businesses, and our planet—this seems an abysmally small number.

It's no wonder, then, that year in and year out, the environment ranks near the bottom of issues about which people are concerned. And it explains why environmentally progressive political candidates don't run on those issues—and why conservative politicians, as a rule, can run roughshod over the planet with impunity.

A group called ecoAmerica—"the first environmental nonprofit with a core expertise in consumer marketing," it proclaims—is trying to change all this. Armed with a half-million dollars in market research and out-of-the-box—for "enviros," at least—thinking, the group has been attempting to engage "environmentally agnostic" consumers to support green causes "as a personal and public policy priority."

In 2006 and again in 2008, ecoAmerica and SRI Consulting conducted a 240-item mail survey that focused on measuring citizens' attitudes about the environment—how they value it, how they think it should be protected, the role they are willing to play, and related questions. It used the aforementioned Values and Lifestyles (VALS) classification system to categorize them. The purpose of the survey was to help environmental organizations better market themselves, but the findings are of value to any organization seeking to address individuals on environmental issues. Among the takeaways:

- *There is no common agreement on what environmental concern means or what to do about it.* To the extent that people are concerned, they are concerned about widely divergent environmental issues, from global problems to local ones to global ones. This diffusion of knowledge, perspectives, and interests makes it hard to gain credibility, let alone achieve consensus on most issues.

- *Libertarian values trump communal ones.* Jaren Bernstein of the Economic Policy Institute has described two competing mind-sets that affect politics and the environment: "We're In This Together," or WITT, and "You're On Your Own," or YOYO. (Linguist George Lakoff describes a similar divergence between the conservative right, which values self-reliance and self-responsibility, and the liberal left, which favors caring, empathy, cooperation, and growth.) The environmental community—and most green marketers—lean pretty strongly toward the communal, WITT side of the house, a position at odds with the political zeitgeist, at least as practiced for the past quarter century by the YOYO Republican Party. Clearly, there's a need for more "macho" (in Lakoff's terms) marketing—the notion of man as protector and of personal responsibility to protect families, communities, and the planet.

- *Environmental complexity is paralyzing.* In the early days of the modern environmental movement, ecological issues were pretty easy to understand: A company spewed waste into a river. You could see it and smell it, and the impact was local, immediate, and often acute. Today's biggest environmental problems—climate change, species extinction, depleting fisheries, etc.—are quite the opposite: They are hidden, global, long-term, and chronic. And many environmental challenges involve multiple steps: Droughts cause a species to migrate, causing a chain reaction resulting in the death of a forest, for example. Those cause-and-effect relationships are tough to grok, even for the knowledgeable. As a result, activists and marketers need to shun intellectual discussions and not expect people to make big behavioral changes today in order to gain environmental benefits tomorrow. It's important to demonstrate the "cost" of environmental problems to individuals, families, and communities and to show how problems can be addressed through simple, incremental changes in behavior—if, indeed, that is a realistic solution.
- *Pocketbook environmentalism is powerful.* Consumer behavior, not political behavior, may be an easier route to get buy-in and to change environmentally damaging behaviors. Unlike pure environmental appeals—which often bump up against everything from ignorance to apathy—there is immediate understanding and concern about things that affect our pocketbooks. Sad to say, any product, action, or behavior that potentially can save money is a far bigger motivator than one that can save the planet.

One potential pathway for messengers and marketers is to help consumers understand the hidden costs in products and services that are not environmentally friendly, such as incandescent light bulbs or inefficient cars. This is admittedly tough—it's harder to sell something by pointing out the shortcomings of the competition—but it could help to make environmental issues relevant and understandable.

ecoAmerica found that even the most environmentally sympathetic consumers have competing priorities, that environmentalism is hampered by antiscience and anti-intellectual attitudes, and that men and women have very different environmental concerns—three additional challenges for those trying to reach buyers with environmental messages.

The bottom line, says ecoAmerica: "We have an image problem." Environmentalists seem disconnected from most people. Indeed, many consumers view the environmental movement as traditional, dated, and somewhat out of touch with current society.

The obvious question, then: If consumers see environmentalists as out of touch, how will they view your green-minded company or product? Will it, too, be tarred with the same brush?

# Chapter 11

# The "Greenwasher" in All of Us

The growth of the green economy in recent years has brought about a renewed focus on "greenwashing"—"what corporations do when they try to make themselves look more environmentally friendly than they really are," in the words of the watchdog group Sourcewatch. The increased scrutiny isn't necessarily a bad thing. Companies should be held accountable for what they say and do. With little government oversight, we the people—whether your customers, your competitors, your employees, or even yourself—have assumed the role of green police, determining who's naughty and nice from a green-marketing perspective. With the help of blogs, wikis, social media, and good, old-fashioned protests and press releases, a disparate corps of activist groups and self-styled experts are exercising their constitutional right to have a point of view on the topic—and to broadcast it far and wide.

Is it a blessing or a curse? Probably a little of each. For starters, there's far from unanimity of opinion. Do BP's, or Wal-Mart's, or General Electric's green initiatives render them benevolent leaders or malevolent "greenwashers"? You can find passionate opinion claiming both.

While it's generally a good thing to maintain high standards for companies' seeking to claim environmental leadership, I can't help but ponder the hypocrisy of it all—how much more we expect of companies than of ourselves.

When I speak to business audiences, I sometimes conduct an informal poll to see how audience members behave in their personal lives—how many drive hybrids or carpool to work or are simply driving less, how many have installed solar panels or purchase green energy for their homes, how many use organic or low-toxic gardening products and techniques, how many seek out locally produced goods, how many have taken the basic measures at home—installing energy-efficient light bulbs and appliances, water-saving devices, insulation and weatherstripping, and the like.

Some audiences are more tentative than others in volunteering answers, but even the most enthusiastic groups tend to have only a handful of members who appear to be taking more than a few token actions. That is, few of us have gone very far out of our way to make changes that we all know are necessary to address today's environmental challenges.

This admittedly unscientific research has limited value, of course, except to raise the inevitable question: Why aren't most individuals willing to do what they're asking companies to do?

I'm guessing that in the few seconds it took for you to read the preceding sentence you've already formulated some kind of answer for your own household: "It's hard to do everything right," "It takes too much time and costs too much," "I want to do these things but never seem to get around to them," "My spouse/partner/friends don't share my interest in being environmentally responsible," "I'm not sure which products and companies are truly the good ones," or "I have doubts that if I do these things that it'll really make a difference."

Sound even a little familiar? Does this make you malevolent? Probably not, although reasonable minds will disagree.

One need modify the preceding statements only slightly to make them appropriate for companies. As I've found over the years of engaging CEOs and line employees of both large and small companies, they, too, find it hard to do everything right and sometimes to do anything at all. And while their intentions may be honorable, there always seem to be competing priorities. It may be that few of their competitors or trading partners are acting green, and being a pioneer can be lonely, not to mention setting oneself up as a target for all kinds of slings and arrows. And business people often wonder whether one little old business can really make a difference.

I'm not for a minute suggesting that companies be let off the hook. Companies—all of us—need to be held to high standards. But all of this begs a question that I've been asking audiences and discussing with hundreds of people over the past few years: What must a company do to be considered "green"? What is the minimum level of policies, programs, performance, and progress that a company must exhibit to be seen as green? How good does a company have to be to be considered "good"? How good must it be to even have permission from the marketplace to make green claims without being laughed at or worse?

I don't have an answer to these questions—none of us does, and that's a problem. As the PR machines of companies push out countless campaigns, products, announcements, and self-promotional consumer tips, we'll no doubt see growing charges of "greenwashing"—tales of companies that, despite their green-minded statements or claims, are far from perfect. As we watch and read these stories and, perhaps, proffer some inner expression of support—"Attaboy! Nail those bastards!"—it may well be worth committing a split second or two to self-reflection: "Am I really doing all that I can to address the environmental problems that concern me most?" "Do I profess one thing and do another?" "Do my friends think I'm greener than I really am?" "Am I holding others to a higher standard than myself?"

And in the process perhaps acknowledge that there is, indeed, a little "greenwasher" in all of us—even those of us with the best of intentions.

# Chapter 12

# Eco-Literacy and Our Nature-Deficit Disorder

It's axiomatic that the more people who truly understand something, the better able they'll be to create informed opinions and decisions. And in the case of environmental literacy, what we don't know truly could hurt us. This is why research on eco-literacy is so humbling.

Consider a 2005 report from the National Environmental Education Foundation (NEEF), a nonprofit chartered by the U.S. Congress to promote "environmental education in its many forms." The report, by NEEF's then-president, Kevin J. Coyle (now vice president for education at the National Wildlife Federation), represents an analysis of nearly a decade's worth of research on Americans' environmental literacy, conducted by NEEF in partnership with the Roper Public Affairs unit at GfK NOP, which also conducts the Green Gauge survey.

The bottom line, according to the report: "Most people accumulate a diverse and unconnected smattering of factoids, a few (sometimes incorrect) principles, numerous opinions, and very little real understanding. Research shows that most

Americans believe they know more about the environment than they actually do."

Suffice to say, this is a problem for any company seeking to address its customers, suppliers, employees, or the public at large on environmental issues.

According to Coyle's survey, some 45 million responders think that the ocean is a source of fresh water; 120 million citizens think that spray cans still contain ozone-depleting chlorofluorocarbons (CFCs), even though CFCs have been banned since 1978; another 120 million people think disposable diapers are the leading problem with landfills, when they actually represent about 1 percent of the problem; and 130 million people believe that hydropower is the top energy source, when it actually accounts for just 10 percent of the total.

There's more. Few people understand the leading causes of air and water pollution or how they should be addressed, says Coyle, adding that his years of research have found "a persistent pattern of environmental ignorance even among the most educated and influential members of society."

Coyle lays the blame in part on what family expert and author Richard Louv calls our "nature-deficit disorder"—unprecedented pattern changes in how young people relate to nature and the outdoors. "As kids become more 'wired' than ever before, they are drawn away from healthful, often soul-soothing, outdoor play," explains Coyle. "The age-old pattern of children spending hours roaming about and playing outside is becoming close to extinct due to a combination of electronics, cyberspace, and parental efforts to keep their children indoors and, in their minds, safer."

(In response to the nature-deficit disorder, U.S. Senator, Jack Reed, and Representative, Paul Sarbanes, introduced the No Child Left Inside Act of 2008—legislation to strengthen and expand environmental education in America's classrooms. The bill would, among other things, provide federal funding to states to train teachers in environmental education and to operate model environmental education programs. As of mid 2008, it was still pending.)

Coyle's and others' research has found that environmentally knowledgeable people are 10 percent more likely to save energy in the home or purchase environmentally safe products, 50 percent more likely to recycle or avoid using chemicals in yard care, 30 percent more likely to conserve water, and twice as likely to donate funds to conservation organizations.

Coyle promulgates an "environmental literacy index" that attempts to monetize the value of a better-informed, eco-literate society. Using an admitted back-of-the-envelope calculation of what an improved level of environmental knowledge might mean for savings in the national economy, he came up with the following examples:

- The U.S. Department of Energy estimates that home electricity use in America costs about $233 billion per year. Increased environmental knowledge that led to a 5 percent reduction in home electricity use would generate annual savings of $11.5 billion.
- Similarly, gasoline use accounts for $137 billion per year and a sizable percentage of our petroleum usage. A 5 percent savings in gasoline brought about through improved fuel efficiency and driving habits would save nearly $7 billion per year.
- A 5 percent reduction in domestic water use would save $14.2 billion and trillions of gallons of water.

Coyle found another $25 billion in savings from small businesses reducing overhead costs by 5 percent and $18 billion in savings resulting from a 2 percent drop in home and office hazard costs as the result of increased environmental knowledge—a grand total of $75.5 billion in direct savings to the public for just five outcomes.

Economists and others might find such calculations overly simplified, and sharper pencils would no doubt yield better data. Along the way, though, all of this leads to an inescapable conclusion: Even incremental improvements in the public's environmental literacy can lead to small changes by large populations that can have significant positive economic, environmental, and public health impacts. Put in business terms, the financial dividends for investments in increased public eco-literacy can be substantial.

The question, of course, is, Who's going to lead—and pay for—this eco-literacy crusade: Government? Companies? Schools? Activists? All these institutions have a unique role to play, and all could benefit from a better-informed populace.

What's the value of a more eco-literate populace to your company? How would your company benefit if your customers and potential customers were to become smarter about the environmental impacts of their lives—and started turning that knowledge into action? Would what you sell be seen as part of the problem or the solution?

# Chapter 13

# What's in It for Me?

Ted Levitt, the Harvard marketing professor whose name is often preceded by the word *guru,* famously said: "People don't want to buy a quarter-inch drill. They want a quarter-inch hole." Levitt's point is that people usually buy things because they have needs or desires that demand solutions or fulfillment. Rocky Mountain Institute cofounder Amory Lovins, one of the pioneers and innovators in energy efficiency and conservation, expressed the same sentiment: "People don't want heating fuel or coolant; people want cold beer and hot showers." That is, their interest is less in products than in the benefits those products provide.

When it comes to the environment, hardly anyone shops with a mind-set to "save the planet," despite what many marketing professionals seem to think. They want what everyone in developed economies want: comfort, security, reliability, aesthetics, affordability, status, and pleasure.

And yet, so many green-minded companies end up selling "quarter-inch drills." They'll explain

- Why the world needs their drill ("The polar bears are dying!" "We're running out of resources!")
- The benefits of their drill ("Uses less energy and emits fewer toxic emissions." "Recyclable, so it won't end up in landfills.")
- The drill's technical makeup ("Made of 100% plant- and mineral-based ingredients." "Uses 20 percent less energy than the competitor.")
- What the drill doesn't contain ("No petroleum-based products or artificial dyes or preservatives.")
- How it's better than competitors' drills ("The highest percentage of recycled material on the market." "Available wherever you buy organic foods.")
- The benefits to the planet if everyone bought their drill instead of the competitors' ("We'd reduce greenhouse gas emissions by the equivalent of taking 135,000 cars off the road." "We would save 11 million gallons of water, 23,000 acres of trees, and enough energy to power Toledo for a month.")

But little or nothing about the quarter-inch hole—about how this product will get the job done, whether the "job" is cleaning my house, transporting me from hither to yon, satisfying my hunger, or making me feel attractive and cool.

Much of environmental strategy and marketing seems disconnected from most people's lives. Indeed, research shows that many shoppers view the environmental movement as traditional, dated, and somewhat out of touch with current society.

This is ironic perhaps. Many environmentalists I know believe that they have a better understanding of the state of the world than do other people. And they might. But that's of little consequence. The millions of "Security Moms" and "NASCAR Dads" who haven't yet tuned into how climate change and fisheries loss might mess with their kids' future aren't about to be beaten into submission by the latest technical arguments or evidence. They're not about to make purchase decisions based on a maybe-someday rationale for stemming environmental problems. They want to know: *What's in it for me, today?*

So, big news: Most consumers may be shallow, misinformed, self-interested, and unsophisticated, but they're also our neighbors, colleagues, and relatives. And they're likely your clients, customers, or employees. If you want to move them toward greener behaviors and actions, you'll need to deal—carefully and creatively—with all the sobering reality of the green economy—that the overwhelming majority of shoppers in developing countries are, to put it mildly, self-absorbed. They want what they want—a safe and cleaner world, of course, but also a life filled with comfort and joy. No matter that the former may be directly linked to the latter. In the day-to-day struggles of work, family, finances, and all the rest, most people can't be bothered with the bigger picture—shifting social mores, political trends, changing family values, or the declining fate of the Earth. They're important, to be sure, but for most folks, *saving the planet* usually takes a back seat to *saving the day*.

Consumers find no irony in jumping into a sports-utility vehicle with underinflated tires and driving several miles out of their way to buy their favorite brand of recycled toilet paper. It eludes them that the environmental impacts of getting to and from the store might outweigh any of the green choices they can make up and down the aisles.

We want it all: inexpensive products made by companies that don't pollute and pay their workers well; luxury without guilt; safe, roomy, classy cars that don't use much gas; wind and solar power plants, as long as they're not nearby or in view; simple solutions to complex problems; and changes without changing.

Some of this is possible, technically speaking. We may yet reach the day when vehicles are powered by sunlight and oxygen, emitting nothing but air and water. We may clean up conditions in factories in the developing world—the ones that manufacture our dirt-cheap goods—without raising the prices of the things they produce. We may reinvent our manufacturing systems so that they use renewable resources and closed-loop systems, eliminating smokestacks, drainpipes, and dumpsters. We may even curb rampant consumption, somehow deciding that less is more and that the lavish lifestyles of a relative few are bad for us all.

Maybe. But the road to a greener, cleaner economy will be long and arduous, with roadblocks, speed bumps, and detours at every turn. It will be more evolutionary than revolutionary, and we may never reach the state referred to as *sustainability,* in which we are able to conduct our affairs and live the way we do for eternity while ensuring quality lives for others.

But we'll try, and smart companies will prosper in the process.

# PART 3

# How Good Is "Good Enough"?

Efficient markets demand norms, conventions, and standards, from generally accepted accounting principles, to your computer's USB plugs, to the red-yellow-green convention of our traffic signals. We rely on these things, usually unconsciously, to get us through the day.

In that light, the green marketplace is anything but efficient. There are few standards—implied or explicit—about what it means to be a green, sustainable, or environmentally responsible business, let alone how those monikers apply to individual products and services.

This is a big problem. Lacking definitions, anything can be deemed green—and just about anything, it seems, is, thanks to overzealous PR and marketing professionals eager to tap into the growing environmental consciousness. Oil companies, nuclear power plants, chemical companies, insurance companies, and manufacturers of everything from carpets to car parts have promoted themselves as environmentally responsible. And, perhaps, some are, relatively speaking. But there's no real way of knowing.

Because of the lack of standards, most companies don't know how to answer a seemingly simple question: "How good is 'good enough'?" It's a vexing issue that stymies many companies. Some of the more environmentally proactive firms are reluctant to talk publicly about their initiatives for fear that they are imperfect, likely inadequate, and could bring unwanted attention. After all, if your company isn't in the crosshairs of customers, activists, or inquiring reporters, why bother promoting your good, green actions? After all, once you start talking about what you're doing right, you risk unwittingly illuminating what you're not yet doing right and may even raise problems the public didn't know you had. For many companies, the result is paralysis—an inability to communicate their progress toward being environmental leaders or at least "good" companies. It also represents a lost opportunity to turn those efforts into competitive advantage and to communicate that to their customers and the world at large.

Some companies do the opposite: They promote small, relatively insignificant advances without regard for whether their efforts represent genuine improvements worth touting—that is, whether they truly are "good enough"—or just an attempt to "green up" an otherwise unremarkable company or product. In doing so, many of these firms set themselves up for criticism by activists or the media and cynicism on the part of current and would-be customers.

Is your company "good enough"? Of course it is. But is it really?

# Chapter 14

# The Lowdown on Labels

Since the early 1990s, a number of nonprofit and for-profit entities have tried to define what is and isn't environmentally responsible. The underlying assumption is that a universally accepted label would help to steer customers toward environmentally preferable products and companies.

What's needed is something akin to a Good Housekeeping Seal for the environment. The Good Housekeeping Seal, introduced in 1909, when there was little regulatory oversight of consumer products, represented an audacious marketing promise from its namesake magazine: If a product bearing the seal proved defective within two years, the magazine would replace it or refund the purchase price.

Ironically, the Good Housekeeping model wouldn't likely pass muster with most environmental activists in large part because of it's a pay-to-play proposition: To advertise your product in *Good Housekeeping* magazine, it must qualify for the seal, and to get the seal, a product must advertise in the magazine (and usually agree to buy a minimum number of ad pages). Still, the reference to the century-old Good Housekeeping Seal is apt because the seal bestows confidence on a product or company. For decades, the Good Housekeeping seal was the "gold standard" of quality, a universally accepted endorsement that a product would live up to its billing. This is exactly the kind of assurance needed in the green marketplace.

Could a green label do the same thing for our planetary home that Good Housekeeping's did for our personal homes? This has been the hope. But the quest for an environmental seal of approval has been long, arduous, and largely unsuccessful.

In 1989, a group of environmental activists and concerned individuals gathered at the Cosmos Club in Washington, DC, to discuss the notion of launching a U.S. green labeling program that mirrored those already underway in other countries, such as Germany's Blue Angel, Canada's Environmental Choice, Japan's and India's Ecomark, and the Nordic Swan used in Denmark, Finland, Iceland, Norway, and Sweden. The time was ripe. Earth Day 1990 was around the corner, and people were awakening to the planet's environmental challenges. The past decade had seen a string of media-fanned environmental moments that, collectively, galvanized activists, school kids, politicians, and others: the 1979 nuclear accident at Three Mile Island in Pennsylvania, which initiated a protracted decline in the public acceptance of nuclear power; the 1984 chemical disaster in Bhopal, India, in which a facility operated by Union Carbide leaked 40 tons of deadly methyl isocyanate gas, killing between 2,500 and 5,000 people; the *Mobro,* a barge made famous in 1987 for hauling the same load of trash from New York to Belize and back before a way was found to dispose of the garbage; and perhaps most famously, the 1989 Alaskan oil spill caused by the collision of the *Exxon Valdez* into Prince William Sound's Bligh Reef.

Suffice to say, millions of consumers, seeking solutions, were primed to find a way they could help—preferably a simple way that demanded little or no cost, time, or personal lifestyle changes. An eco-label separating the "good" products from the others seemed just the ticket.

The Cosmos Club event, which I attended, signified the launch of the nonprofit group Green Seal. The organization entered the world in June 1990 with great fanfare and a noble promise: an efficient means for identifying products that meet comprehensive standards established by an authoritative group of stakeholders representing industry, activism, and science. The goal was to create a trusted mark with the authority of a kosher, Underwriters Laboratory, or Good Housekeeping seal. Green Seal's credibility was buttressed by the fact that its leader was Denis Hayes, the impresario of the first Earth Day in 1970 and its high-profile successor in 1990. Hayes' board of directors included leading lights in the worlds of environment, consumer affairs, education, and religion.

Green Seal wasn't the only green seal. There was also Green Cross, created by Scientific Certification Systems (SCS), a California company that already had established itself certifying produce as being free of pesticide residues. SCS's Green Cross label (the name was later dropped after complaints by Green Cross International, the nonprofit organization founded in 1989 by former Soviet Union President Mikhail Gorbachev) had a similar but different methodology than Green Seal, the details of which are of interest only to technical types. One of the things that distinguished Green Cross from Green Seal was the former's for-profit status. At the time, the idea that a money-making business might rate other companies' products on environmental performance struck some hard-core activists as unseemly, if not unethical.

Green Cross had its adherents, namely, several supermarket chains that adopted the label as their internal standard of greenness, including Ralph's Grocery Company in southern California, Raley's in northern California, Fred Meyer, Inc., of Portland, Oregon, and ABCO Markets of Phoenix. The problem was that the big consumer packaged goods companies—Colgate-Palmolive, Kraft, Lever Brothers, Procter & Gamble, and the like—balked at both organizations' seals. They simply didn't want anyone else telling them how to design and market their products. And smaller firms were coming into the market with alternative products boasting self-certified green claims that weren't necessarily, well, kosher. Moreover, companies that were making bona fide green products often recoiled at certification's high price tag—upwards of $25,000 for a single product, with no guarantee that the product would even qualify.

Amid all this, marketing claims were flying willy-nilly, often raising more questions than answers. *Made from recycled material* (Is it 1 percent or 100 percent?). *Won't harm the ozone layer* (But does it contain other pollutants?). *Biodegradable* (Perhaps, but probably not for hundreds of years). *Recyclable* (Where, how easily, and what happens to it then?). *Nontoxic* (Perhaps when you use it, but what about when it is manufactured?). *Safe for the environment* (What on earth does this mean?).

Retailers got into the labeling game, too. In 1989, Canadian supermarket chain Loblaw's introduced a line of green-branded products called Nature's Choice that included claims about disposable foam plates, a dishwasher detergent, and a motor oil. In an unusual move, environmental groups received royalties on sales of the Loblaw's labeled products. Within the first few months, sales of the Nature's Choice line exceeded $5 million, more than double its projections.

And then there was Wal-Mart. In mid–1989, the company, at the time the number-three retailer in the United States, purchased full-page ads in the *Wall Street Journal* and *USA Today* to announce that it was challenging manufacturers and suppliers to seek "more merchandise and packaging that is better for the environment in its manufacturing, use, and disposal." It was a bold move, backed by an ambitious campaign to provide shelf labeling in the company's stores highlighting products deemed "better for the environment."

But the campaign was flawed to the point of being silly. For example, as I strolled the aisles of a Wal-Mart in Winchester, Virginia, in early 1990, I encountered a roll of Bounty paper towels—64 square feet of nonrecycled, chlorine-bleached paper packaged in plastic—sporting a "shelf talker" attesting to its environmental advantages. Specifically: the product's inner-core tubes were made with 100 percent recycled paper! I also found a plastic canister of Turtle Wax car polish, singled out by Wal-Mart because its container included the Society of the Plastics Industry resin recycling code—the number 5 placed inside a triangle. Never mind that number five plastic, polypropylene, was not recyclable. Yet another celebrated product was a package of polystyrene foam coffee cups, honored by Wal-Mart because the cups were made without ozone-depleting chlorofluoro-carbons (CFCs), despite the fact that CFCs were never used to make foam coffee cups and had been banned in the United States since 1978. It all would have been laughable if it wasn't so maddening.

When I contacted Wal-Mart that year to ask about these things, their spokesperson, Brenda Lockhart, wouldn't reveal how products were chosen for green labeling, calling the details "proprietary." The program, she told me, "is a very simple one in that we don't get caught up in the rules and regulations. We're caught up in the cause itself."

And so it went. The cure, in this case, seemed worse than the disease.

Where are we now? Things have improved a bit, but not much. Today, Scientific Certification Systems has abandoned its all-purpose eco-label in favor of auditing and certifying specific claims, such as nutrition and antioxidant content in food, pesticide-residue-free food, sustainably managed fisheries, flowers and potted plants produced through environmentally and socially responsible methods, organic food, and the amount of recycled, reclaimed, salvaged, and bio-based content in materials. And Green Seal continues to survive, if not thrive, in the marketplace. The group has promulgated standards for about 30 product categories from paints to paper products to pow-ered laundry bleach. All told, just over a thousand products have been certified, many of them intended for institutional buyers, such as cleaning services, users of commercial adhesives, and fleet vehicle maintenance. With the exception of household cleaners, however, where seven products have achieved the Green Seal logo (there are many other certified cleaners, but for institutional use), individual consumers would be hard-pressed to find a Green Seal logo in local supermarkets, hardware stores, department stores, or anyplace else.

There are scads of labels addressing individual attributes of a prod-uct. The Web site *www.ecolabeling.org* lists nearly 300 eco-labels from every corner of the world, from Austria to Zimbabwe. These single-attribute labels can be helpful, but they aren't without problems.

For example, the Forest Stewardship Council—an international standard bearer for sustainable forestry whose tree-with-a-checkmark logo adorns products for sale at big retailers, including Home Depot, Lowe's, and IKEA—admitted in 2007 that some companies using its label were destroying pristine forests, although it vowed to overhaul its rules.

Meanwhile, the quest for a universally accepted green standard continues. How would your company benefit from such a standard? Would it level the playing field or put you at a disadvantage? Would your products no longer be able to be sold in some parts of the world if a reasonably stringent standard existed, or would you be at a competitive advantage because your goods already far exceed any likely standard?

Increasingly, companies are "complying" with the toughest standards, even if they aren't required to legally. For example, many electronics companies are hewing to the European Union's Restriction of Hazardous Substances (RoHS) standard, which places tough limits of certain toxic chemicals in electrical and electronic equipment, for all products wherever they are sold. Other companies are complying with their home country's environmental regulations globally, even if they exceed local standards.

It makes sense. If a standard is good enough for the country where you're headquartered, it should be good enough for the country where you are, in essence, a guest.

# Chapter 15

# The Rise of Ratings

The lack of universal eco-labels has left a void that seems to be filled by just about any group with a list of companies, a checklist, and a Web site. You can find ratings, rankings, and top-ten lists of companies across a spectrum of sectors and subjects, from cars to computers to cosmetics. The public and the media love these quantitative and qualitative listings, especially anything that includes the words *best* and *worst* (or better yet, *green* and *greenwash*). Companies, of course, hate these lists, bemoaning the raters' cavalier methodologies and slipshod accounting—except, of course, those companies that rate highly, in which cases the methodology and accounting are just fine.

If you fear environmental ratings, you're in for a rough ride. The number and scope of ratings and rankings are sure to rise in the coming years, filling in for more comprehensive product and company ratings. As the environmentalists like to point out, when it comes to healing the planet, a little sunshine is often the best disinfectant.

To get a peek into the brave new world of ratings, consider Climate Counts, a nonprofit on whose board of directors I sit. Climate Counts was the brainchild of Gary Hirshberg, the idealistic and iconoclastic "CE-Yo" of Stonyfield Farm, the organic yogurt company that is majority-owned by the French food giant Danone. Hirshberg is a long-time activist who cofounded Stonyfield in 1983, after years promoting renewable energy. I first met Hirshberg a decade later, in 1993, when researching my book about corporate social responsibility, *Beyond the Bottom Line.* I recall being impressed at the time by his passion and commitment, but also by his humbleness and honesty. "I think whatever your definition is of social responsibility," he told me at the time, "if the message is, 'Look how great we are,' then you're missing the boat." It was a refreshing change from so many companies' arm-waving, self-congratulatory approaches to social responsibility, both then and now.

From the beginning, Hirshberg infused his yogurt company with a culture of activism, often flying in the face of conventional business wisdom. For example, Stonyfield pays some farmers almost twice as much as necessary to encourage them to engage in sustainable practices. The company does almost no advertising. In fact, it promotes other's causes on its packages, devoting precious "real estate" on yogurt lids to advance environmental causes. None of this has seemed to dampen sales or profitability. The company has enjoyed 27.4 percent compound annual growth since 1990, and its sales of more than $300 million make it the third biggest yogurt brand, after Yoplait and Dannon. Stonyfield's Profits for the Planet program has given 10 percent of company profits to organizations "that help protect and restore the environment." (Hirshberg got Danone to agree to maintain the program for at least 10 years after he leaves the company, whenever that is; at present, he has no plans to do so.) And he has funded his own activist campaigns.

Climate Counts is one of those campaigns, launched in 2007 to rate companies on their climate-change commitment and performance. It basically set out to answer the question, as Hirshberg put it, "Who's with us and who's agin' us on climate change?" Working with the consultancy GreenOrder, Climate Counts devised a 100-point score-card on more than 20 criteria in four categories: How well does the company measure its climate footprint? How much has the company done to reduce its greenhouse gas emissions? Does the company explicitly support (or express intent to block) progressive climate leg-islation? And how clearly and comprehensively does the company pub-licly disclose its climate-protection efforts? (You can view the entire scorecard at *www.climatecounts.org*.)

The Climate Counts methodology calls for a group of researchers to dig up as much publicly available information as they can to answer the scorecard questions for each rated company and then to submit the com-pleted scorecards to the respective companies, asking them to verify, cor-rect, or supplement the information as appropriate. So far, so good.

Problem was that the completed research—which was sent by reg-istered mail to the senior environmental executive at each company—often got lost, misrouted, or in some cases ignored. In other cases it was shuttled off to the communications or legal department, where it ended up, by design or circumstance, at the bottom of the heap (or, perhaps, in the recycling bin). For whatever reason, roughly half the 78 companies contacted initially never responded. While there was no correlation between ratings and response—some of the companies that didn't respond rated highly, and some that did respond fared poorly—there was hell to pay at many of the bottom-ranked companies. The day the ratings were released—and covered in the *New York Times,* *Wall Street Journal,* and *Fortune,* as well as on CNN and the major wire services—I received calls from environmental managers at two low-ranked companies offering tales of woe about calls from their superiors demanding explanations for the low ratings. One individual who called, from a global apparel company, said, "Well, it worked. You got my company's attention. What do I do now?" She proceeded to explain that the company was doing far more than it was talking about publicly, so it wasn't getting the credit it deserved. I explained that being humble was no longer an asset and that her company might con-sider being more public about its policies and progress. At last check, the company was working on it.

The fact is that many of the low-rated companies were doing a lot—they just didn't know it, and neither did anyone else. For example, it turned out that the apparel company already had a series of climate-related initiatives in place, from improving the energy efficiency of its Asian manufacturing facilities, to consolidating shipments to reduce emissions (and costs), to retrofitting its headquarters with more efficient lighting. There also were efforts to inventory the company's climate emissions across its supply chain, but it was still not complete.

If only this company knew what this company knew.

I've seen this a great deal. Many big companies are more environmentally proactive than anyone inside the organization even knows. There's often too little information sharing and awareness about initiatives taking place at disparate facilities or operating units or even at headquarters. Often, different parts of the company are inventing the same "wheel," simultaneously figuring out, say, how to increase recycling, reduce waste or emissions, or find a less-toxic substitute for some problematic ingredient.

The smartest companies don't just communicate well internally; they also go beyond that, staying one step ahead of their critics, rating themselves before others do. Some of these companies are devising sophisticated metrics that measure, and thus manage, the life-cycle impacts of their products: what's in them, where the materials come from, how and where they're manufactured (and under what conditions), how they're transported to market, and what happens to the products after they are used up or no longer of service.

In 2002, for example, Norm Thompson Outfitters, a Portland, Oregon–based mail-order company, set out to help its suppliers improve the environmental attributes of their products, an assortment of offerings, from clothing to furnishings to personal-care products. To do this, it created an innovative "toolkit" that allowed its own buyers to rank the environmental impact of finished products based on a simple scorecard methodology. The scorecard—invented by Brown & Wilmanns, a consultancy founded by two ex-Patagonia environmental managers—allowed Norm Thompson's suppliers to be accountable for their sustainability progress while maintaining flexibility about how they met the mail-order company's environmental goals.

The toolkit Brown & Wilmanns produced for Norm Thompson is a colorful and visually engaging document. It assigns a rating to dozens of materials and processes that make up the bulk of products sold by Norm Thompson. However, rather than conduct a full life-cycle analysis of all these materials and processes—a prohibitively expensive and time-consuming proposition—it created a simplified version that was nearly as accurate at a fraction of the cost.

Each page of the toolkit covers a topic that represents a significant component of Norm Thompson's purchasing decisions. Thus, for example, for an article of clothing, the toolkit highlights the impacts from obtaining the raw materials for the fiber (e.g., cotton growing, oil production), from manufacturing (e.g., dyeing, fabric scrap), from consumer use and maintenance (e.g., laundering, dry cleaning), and what happens at the end of the item's useful life (e.g., recyclability, disposal). Each option is listed based on whether it is a good (green light), adequate (yellow light), or poor (red light) choice for the environment. The toolkit then assigns a rating scale of +3 to −3 to each of the characteristics it chose to judge. Therefore, for example, in the section on polyester, a green light (+3 to +2 on the scorecard) is given to recycled polyester and to material made without the toxic chemical element antimony. "Common" polyester gets a yellow light (+1 to −1), whereas polyester made with chlorinated "carriers" in the dyeing operations is given a red light (−2 to −3). Accompanying explanations tell why a given material is good or bad.

The toolkit's methodology may not represent the "gold standard" of materials and product rating, but its results may be just as useful, in that it gives companies useful guideposts in an easy-to-understand manner, allowing them to make changes that most likely will yield the same results as more conventional life-cycle assessments, and to do so in a way that doesn't compromise product quality or performance. Over time, Norm Thompson was able to help suppliers move up the scale, substituting green-light materials for yellow and red. The company didn't reveal these ratings to its customers; they were an internal tool. And Mike Brown and his team subsequently used the methodology to develop rating tools for other companies.

Norm Thompson isn't alone. A growing number of others are developing scorecards, metrics, and other means of better understanding the impacts of what they do and sell and to make continual improvements, often reducing costs or improving products along the way.

Some companies have mandated that every new, revamped, or reformulated product go through this process. For example, Herman Miller, the Michigan-based furniture company, uses a scorecard system to rate every component in its products. The idea, says Scott Charon, who manages the company's Design for the Environment program, began with customers' growing questions about the environmental attributes of products. "We wanted to develop a tool to bring products to market that customers are asking for," he told me. "This is an area where we wanted to be a leader." Charon noted that some large customers are now putting environmental considerations ahead of cost.

Under the company's design protocol, each product is rated in three areas—disassembly, material chemistry, and recyclability. In each of these areas, designers assign a series of credits related to various design factors. Thus, if a product can be completely disassembled down to its individual components, it gets a "credit" of 100 percent. A component that cannot be disassembled easily, such as a glued assembly, receives a 0 percent rating. Similar ratings are given for "material chemistry," the human health and environmental factors associated with each product component. Every material contained in a product is rated on a green-yellow-red color scheme and assigned a corresponding credit, which is weighted based on the amount of that material in the product. The third rating is given each material based on its recyclability, along with the material's recycled or renewable content. Finally, the three scores are compiled, and the product is given an overall score.

Herman Miller now uses the sustainability tool to assess all new launch products—dozens of products with hundreds of related components—as well as existing products as they are updated and relaunched. The overall goal is to continually improve each product's score by finding better alternatives to problematic components—less-toxic dyes, for example, or reduced volitile organic compound (VOC) particleboard.

But it's not all about numbers. Another leading furniture company, Steelcase, creates "environmental product declarations," four-page documents that summarize a life-cycle assessment of its major products, and a two-page "product environmental profile," used with smaller-volume products. The purpose of these, says Angela Nahikian, manager of global environmental strategy, is to "communicate clear and transparent information about a product's environmental impact at every stage of its life cycle." The documents contain information about the types of materials used in a product, each material's origin and certifications, the percentage of recycled content, plant certification and manufacturing processes, and the recyclability of the product and its packaging. In addition to all this, the documents help designers to identify how Steelcase products can contribute to rating points earned under the LEED Green Building Standard.

In yet another example, General Electric (GE) uses scorecards to certify products that qualify for "ecomagination" status and as the basis for communicating those messages to its customers and other interested parties. The moniker came from the company's launch, in 2005, of a major strategic initiative. At the time, GE was far from an environmental leader—its environmental credentials rested largely on the toxic polychlorinated biphenyls (PCBs) it routinely dumped in a 200-mile stretch of the Hudson River between the mid–1940s and mid–1970s. GE had used PCBs as an insulating fluid in electrical capacitors manufactured at plants along the river.

GE's environmental reputation left a lot to be desired, but it nonetheless had a good story to tell. Soon after Jeffrey Immelt took over from Jack Welch as GE's chairman and CEO in 2001, he sat down with the heads of GE's various business units, a regular event called the *Growth Playbook,* in which division heads report on how things are going, as well as on what they see over the next three to five years for their business. Their reports mirrored what Immelt was hearing from GE customers, including the major electric utilities, railroads, and airlines. As Peter O'Toole, GE's director of public relations, recalls, "Jeff kind of looked around the portfolio and said, 'We're in the wind business. We've got a new super-efficient jet engine coming out, the GEnx. We've got a new efficient locomotive called the Evolution. We're Energy Star Partner of the Year from the EPA and the Department of Energy on our appliances and our lighting products. Maybe there's something more here if we put all of those together.'"

Immelt saw an opportunity to change GE's environmental story to the public and its customers, and "ecomagination" was the result. In mid–2004, the company approached my colleagues at GreenOrder to help GE position the initiative and make sure that it was credible. The first task was to focus "ecomagination" as a customer-focused initiative that was unabashedly about financial growth as well as solving environmental problems. To demonstrate that GE's environmental innovation could produce real business results, the company needed concrete goals—including a revenue growth target for relevant products, which Chairman Jeffrey Immelt initially set at $20 billion by 2010. Thus, "ecomagination" would become not just a name for GE's commitment to environmental leadership but also a subbrand applied to a select group of "certified" products and services whose sales would be tracked.

But which products across GE's diverse businesses—from energy and water to lighting and commercial finance—would be included, and how would that be determined? It turned out that it wasn't feasible to pick a single standard to define an "ecomagination" product—one that was, say, 10 percent more efficient than the state of the art. Ten percent improvement wasn't a big deal for a light bulb—but 2 percent was a very big deal for a locomotive engine. GE needed a certification standard that was broad and flexible enough to encompass its varied offerings.

Ultimately, GE defined an "ecomagination" product as something that would significantly and measurably improve a customer's environmental and operating performance. To determine which products would qualify, GreenOrder helped GE develop a scorecard system to measure the environmental and performance attributes of products. The scorecard took into consideration the state of the art, competitors' best products, the existing installed base, relevant regulations, and historical product performance. The scorecards produced compelling claims and proof points that would be used in marketing and sales, as well as to show interested parties—activists, journalists, and others—that "ecomagination" had substance behind it. "GE knew that ecomagination had to be bulletproof, grounded in real facts and sound science, not just slogans and promises," says GreenOrder CEO Andrew Shapiro. The scorecard system provided that security and encouraged GE businesses to identify—and create—products that could measurably, as Shapiro puts it, "out-green the competition."

Ultimately, what started out largely as a marketing exercise turned into a game-changing business strategy by the time it launched in May 2005. Immelt recognized that, in effect, his company's growth hinged in part on GE's ability to make its customers cleaner and more efficient.

It's not just big companies that can do this. Smaller companies also create metrics that help their customers understand and value the environmental attributes of their products. New Leaf Paper, an innovator in creating environmental printing paper, provides its customers with an "eco audit" that attests to the environmental benefits of printing on New Leaf stock. Thus, for example, when Raincoat Books published *Harry Potter and the Order of the Phoenix* for the Canadian market using New Leaf's EcoBook 100 Natural, a 100 percent, postconsumer, chlorine-free recycled paper, the roughly 955,000-copy print run and reprints of the 768-page tome saved roughly 39,320 trees, 16.7 million gallons of water, 1.8 million pounds of solid waste, 3.6 million pounds of greenhouse gases, and 27.3 million British thermal units of energy, according to New Leaf's "eco audit." The accounting, which appears on many of the books, brochures, and other things printed on New Leaf stock, gives customers fact-based bragging rights, stated by a third party, about their environmental commitment.

A different approach comes from Timberland, the often-maverick maker of footwear and apparel, which in 2006 unveiled a self-described "nutritional label" intended for use on all its shoeboxes. It represented the first time a footwear or apparel company sought to label its products with information on its environmental and community impacts. The label, modeled after the ubiquitous (and federally mandated) food nutrition labels, aims to give consumers information "about the product they are purchasing, including where it was manufactured, how it was produced, and its effect on the environment," according to company literature. Specifically, it offers data on two aspects of Timberland's environmental impact—the energy used to produce the shoe and the company's purchases of renewable energy—and three aspects of its community impact—the number of hours served by Timberland employees in community service, the percentage of its factories "assessed against a code of conduct," and the child labor employed in making the shoe. It also tells where in the world the shoe was manufactured.

Why do this? "We thought the packaging we had was not a reflection of who we are as a brand—that communicated the commerce and justice aspects of the brand," Tracy Stokes, Timberland's senior director of global brand management, explained. The label, she says, is an attempt to "bring those values to life in a very transparent and direct way to the consumer."

The label is a step in the right direction, although it raises more questions than it answers. For example, it's interesting to know the amount of energy required to produce the pair of shoes in the box—two kilowatt-hours on the sample label provided by the company—but what does it mean? Is it a little or a lot? How does 2 kilowatt-hours compare with industry averages? And the renewable energy statistic reflects only the amount purchased for Timberland-owned facilities, not for its factories, which Timberland does not own. Thus the metric is somewhat misleading—the renewable energy was used to run offices and other company facilities, not the factory that made the shoes in the box.

And what about other aspects of the shoes' environmental footprint—the nature of the materials, for example? What, if anything, is Timberland doing to reduce the use of chromium and other toxic chemicals in tanning leather? What percentage of the shoe contains hazardous solvents or glues? Do the shoes contain any organic, recycled, or bio-based materials? And what about the shoe's probably largest environmental footprint: the climate emissions from shipping it from factories in Argentina, Bangladesh, Brazil, China, Egypt, India, Turkey, or any of a dozen other countries (as well as shipping all the shoes' component parts to the factories from around the world)? We don't know.

Still, I love the fact that information about a company's social and environmental responsibility appears on 30 million shoeboxes a year—presumably, for years to come. Product packaging is a vastly underutilized vehicle for educating consumers about a company's environmental and social performance, a missed opportunity for most companies. Indeed, I view Timberland's label as a gauntlet thrown down for other companies—and not just those in the footwear and apparel sector—to similarly disclose to consumers what they're doing to address their impacts.

It's all part of the new way—transparency, accountability, and reporting. Customers want to know what you're doing and not doing, how that syncs with their values and aspirations, and how that affects their efforts to reduce their own environmental impacts. In the age of disclosure, there are fewer places to hide. Over time, companies in a wide range of sectors will be expected to provide more and more disclosure, perhaps in a format not of their choosing. What will the information about your company and products look like? How will that information compare with that of your competitors? Are you prepared to let it all be known?

To quote Don Tapscott and David Ticoll, authors of *The Naked Corporation*, "If you're going to be naked, you'd better be buff."

# Chapter 16

# Context Is King

During the dot-com boom of the 1990s, one of the many bits of conventional wisdom was that "Content is king." This phrase, which rose to cultlike status for a time, implied that those who own "content"—intellectual property, such as books, articles, databases, news stories, images, videos, music, and the like—would call the shots, whereas the folks who delivered it—the builders of Web sites and the technologies behind them—would be mere messengers, relegated to delivering services at barely profitable margins.

That turned out to be flat-out wrong. Some of the most successful and profitable Web sites—Craigslist, eBay, Facebook, Google, LinkedIn, and YouTube—own relatively little content, profiting instead from their messenger-enabling platforms that allow others to produce and distribute just about everything you can imagine.

It turned out that *context*—the ability to organize, sort, filter, and make sense of a continuous tsunami of information—trumped the content itself. Without context, every bit of information is as important as the next, making none of them particularly important.

Context is often a missing ingredient in the green economy. We see a great deal of data—on environmental issues, company performance, consumer behavior, and more. We hear facts repeated so often that they become gospel, never mind that conventional wisdom sometimes changes when put into perspective: Local is not always better than imported. Paper may not be better than plastic. Packaging isn't always bad. Recycling isn't always good. Each of these and many other environmental statements can be true, but it depends on the circumstances. For example, locally produced foods can have a larger environmental footprint than those grown elsewhere, even overseas. Plastic packaging can play a critical role in safety, security, freshness, and communication. Recycling something can consume more resources than it saves. You get the idea: It depends.

"I don't know that anybody understands what is good or bad for the environment," says Bob Langert, vice president of corporate social responsibility for McDonald's, the company's environmental spokesman for nearly 20 years. "I dedicate every day to figuring these things out, and they're confusing. My theory is that people kind of give up on it."

Langert's got a point. Most environmental issues aren't simple—far from it—and even the so-called experts don't agree on some seemingly simple choices, such as paper versus plastic bags, cloth versus disposable diapers, or ceramic versus polystyrene foam coffee cups. There's no conclusive agreement as to which of these choices is better for the environment. You can find detailed and authoritative research proving each of them creates less pollution, requires fewer resources, or is less troublesome in a landfill. All too frequently, the "right" answer is, "It depends."

Home Depot found this out when it launched its Eco Options labeling program in 2007. The program, which highlights environmentally friendly products on store shelves, actually began in Canada in 2004, and its success brought it south to the United States after three years. When Home Depot invited its suppliers to submit green products for the program, 60,000 products showed up—roughly a third of the 175,000 or so products the company carries. As the *New York Times* reported, "Plastic-handled paintbrushes were touted as nature-friendly because they were not made of wood. Wood-handled paintbrushes were promoted as better for the planet because they were not made of plastic." Ron Jarvis, Home Depot's vice president of environmental innovation, told the *Times,* "Most of what you see today in the green movement is voodoo marketing." And so it goes. These days, it seems you can paint anything green. Determining whether it actually *is* green often results with the conclusion, "It depends."

This means that in a world with so much complexity and so little certainty, you can't pretend to have all the answers because you don't—no one does. You can make claims, and they might pass muster, but there's a chance that they won't be "good enough," perhaps seen as too little, too late, or too irrelevant to an individual purchase decision. Do I really care that a paintbrush handle is made of wood or plastic as long as its price and quality meet my needs? Well, it depends.

It takes more than a few swift brush strokes to paint a green image. People want the facts, but they want a good story, too. They want to know what the facts mean, why they're important, and how they will improve their lives while contributing to a better world. In short, they want to know why your product or company should stand out in a world in which just about everyone, it seems, is waving the green flag.

There's a temptation to want to ply customers with facts, often explaining why something is less bad than competing products. It is increasingly common to see labels, advertisements, and other marketing materials that contain lengthy lists of environmental improvements for a single product—the savings in energy, trees, water, waste, greenhouse gases, and other resources and emissions. Often, these come with comparisons—the equivalent in land area ("enough trees to cover a state the size of Rhode Island") or an extrapolation of what would happen if everyone bought this compared with the competition ("enough aluminum to build 3,416 Boeing 747s").

These can be helpful, but they're not very compelling, and they sometimes raise suspicions. We learned in the world of nutrition labeling that marketing claims can be spun in misleading ways. For example, just because something is "fat free" doesn't mean it isn't laden with copious calories. Moreover, environmental issues are generally more impersonal than the food we put in our bodies, so there's less of an emotional connection with, say, a product releasing fewer volatile organic compounds (VOCs, a principal ingredient in urban smog) compared with, say, eating food containing less salt or cholesterol.

Making the case takes more than facts. It takes context—the story that makes the facts make sense. People want to hear a good story, one they can quickly understand and perhaps share with friends and loved ones. They want to you to make a clear and compelling case that will help them to feel good about what they're buying, that it's making a difference—and they want the facts to back it up. They want third-party validation or other expert opinion that undergirds your claims.

It's a balancing act, to be sure—content and context. But finding the right balance can tip the scales in your favor.

# Chapter 17

# Coke, Levi's, and the Tyranny of Brand Leadership

Being an environmental leader can be a double-edged sword, particularly if you're one of the world's best-known brands. On the one hand, it can help you to cut through the media clutter to distinguish your company. On the other hand, it can cut to the heart of your company's environmental challenges, often illuminating environmental challenges the public didn't even know you had.

Case in point: A few years ago I learned that Levi Strauss & Co., at the time the largest buyer of cotton in the world, had quietly started sourcing 2 percent of its annual cotton buy organically. The company didn't announce the initiative or have plans to launch a line of organic-cotton clothing. (They'd been there, done that: In 1991, it had launched a line called Levi's Natural that didn't do so well. Levi's marketers pulled the plug, lest they lose their shirts.) Rather, the company planned to blend the organic cotton with conventional cotton, much the way paper companies blend recycled pulp with virgin pulp to make a partially recycled paper product. The hope was, over time, to gradually increase the percentage of organic cotton.

Why bother? Levi's has a long history of social responsibility. ("It's in our jeans," is the unofficial, tongue-in-cheek company motto.) It has on numerous occasions gone well beyond societal demands in such areas as community engagement, human rights, and philanthropy. In this instance, Levi's wanted to help expand the burgeoning market for organically grown cotton—and, along the way, to garner experience in sourcing and working with this material that could help it gain competitive advantage as organic cotton became more widely understood and demanded by consumers.

At the time, no major apparel company had publicly moved toward organic cotton. Only Patagonia, the relatively small but bold marketer of specialty outdoor wear, had embraced organic cotton. When I learned about Levi's organic cotton commitment, I figured that it was a good story for the newsletter I wrote at the time, so I called the company to learn more. The company declined to talk about it on the record. Indeed, the company had not issued any press releases about its move to organic cotton and was not identifying the organic material on product labels.

I persevered, working through contacts there, and eventually prevailed. Clarence Grebey, Levi's director of global communications at the time, reluctantly agreed to be interviewed on the record.

Of course, one of the first things I asked him was, "Why don't you want to talk about this? This seems like a big deal. The world's largest cotton buyer is going organic."

"Look at it from our perspective," Grebey replied. "If we start promoting this, we'll need to explain why—that fully a fourth of all pesticides in the world are used on cotton, and the resulting impacts on groundwater runoff, worker health and safety, and the birds and the trees. If we do that, we risk our customers saying, 'So, 98 percent of what you buy is bad for people and the planet?'"

Grebey didn't need to go on. I knew the story line from there. Activists might demand to know, "Why only 2 percent? Why not 5 percent? Hey, we'll be conducting campus boycotts of Levi's products until you commit to 10 percent organic cotton!" At the time, given the vagaries of the nascent organic cotton market, Levi's didn't know whether it could sustain even 2 percent from year to year. One modest drought or insect infestation, and the supply of organic cotton could shrink faster than a pair of 501's in hot water. Thus Levi's reluctance to tout its organic cotton initiative was understandable, even though it was passing up an opportunity to garner some green cred.

Levi's knew what it was doing. Brand leaders in particular need to be careful because activists love to make an example of them. Think about the targets of the biggest environmental activism campaigns of the past 15 years: Citigroup, Dell, Home Depot, McDonald's, Nike, Staples, Starbucks, and Wal-Mart—brand leaders all. (It's no coincidence that, to their credit, all these companies eventually became environmental leaders in their respective sectors, even if they were initially dragged kicking and screaming to the party.) The activist community has a great knack for turning a well-liked brand into a poster child for evil, and the news media and blogosphere are only all too happy to go along for the ride.

So it wasn't surprising a few years back to hear that Coca-Cola, perhaps the biggest global brand around, had been targeted by recycling groups on charges that it had backtracked on a promise to include more recycled material in its plastic beverage containers. It was a classic case of No Good Deed Goes Unpunished.

In 1990, in the aftermath of the media frenzy commemorating the twentieth anniversary of the first Earth Day, during which "overflowing landfills" were viewed (erroneously, it turned out) to be one of the planet's principal environmental ills, both Coke and Pepsi announced that they would begin selling beverages in plastic bottles made with up to 25 percent plastic recycled from used bottles. Actually, it was more than that: Each promised that it would outgreen the other, being the first to reach this goal. It was a big deal for these stalwart beverage companies. The move was lauded by recycling advocacy groups—which, in their typical understatement, viewed it as *maybe* a step in the right direction.

But neither Coke nor Pepsi succeeded in meeting the goal, earning the rage of these same activists, in particular a small but vocal group called the Grassroots Recycling Network (GRRN). By decade's end, with both companies struggling to get their share of recycled plastic out of the single-digit range, Coke and Pepsi agreed with activists to a downsized goal of using 10 percent recycled plastic in their bottles.

In retrospect, making a promise it wasn't in a position to keep might not have been the smartest move. Coke, for its part, doesn't own three-fourths of its bottlers, which are independent franchises. And the market for recycled plastic is affected by things outside the company's control—such as the price of virgin plastic, which can hinge on the fluctuating price of oil. When oil prices are high, virgin plastic becomes more expensive, making recycled plastic more attractively priced. When oil is cheap, recycled plastic is more expensive than virgin. It also varies geographically. Some regions have a more robust plastic recycling infrastructure than others.

During this period of the 1990s, plastic bottles were garnering an ever-greater share of the beverage market, thanks in part to the introduction of 20-ounce plastic bottles of most carbonated beverages, as well as the growing popularity of individual-serving water bottles. With a limited availability of recycled plastic, the beverage companies were getting farther and farther behind their goals. Thus activist groups attacked the brand leader, waging a nationwide boycott of Coke products. They purchased ads in the *New York Times* and *Wall Street Journal* urging consumers to "Think before you drink Coca-Cola" and asking them to mail crushed 2-liter bottles back to the company with the message, "Use it again!"

Talk about a message in a bottle.

Others piled on. The politically progressive long-distance phone company Working Assets (subsequently rebranded as CREDO Long Distance) sent an alert to more than 300,000 customers, generating more than 40,000 letters, e-mails, and phone calls to Coke's CEO. Local governments in Florida, Minnesota, and California passed resolutions targeting Coke's recycling waste.

Eventually, the GRRN campaign faded away, but the activism mantle was picked up by two shareholder groups, As You Sow and Walden Asset Management. For several years, the two organizations partnered to press Coke to set high levels of recycled content for plastic soda and water bottles and to develop strong container recovery goals. The two groups withdrew a shareholder proposal on beverage container recycling in 2007 after Coke promised to take substantive steps. In September of that year, the company announced plans to step up its recycling efforts with a $60 million recycling plant described as the world's largest, with the ambitious goal of recycling or reusing all the plastic bottles it uses in the U.S. market. A few months later, in early 2008, it added aluminum cans to that commitment.

Why target Coke and not Pepsi? Coke's brand leadership made it an obvious target. In a 2002 "fact sheet," the GRRN explained:

> The Coca-Cola Company is the overwhelming soft drink industry leader, with 44 percent market share in 1997. If Coke chooses to act responsibly, Pepsi and other soft drink companies will follow. Coke is a highly profitable company that industry sources say is reaping windfall profits from increasing reliance on plastic packaging in the U.S. If any company has the resources and the capability to take responsibility for its products and packaging, it is Coca-Cola.

It's not simply profitable brand leaders who are at risk, of course. Any brand could become a target of disgruntled customers or activists. And competitors could get tarred with the same brush. If Coke and Pepsi are seen as eco-villains, the sentiment could bubble up to all beverage companies.

The Coke and Levi's stories represent different sides of the same coin. In one case, a company kept its good deeds quiet for fear it would raise a red flag about a problem that hadn't been on consumers' or activists' radar screens. In the other, a company raised activists' expectations about commitments the company had made but couldn't fulfill. Both cases suffered from a lack of definition about what reasonable expectations should be. Was 2 percent organic cotton a little or a lot? What percentage would be necessary to create a robust, profitable market for organic cotton? Should it be Levi Strauss's responsibility to create that market? And what percentage of recycled plastic could Coca-Cola, or any other company, reasonably achieve, given all the external forces governing supply and demand? Could Coke, for one, make a significant impact on landfills simply by using 5 percent recycled plastic, or would it take 50 percent or more?

In short, both cases begged the question, "How good is 'good enough'?"

Both companies might have mitigated these risks by providing a little context. For example, Levi's could have chosen to go public with its initiative, sharing its concern about cotton's environmental impacts and how it was working to reduce them. The company might have invited or even challenged its competitors to match its actions. (Of course, this strategy had a potentially downside, potentially raising the costs of organic cotton for everyone, as demand would no doubt outstrip supply.) It could have demonstrated its commitment to changing the cotton market by subsidizing farmers willing to incur higher prices associated with going organic or by partnering with a respected university or research organization to find ways to transform the cotton market. It could have partnered with an activist group concerned about pesticides or farmworker health to do research or educate farmers. By being seen as publicly proactive, and by explaining its vision for a greener cotton industry, Levi's might have garnered respect and credit for its own leadership actions, buying reputational capital that could have reduced the risk of criticism or backlash.

What about Coke? In their otherwise admirable race to outgreen each other, Coke and Pepsi inflated expectations and failed to mitigate risks. Coke could have invited GRRN or other activists to help it transform the market, directing its resources toward educating consumers or pressuring its bottler franchises to use more recycled plastic. The beverage company could have better explained what influenced its ability to cost-effectively use recycled plastic, such as the price of oil. It could have worked with local governments to launch or improve plastics recycling operations. And it could have enlisted the activist groups to help, thereby spreading the responsibility—and the risk. To its credit, Coca-Cola executives seem to have recognized that recycling can do more than simply stave off critics. In 2008, Sandy Douglas, president of Coca-Cola North America, told the National Recycling Coalition, "We envision a world in which our packaging is no longer seen as waste, but as a valuable resource for future use." For a company whose product is enjoyed globally 1.4 billion times a day, that's a lot of potentially "valuable resources."

Consumers, even activists, can accept imperfection and incremental solutions when they know that the company understands the issue at hand, is sufficiently concerned, and is taking adequate steps to change things, including influencing others—suppliers, competitors, and legislators—to join them in becoming part of the solution. But when these influencers don't understand the full picture, they can get ornery and downright dangerous.

By the way, there's an interesting coda to the Coke story. The GRRN's nationwide boycott campaign against the company had no discernable impact on sales—it wasn't even a blip on Coke's radar. In 2000, however, the group added a twist to its campaign: the "Dirty Jobs Boycott." It urged U.S. college students to shun Coca-Cola's recruiters when they came to campus to do interviews.

This changed the game. Even a small drop in the number of new recruits hits companies where they live. Big companies need a steady stream of the best and the brightest talent knocking on their doors, and activists understand this. When Coke's recruiters reported the drop in campus interest, that got management's attention. The environmental department heard from company brass, demanding answers.

# Chapter 18

# How Starbucks Met Its "Challenge"

It's axiomatic in today's hypercaffeinated online world of blogs, wikis, and other social media that consumers hold the power. Their rants and raves can make or break everything from TV shows to tech toys to travel destinations—all in a matter of days. Some companies wilt under such scrutiny or at least get defensive, sounding more like a beleaguered White House press secretary than a company seeking to earn the trust and goodwill of its customers.

Starbucks demonstrated that being in the cyberworld hot seat doesn't necessarily require turning on the PR fire hose. Sometimes all it takes is a little low-tech communication.

In 2005, a 26-year-old University of Southern California (USC) grad student who blogs simply under the name Siel helped launch the "Starbucks Challenge." Her blog, Green LAGirl, along with an allied London-based blog called City Hippy, asked readers around the world to hold Starbucks accountable to its policy of making fair-trade coffee available in all its stores every day.

Starbucks has ramped up its purchases of fair-trade coffee over the years, largely in response to customer and activist demands, and it claims to be the largest purchaser, roaster, and distributor of Fair Trade Certified coffee in North America and one of the largest worldwide. In fiscal year 2007, Starbucks purchased more than 20 million pounds of fair-trade coffee. According to the company, it paid approximately $8 million more to fair-trade cooperatives than they would have received if they had sold their coffee at "C market" prices, the worldwide reference used by coffee traders. The company says that this is similar to the premiums that Starbucks typically pays above the commodity price for other high-quality coffees.

According to its own stated policy, Starbucks will make a cup of fair-trade coffee for you any day of the week in 21 countries—Australia, Austria, Canada, China, France, Germany, Greece, Hong Kong, Indonesia, Japan, Korea, Malaysia, New Zealand, the Philippines, Singapore, Spain, Switzerland, Taiwan, Thailand, the United Kingdom, and the United States. If it isn't brewing fair-trade coffee as one of its "coffees of the day," a Starbucks barista is supposed to, on request, make a pot using one of those French press plunger devices.

Given this policy, wondered Siel, "Just how easy is it to get a fair-trade cup of coffee in a Starbucks in one of those countries?" She launched the Starbucks Challenge to find out, unleashing her readers around the world to visit their local Starbucks store and report back.

She caught a viral wave. In just over a week, a couple dozen or so other blogs and Web sites promoted the challenge, asking readers to check out their local Starbucks, order a cup of fair-trade java, and record and report their experiences. The self-appointed investigators found that most Starbucks fulfilled the company's commitment, but not all—and getting a cup of fair-trade coffee in some stores took a bit of effort.

So how did Starbucks respond to all this high-tech networking? Simple: It picked up the phone.

Starbucks' Cindy Hoots contacted Siel to talk coffee and to find out what the Starbucks Challenge was revealing. Their friendly, wide-ranging conversation covered fair-trade coffee, Starbucks' other socially responsible coffee-related initiatives, Siel's Starbucks Challenge, and life in general. As Siel, who studies literature and creative writing at USC, subsequently blogged:

> Cindy's sweet. At the end of our chat today, we started talking about ourselves. She's a theater major who once "wanted to change the world through art." Now she's older and money-wiser and works within a different medium—Starbucks' Corporate Social Responsibility Department.

> "I honestly think it's cool," Hoots said about the Starbucks Challenge. And she said that once we finish tabulating the results and stuff, she'd love to follow up with us.

Siel wasn't entirely convinced, however. "I really got the impression that Cindy really cared a lot personally and wanted to work from within," she told me at the time. "But I wasn't as sure, aside from giving me some additional information about Starbucks' policy, how connected she was to the actual practices of the company. I'm sure she was motivated by the same concerns as I am. I'm just not sure how much Cindy's caring attitude about this will get translated into the actions of the company as a whole."

Now, all of this may seem a tempest in a coffeepot—after all, at its essence the question being examined by the Starbucks Challenge is whether Starbucks is being perfect or merely admirable. But the lesson here isn't about fair trade or even about corporate responsibility. It's about companies engaging, even embracing, their critics and skeptics to fully understand their environmental and social concerns and help them to understand how the company is responding. It's about the power of personal, one-on-one communication in a world in which public relations is all too often reduced to digital transmissions, however creatively produced and disseminated.

Reaching out doesn't always work. But I've seen precious few cases where such engagement did more harm than good. In the world of green, in which politics mixes seamlessly with passion and pragmatism, the personal touch can go a long way to diffusing a potentially problematic situation.

Indeed, several companies have found that engaging critics can go a long way toward neutralizing them, even if the critics' demands or needs aren't fully met. Critics—whether organized activist groups or concerned individuals—often expect companies, especially big ones, to dismiss their criticisms or challenges. When companies actually listen and respond thoughtfully, even the harshest critics can take a more reasonable stance. Ironically, it can be the most progressive companies—Starbucks, Stonyfield Farm, and Patagonia, among others—that are held to higher standards, often by their most loyal and passionate customers. This is an unfortunate reality of the green economy: Being a leader sometimes can set you up as a target.

But Peter Tremblay, Starbucks' director of public affairs, told me that his company is better off for having been challenged. "We don't mind," he said. "We want to learn. We want to try to do the best we can. The Starbucks Challenge—we want to be partners with them. It helps us figure out where we have opportunities to improve. The fair-trade movement and Starbucks have common goals."

Meanwhile, Siel, for all of her healthy skepticism, continued her dialogue with Cindy from Starbucks' Corporate Social Responsibility Department. "I don't think they're the evil empire by any means," she says of Starbucks. "I just think that if they claim to be doing something, they need to be doing it."

And with a little prodding from the blogosphere, they are.

# Chapter 19

# Clean Energy: It's Not Just the Environment, Stupid!

I f you could pay an extra five or ten bucks a month to help reduce global warming, childhood asthma, energy shortages, the national debt, and the threats of al-Qaeda, would you bother? I'm guessing that you'd think this a no-brainer.

So why aren't more of us buying clean energy?

Today, electricity from renewable sources such as solar and wind represents a tiny fraction of our total energy use. The combined output of geothermal, wind, and solar electricity generation—the three principal sources of renewable power— accounted for approximately 1 percent of global electricity generation in 2007, according to data provided by BP.

One reason for the slow growth has been tepid demand on the part of both consumers and businesses. Understanding the lack of enthusiasm has befuddled everyone from environmental activists to utility executives. Nearly everyone, it seems, understands that generating electricity from the sun, the wind, the earth's heat, or gases generated by rotting waste or plant matter is good news for everyone—the planet, people's health, national security, and the economy.

As with so many other green products, consumers tell market researchers overwhelmingly that they want clean energy. A 2007 poll conducted by IBM found that two-thirds of energy consumers in six industrialized nations expressed willingness to pay extra for environmentally friendly energy despite the fact that prices for conventional energy already were high. But, the survey found, only a quarter of respondents are purchasing renewable energy options available to them.

The frustratingly slow rise of renewable energy underscores the challenges that good, green products and the companies that sell them can face when asking their customers to take a chance and switch to their product or brand from the old reliable one they've been buying. It also shows that despite consumers' seemingly strong desire to make greener buying decisions, they're not always willing to do so, even when it requires little or no effort or change of habits.

What's the problem with clean energy? People overwhelmingly understand its benefits. But it turns out that most people just don't think it works. This was the finding of Connecticut-based SmartPower, a nonprofit that has engaged in a market research and advertising campaign of Madison Avenue proportions. Armed with nearly $2 million in funding from five foundations, SmartPower partnered with the Clean Energy States Alliance in 2003 to better understand public attitudes about clean energy. This is no simple matter. For years, a succession of opinion polls has consistently demonstrated Americans' desire for cleaner fuel sources, but the gap with actual clean-energy purchases has remained gargantuan.

Working with Gardner Nelson & Partners, a New York ad agency that has represented Southwest Airlines, Chase, and other blue-chip clients, SmartPower conducted focus groups and other research around the United States. For starters, "We wanted to know what people really think about coal and oil," SmartPower President Brian Keane told me. "We, like a lot of other people, started with the notion that coal and oil are bad."

But that's not how most others see fossil fuels, as Keane's group learned from an "obituary exercise" it conducted. Explains Keane, "If you want to know what someone thinks about something, take it away from them." Therefore, even before the focus groups actually met, while the participants were still in the waiting room, they were informed, "Fossil fuels have died. Write the obituary."

What resulted was an eye-opener. Wrote one:

It is with *great sadness and regret* that we announce the demise of fossil fuel. After hundreds of years of supplying the population of Earth, the resource had been depleted. It will be remembered for the *warmth, comfort and pleasure* it provided to living things. There will be a great void that needs to be filled perhaps through wind and solar power. It will be *sorely missed* by all beings that depended on it to warm them, supply their transportation, power their equipment and support all the resources necessary for a *safe and comfortable life* [emphasis added].

Wrote another:

Fossil Fuel died after a long, slow illness called greed. Fossil has left the family of the Middle Eastern nations and former President George W. Bush and his cabinet members. Currently, the world is adjusting from heating by oil and illuminating by electricity to solar and wind mill sources. *There are several kinks to be worked out and roadblocks to conquer. Will we ever be warm again? Miss you, Fossil Fuel* [emphasis added].

"In obituary after obituary, what kept coming through was that fossil fuel has kept this country warm and strong and that there was nothing to take its place," says Keane. "And that solar and wind were not ready for prime time. They said that fossil fuels were a necessary evil."

It wasn't all bad news. Every single respondent knew exactly what clean energy is, and they absolutely want it to work. They could discuss it confidently, without hesitation. Many had heard of fuel cells.

They believed that it would be a better world if we developed more clean energy. They believed that it would be better for their health and their environment.

But the misconceptions and misinformation turned out to be rampant. The researchers found that while most people understood clean energy's benefits, they thought it would require them to have wind turbines on their homes, or that the power would go on and off on cloudy or windless days, or that it was ultimately all about tradeoffs, such as using less heat or air conditioning.

"No one's talking about it on television," was another comment Keane recalls hearing. "They could actually live with the fact that no one in their neighborhood has a solar panel," says Keane. "But if they saw it was on television, they could understand its potential. TV is the great validator of the day."

Keane's group tested a series of messages reflecting patriotism, security, jobs, and other themes. The one that overwhelmingly migrated to the top was the one that featured an image of the skyline of Chicago. The caption:

America already produces enough clean energy to supply all of Chicago's power requirements. Not to mention New York, L.A., Boston, Philadelphia, Phoenix, San Diego, Dallas, and San Antonio, too. Let's make more.

This did the trick. People responded, "I had no idea. Is that true?" They concluded that if clean energy "already" makes enough to power big cities like Chicago, with all the lights and technology they require, then it must be a lot closer than people think. We should be doing more of that!

Keane's group realized they had hit a nerve. *People don't really understand or appreciate that clean energy is here and that it works.* The result was a series of slick and powerful print ads and billboards, along with TV and radio spots, featuring strong, authoritative voices.

It turned out that everything we "experts" thought we knew about clean energy was wrong. We assumed that if we just could explain the benefits, everyone would want it. But that is not the case. Says Keane, "All survey research indicates virtually every American agrees the environment is important. In the past, clean energy advertising has leaned on the environment. It hasn't been effective—but not because people think it's not important. The problem? It's old news, and no longer very motivating. The environmental story is already well understood. It will take a new message to break through."

So it's *not* the environment, stupid. Says Keane, "We talked to a lot of environmental groups and learned that pushing this as an environmental issue is not even winning over the environmentalists. They know clean energy is good to the core. They just don't think it works."

Since that original research, Keane has continued to conduct focus groups every six to eight months. And despite the growth of attention paid to energy in general, and to solar and wind energy in particular, the barriers for consumers to switch persist. There are four main barriers, says Keane. The first continues to be clean energy's perceived lack of reliability. But even after you can convince them that it actually works, people often are hard-pressed to figure out where to buy it. "If you go to the Yellow Pages, do you look under 'clean energy' or 'renewable energy'?" asks Keane. "Do you look under 'solar' or 'wind' or 'hydro'? Or do you look under 'plumber'?"

The third barrier is cost, whether it's the added premium most utilities charge for their "clean" option, in which utilities buy a percentage of energy from renewable sources, or the considerable investment required to install rooftop solar panels.

The fourth barrier took me by surprise: Many people feel that if they buy clean energy, they're somehow adopting an "alternative" lifestyle to which they're not ready to commit. As Keane explains, "The perception is still that clean energy is an environmental product used by environmentalists—people who eat organic, dress in hemp—and many people don't want to have to buy into that way of living. They say, 'Hey, I'm busy enough. I've got a job, I've got kids, I've got the house. What am I supposed to do? I don't have time to actually buy into a cause like this.' And it conjures up the most negative impressions one has of the environmental movement."

However, there's a countervailing force. "When you tell a consumer that their tiny little action has huge ramifications," says Keane, "they will actually take that tiny little action. So, when I tell them that if they unplug their cell phone charger from the wall, they actually not only save their household fourteen dollars a month, but they also cut down on greenhouse gases by about four tons a year, that really matters to them. And that gives them a little control over climate change, which is a problem that they feel they have no control over."

In other words, the more powerful you make someone feel, the less power he or she will use.

Concludes Keane, "On energy efficiency, there seems to be a much more willingness to be a part of a solution, provided that solution doesn't crimp on their lifestyle."

The lesson for business strategy makers is implicit, if not explicit: The assumptions you make about what customers know and feel about your product or service may not synch with reality. If you focus exclusively on all those polls and surveys that report conclusively that some overwhelming percentage of consumers say that they want or are willing to buy what you are selling, you may be in for an unpleasant surprise. You need to dig deeper—much deeper. Take the time to understand the depth and breadth of customers' interest and the myths and misunderstanding they bring to market with them. You may learn that while your product has a lot of appeal, it also has some perceptual problems, not necessarily of your making, that could become a show-stopper.

This is particularly true with products made from recycled paper—tissues, toilet paper, copier paper, and others—which have suffered images of inferior quality, high prices, or hassles in the past. Those perceptions die hard. And even though what you offer may overcome past problems, it will require a deeper level of engagement with consumers to get them to take another look. Rooftop solar panels, rechargeable batteries, compact fluorescent light bulbs, green cleaning products, organic fiber clothing—all these entered the marketplace with products that couldn't compete favorably with the reliability, affordability, aesthetics, or ease of use of their conventional counterparts. All have come a long way toward overcoming those shortcomings, but they still suffer from those early experiences and impressions.

Clean energy, says Keane, is like vacuum cleaners of 40 years ago. Back then, a vacuum cleaner salesman would knock on the door, the woman of the house would answer, and the salesman would say, "I'm here to sell you a vacuum cleaner." The woman likely had heard about vacuum cleaners, but she didn't have one and possibly didn't trust that it would clean to her standards. So the salesman would toss dirt on her floor and vacuum it up to prove that it worked. It was a dramatic but effective sales tactic. The salesman then would go to the next house, throw dirt on the floor, and move on down the block. Today, of course, we don't have door-to-door vacuum cleaner salespeople. You can buy vacuums in any of dozens of stores or on the Internet. Every home has one or more of the machines.

Today's clean energy market is similar to the vacuum market of yore. Salespeople literally go door to door in some communities, attempting to convince homeowners that clean energy actually works. But it's harder to show them how energy works—to vacuum up the dirt, in effect. So the challenge is to find a way to demonstrate clean energy's potential in order to remove all doubt by letting the home-owner see it with his or her own eyes.

"To understand clean energy," says Keane, "consumers need to see it in their community. They need to go to city hall, to Wal-Mart or Staples, to see it in action. That says to them, 'If Wal-Mart trusts that this stuff actually works, it must be good enough for me.' And so it starts to get into them, and then you can get them on the marketing food chain. Eventually, you can get them to actually buy clean energy."

Keane's approach to engendering changes in consumer perceptions of green products makes good sense: By holding their hands, proving that green products work, and asking them to gradually change their green behavior over a reasonable period of time, they're bringing consumers along on a journey, not asking them to accept change for change's sake. Along the way, product purveyors can ramp up gradually, too, creating the sustained, orderly market growth that will lead to a successful market transformation.

It's a conservative, pragmatic approach and a reasonable path to success in the marketplace. And it helps mitigate all those surveys showing that the buying public overwhelmingly wants greener goods and services but doesn't always make the effort to buy them.

It turns out, they just don't think they work.

# Chapter 20

# A Tale of Two Circles

One good illustration of how enduring "facts" sometimes obscure bigger problems—and of the power of context over content—is something I call "A Tale of Two Circles." It offers a good example of how the public and companies can focus on a set of environmental issues or aspects of corporate operations that may not necessarily have the biggest environmental impact. And it offers a warning to companies that have been telling the wrong story when the public's focus changes.

Figure 20–1, the first of the two circles, is a pie chart containing a half-dozen or so "slices" representing the composition of the nation's trash, collectively known as *municipal solid waste* (MSW). You've no doubt seen some version of this. It shows that paper makes up about a third of our nation's trash, nearly as much as yard waste, food scraps, and plastics combined, each of which represents about 12 percent of the contents of landfills. They are followed by smaller amounts of metals, rubber, textiles, leather, glass, wood, and even smaller amounts of assorted other materials.

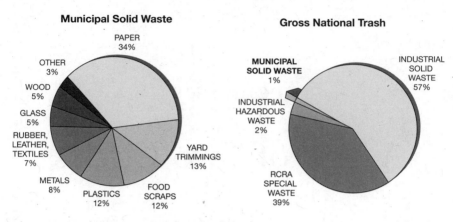

**Figure 20-1** The entire circle on the left represents just 1 percent of the circle on the right.

The MSW pie chart is well known to those in environmental circles and is the grist for a range of claims and disputes. The plastics industry, for example, uses it to "prove" that plastic packaging and bags are less of an environmental problem, at least a solid-waste problem, than their paper and cardboard counterparts. Everyone, it seems, finds some solace in the numbers.

But there's another circle that no one ever sees or discusses. This second circle is much, much bigger, totaling about 13 billion tons of waste a year, or roughly 65 times the size of the MSW pie. This circle doesn't have an official name—indeed, it's virtually unknown by most solid-waste experts. I've dubbed it the *gross national trash* (GNT).

The biggest slice of the GNT pie—57 percent—consists of industrial wastes from pulp and paper, iron and steel, stone, clay, glass, concrete, food processing, textile manufacturing, plastics and resins manufacturing, chemical manufacturing, water treatment, and other industries and processes. All this results from fabricating, synthesizing, modeling, molding, extruding, welding, forging, distilling, purifying, refining, and otherwise concocting what are collectively referred to as the finished and semifinished materials of our manufactured world.

A slightly smaller slice, comprising 39 percent, is something called *RCRA special waste,* referring to a category of wastes defined under the U.S. Resource Conservation and Recovery Act of 1976. This includes medical waste, septic tank pumpings, industrial process waste, slaughterhouse waste, pesticide containers, incinerator ash, and a host of other things. This is the daily detritus of our industrial world, the emissions, effluents, dregs, and debris created by industry.

A third slice, about 2 percent, consists of industrial hazardous waste, a witch's brew of toxic ingredients found in paints, pesticides, printing ink, and chemicals used in hundreds of manufacturing processes—nearly 500 such substances, from acetonitrile ($CH_3CN$) to ziram ($C_6H_{12}N_2S_4Zn$).

The final slice of the pie, a miniscule 1 percent sliver of the whole, is municipal solid waste—the entire MSW circle.

GNT doesn't even include the complete universe of waste created by business and industry—it omits, for example, the billion of tons a year of U.S. agricultural waste. Suffice to say that a lot more waste is created than is generally recognized by waste mavens, environmental activists, and the public.

What's the point? It's only a matter of time before the story of GNT gets told, and the public recognizes that for every pound of trash that ends up in municipal landfills, at least 65 more pounds are created upstream by industrial processes—and that a lot of this waste is far more dangerous to environmental and human health than our newspapers and grass clippings. At that point, the locus of concern could shift away from beverage containers, grocery bags, and the other mundane junk of daily life to what happens behind the scenes— the production, crating, storing, and shipping of the goods we buy and use. And interested parties may start asking questions.

This is no fantasy. Communities around the world are, variously, banning or limiting big-box retail stores (such as in San Francisco, Oakland, Austin, Vermont, and Maine), outlawing plastic bags and polystyrene foam take-out containers (for example, San Francisco, Beijing, and Australia), prohibiting waste incineration (Iowa,

Maryland, Massachusetts, Chicago, New York City, the Philippines, and Buenos Aires are among those that have done so), limiting passage of diesel trucks (the ports of Oakland, Long Beach, and Los Angeles, to name three), restricting landfill disposal of electronic waste (such as Illinois, Indiana, Wisconsin, Massachusetts, and New York), and boycotting companies for their profligate water use, resource extraction, carbon emissions, waste disposal, energy demands, land consumption, or pesticide use. And beyond that, communities are penalizing companies that fail to provide the levels of accountability and transparency demanded by those claiming the "right to know."

What will you say when reporters call and camera crews appear, inquiring about the GNT? What will you tell your customers and employees and shareholders? What will you tell your family?

| Chapter 21 |
|:---:|

# Three Keys to "Good Enough"

Given that there's no comprehensive and widely accepted standard for green companies, how do you assess how well you're doing? How do you answer the question, "How good is 'good enough'?"

In the absence of a simple set of requirements that fits companies of all sizes and sectors, here is my high-level framework, born of talking with hundreds of business leaders, activists, regulators, media, and others about their expectations of companies. Essentially, it asks three basic questions about a company and its environmental performance:

1. What do you know?
2. What are you doing?
3. What are you saying?

Let's take them one at a time.

## 1. WHAT DO YOU KNOW?

Few companies fully understand how what they do affects the environment. That is, they may understand their direct impacts, but not the full measure of their environmental footprint upstream—their suppliers and, perhaps, their suppliers' suppliers—and downstream—their customers and customers' customers and beyond that to the ultimate disposition of their products at the end of their useful lives. When they take the time to find out, companies are often surprised that those impacts aren't necessarily where they expected to find them.

Case in point: Several years ago, Coca-Cola undertook an effort to assess its carbon footprint—the various ways in which its operation produced, directly or indirectly, greenhouse gas emissions. This is an exercise being conducted by many large companies, and some smaller ones, as they find themselves pressed to understand, report, and reduce those emissions. So a team at Coke set out to find out.

Carbon emissions were associated with a wide range of Coca-Cola's operations. For example, the company sources lots of containers—plastic, aluminum, and glass, the production of each of which emits greenhouse gases. Plastic [more specifically, polyethylene terephthalate (PET), the plastic used in most beverage containers] is derived from petroleum. Manufacturing aluminum is one of the more energy-intensive industrial processes, and glass is not far behind. The company sold roughly 1.4 billion servings a day globally in 2006, amounting to 100 billion cans and bottles a year. (The balance were served mostly in cups at fountains and restaurants.) Forty-six percent of its packaging was nonrefillable plastic, 15 percent was aluminum, 13 percent refillable glass, 8 percent refillable PET, 1 percent steel, less than 1 percent unrefillable glass, and 4 percent cartons, pouches, and assorted other things. Twelve percent of Coke's packaging went to restaurant fountains, mostly bulk packaging of concentrated beverage syrup.

Manufacturing packaging is just the beginning of the company's carbon footprint. Coke also sources copious quantities of water—290 billion liters for beverage production in 2006—which requires energy to move and purify; in California, roughly a fifth of all energy consumed in the state goes to transport, pump, process, or treat water. (It is important to note that Coca-Cola has pledged, "By the end of 2010, we will return all the water that we use for manufacturing processes to the environment at a level that supports aquatic life and agriculture.") The company takes the water, packaging, and other ingredients to manufacture a variety of beverages, which it then ships via truck and other means to distributors, retailers, restaurants, and myriad other places. Indeed, by Coca-Cola's own reckoning, if you were to assume that each of the 200,000 vehicles in the world that sport a Coke logo was part of its corporate fleet, Coke would have the largest vehicle fleet on the planet. (In reality, most of these vehicles are owned and operated by independent licensees and business partners that distribute Coke products in and around the communities where they are bottled.) Suffice to say that all these vehicles use fuel of one kind or another. Each of these processes—sourcing, manufacturing, and distributing—contributes to climate change.

So what part of Coke's operation contributes the most greenhouse gas emissions?

None of these, it turns out. The largest source of emissions is Coke machines—some 10 million vending machines and fountains in restaurants, along with coolers and other refrigerated sales and marketing equipment.

It isn't just the energy use of all these devices that makes cold drink equipment the largest portion of Coca-Cola's climate footprint. It's also the insulating foam and refrigerant gas used by these and other companies' refrigeration devices. Coke, for its part, uses insulation free of hydrofluorocarbons (HFCs) for all new coolers, thereby eliminating about two-thirds of its direct carbon emissions. HFCs—used both for insulation and as a refrigerant—make up only a small portion of greenhouse gas emissions, but they are extremely problematic because they are more than a thousand times more potent than carbon dioxide in contributing to climate change. The company also has invested about $40 million over the past decade to find ways to use carbon dioxide as a more environmentally friendly refrigerant gas. (Therein lies a bit of an engineering irony: To limit greenhouse gas emissions, the most common of which is carbon dioxide resulting from the burning of fossil fuels to make electricity, modern refrigeration units increasingly will be using the very same carbon dioxide, but as a refrigerant gas to replace HFCs. In that state, it is 1,300 times less potent as a greenhouse gas than HFCs.) Beyond this, Coke has introduced a proprietary energy management system, reducing energy use by up to 35 percent. When you combine these things—HFC-free insulation, HFC-free refrigerants, and the energy management system—Coke says the newest vending machines and other refrigeration units will reduce carbon emissions by more than three tons each over their lifetime.

Granted, Coke didn't come to this on its own, explains Jeff Seabright, Coke's vice president for environment and water resources. "We were challenged, by Greenpeace in part, because we were an early adopter of the Montreal Protocol, a year before it took effect, to phase out HFCs. And being a brand company that lives and breathes on the basis of our brand and reputation, we were an obvious target for Greenpeace at the 2000 Sydney Olympics. They started a campaign around challenging us to get out of HFCs, and we surprised them by saying, 'Okay, we'll do it.' It kind of defanged the campaign prematurely."

Coke isn't the only one working on this issue. Refrigeration is an energy glutton and climate polluter for many companies, including grocers, warehouses, big-box retailers, and food-service companies. Companies are pressing manufacturers to create new technologies to cut energy use and costs. Coke, for its part, is part of a consortium called Refrigerants Naturally!, a partnership that includes its archrival Pepsi, the activist group Greenpeace, and the United Nations Environment Programme, McDonald's, Unilever, and others. The consortium aims to "combat climate change and ozone layer depletion by substituting harmful fluorinated gases . . . with natural refrigerants with a focus on their point-of-sale cooling applications," according to the group's Web site (*www.refrigerantsnaturally.com*).

Here's another example where a little investigation turns up some surprising results. Seventh Generation, the pioneering manufacturer of green household and personal care products, did a life-cycle study of its best-selling liquid laundry detergent. Again, consider the manufacturing process. It involves sourcing various ingredients, mixing them with water, packaging the solution in plastic bottles, which, in turn, are packaged in cardboard boxes, and then shipping the boxes to retailers. The biggest impact? Seventh Generation concluded that "96 percent of all greenhouse gas emissions are associated with the wash stage"—specifically, when the consumer does the laundry using hot water. Therefore, in 2005 it launched a cold-water version of its detergent. Procter & Gamble (P&G) similarly introduced Tide Coldwater after finding that doing the laundry represented far and away the biggest use of energy during the entire life cycle of all the company's products. This means that home laundry exceeded the embedded energy of the materials, manufacturing, packaging, use in the home, transport, and disposal of all of the $90 billion company's roughly 350 consumer products. According to Len Sauers, P&G's vice president for global sustainability, 3 percent of household energy use comes from heating water for laundry. Perhaps most significant for consumers, says Sauers, is that using cold-water detergents could save the typical household about $63 a year in energy costs, potentially offsetting the cost of a year's worth of detergent.

Such investigations are by no means limited to manufacturing or consumer products companies. Many companies have some version of this story—an unexpected source of significant environmental impacts. For some firms, the biggest impacts will be the operations of its buildings and facilities. In others, it's the business travel of its staff or employee commuting. In still others, it's the disposition of its products once they are no longer of value to their end users—whether they are recycled, reclaimed, incinerated, landfilled, etc.

So what's your company's biggest impact? And the ones after that? Are they from your direct operations or the upstream impacts of sourcing raw materials and component parts or the downstream impacts of product sales and use, their end-of-life disposition, or something entirely different?

What do you know?

## 2. WHAT ARE YOU DOING?

Now that you know your impacts, do you have a plan—preferably, a bold, even audacious plan—to reduce or eliminate them? Every week, it seems, one or more companies announce a significant measure to, variously, reduce energy use, invest in new technologies, improve reporting and transparency, green the supply chain, eliminate a waste stream, introduce new products, or some other initiative or milestone. And beyond the steady stream of press releases, there are countless more companies undertaking these things with little or no fanfare. Most of these undertakings are done for more than pure environmental reasons: They cut costs, reduce risk and liability, improve quality, create a more healthful working environment, motivate and delight employees, and provide other tangible and intangible benefits.

Many of these, company commitments are expressed in absolutes—100 percent renewably powered, carbon-neutral, zero waste, and the like. "Zero waste," for example, has become a rallying cry for some companies. There are zero-waste business alliances around the United States, as well as in Europe and Asia, promoting manufacturing processes that eliminate waste going to landfills or incinerators instead employing source reduction, recycling, and closed-loop processes. In addition to zero-waste networks, there are other business consortia focusing on, well, nothing—the Zero Toxics Alliance, the Carbon Neutral Alliance, the Zero Emissions Research Institute, and others. According to the Zero Waste International Alliance, there are zero-waste groups in Australia, Canada, India, Korea, New Zealand, South Africa, the United Kingdom, and the United States.

The idea of zero waste goes back at least a decade. In the 1990s, several American, Asian, and European companies set forth ambitious goals of eliminating wastes of all kinds throughout their products' life cycles. Xerox Corp. set a waste-free factory performance goal back in 1991. Zero-waste goals are still popular among Japanese companies—Hitachi, Kirin, Sharp, and Omron each already has at least one zero-waste factory.

Today, big companies are setting big goals. In 2006, for example, Honda announced that it would build a $550 million zero-waste automobile plant near Greensburg, Indiana. A year later, Coca-Cola committed to recycle or reuse the equivalent of all the plastic bottles it sells in the U.S. market. It announced a $60 million recycling plant that will be the world's largest, to be located in South Carolina. The facility will produce some 100 million pounds of food-grade recycled polyethylene terephthalate (PET) plastic for reuse each year. In 2008, it added aluminum cans to its 100 percent goal. Nike has long-term environmental goals that included zero toxics, zero waste, and 100 percent closed-loop manufacturing systems. General Motors, Subaru, and Toyota are among the automotive companies that have zero-waste manufacturing facilities. Governments are in the act, too: Two California counties have also adopted zero-waste goals, as has Carrboro, North Carolina. Even smaller companies are demonstrating a Zen for zero. In Colorado, for example, the Boulder Outlook Hotel & Suites, which sports a full-service restaurant, 3,800 square feet of meeting space, and 162 guest rooms, pursued a zero-waste goal. One innovation: Every guest room features bags for guests to insert their compost-friendly items—food scraps or tissues, for example. And then there's the Integrated Design Associates' headquarters in San Jose, California, a refurbished bank branch claiming to be a "net zero" building, one of the first of its kind in the United States. The building generates as much energy as it uses, resulting in no net additional carbon dioxide emissions.

Of course, your goal need not be all or nothing—zero or 100 percent. Most companies' environmental goals are somewhere in between, a challenging target that becomes their lodestar for the next several months or years.

In this age of transparency, it may not be enough to set an environmental goal and to announce it publicly. To pass scrutiny among competitors, activists, employees, customers, and the media, you also may need to make public the policies, processes, progress indicators, and performance results that show how you are or aren't reaching your goal. Operating under the Klieg lights of public attention isn't an ideal way to conduct business, and it involves risks if you don't make your goal, although also opportunities for winning favor if you are able to meet or exceed what you set out to do. But you may have no choice but to operate in a public manner.

So what will your company do? What is the goal it will establish that will set it apart from similar companies in your sector, market, or community? And how will that goal be set, measured, and communicated?

### 3. WHAT ARE YOU SAYING?

Time was that being humble and modest about one's environmental activities was seen as an asset. Companies that undertook environmental initiatives with little or no fanfare had little to risk. It wasn't that these companies didn't want the world to know about their good, green initiatives. It's just that the risks of talking often exceeded the benefits of walking, as the Levi Strauss organic cotton story made clear. Companies operated under the aspiration, "Let them catch us being good."

Those days of humbleness as a virtue are ending. Today, customers, employees, activists, and others expect companies to disclose what they are doing to be better environmental stewards. And they want details—commitments, goals, progress, timelines, proof points, and context, ideally verified by some independent third party. It's no longer enough to say, "Trust us. We're working on it."

This is just the beginning. Companies must operate with the highest of stakeholder expectations, often unrealistically, that they will be able to steer themselves toward a greener course, regardless of the business consequences of doing so.

In this context, what's the story you want to tell, and how will you tell it?

A great deal of business success, after all, stems from storytelling—the stories we tell our employees, our customers, and our various business partners and stakeholders. And the stories we tell ourselves about our purpose as individuals and organizations—why we do what we do. Storytelling takes place not just in a marketing and advertising sense, but in fundamental ways—a company's culture and communications style, its vision and values, the promise that it makes to the marketplace, the way it motivates and rewards employees, and more.

When it comes to environment and sustainability, the role of storytelling takes on even greater importance. Think about the topic. On the one hand, it involves scientific complexity about which even the experts don't agree. On the other, it involves our bodies, families, communities, and future. In other words, it involves both head and heart. Clearly, a company's messages can't go too far in either direction—too much "head" will lose people and seem cold and calculated, whereas too much "heart" will come across as touchy-feely, without regard for "the facts."

Storytelling is a powerful tool for combining the two: head and heart, intellect and emotion, facts and feelings. It helps to make companies more human and is the first step toward transparency. Storytelling is simply the best way we know to spread an idea effectively.

Leadership companies find themselves telling their environmental stories in myriad ways to their various audiences and sometimes to the public at large. Those stories are communicated from senior management through line employees and sales staff. And they are authentic and realistic, encompassing not just about the progress being made but also the work still to be done.

In the end, the answers to these three questions—What do you know? What are you doing? What are you saying?—comprise a pretty good gauge of whether a company is on the right track. Companies that can proffer reasonable answers to these questions are likely to be taken seriously—to be seen as "good enough," whatever that means to any particular individual or organization.

This is, admittedly, a pretty low bar. Simply understanding your impact, announcing a plan to reduce it, and talking openly about your commitment and progress is no assurance that your company actually will become significantly greener, let alone poised to prosper in the green economy. Theoretically, your company could accomplish these three things with a handful of reasonably well-written press releases. Of course, any such efforts would have limited benefits and considerable risks. Companies tend to get in trouble, reputationally speaking, when they let perception get ahead of reality.

In the end, this three-part framework is a start, a rough baseline against which to assess the depth and breadth of your company's environmental commitment. And it will help to determine how well positioned you are to develop more robust and impactful strategies—and to seize the opportunities that the green economy offers.

# PART 4

# FROM HERE TO SUSTAINABILITY

The growing green economy exists in countless nooks and crannies—in small, nimble, values-driven companies and large, staid behemoths; in communities of local entrepreneurs and global networks of enterprises; in the passionate department head struggling against all odds to move her company to embrace greener practices and the dispassionate operations manager seeking to improve his factory's efficiency; inside companies that never, ever promote their environmental initiatives; and in those that scream them from the rooftops. It exists in local government officials hell-bent to turn their communities' environmental leadership into an engine of economic and workforce development; in university presidents who view environmental leadership as a means of attracting the best and brightest; in citizens variously concerned, passionate, and image conscious, seeking to align their purchases with their environmental interests and values; and in the mindshare of kids making conscious green choices with their allowances. The green economy isn't always visible during a stroll through a shopping mall, often hidden inside products' provenance: the choice of materials and manufacturing processes used, the quantity and quality of packaging materials, or the efficiency or progressive policies of the company that made it or the retailer that sold it.

But it is there, seen or not. And it is here to stay. The greening of business is a bell that cannot be unrung. As companies squeeze out the waste and inefficiency, the carbon and energy intensity, the toxicity, the overpackaging, and the nonrenewable resources, they aren't likely to revert to old, wasteful ways when energy prices ease or public attention gets diverted elsewhere. The greening of the economy represents an undeniable and indelible revolution.

The question, as with all business revolutions, is who will win and who will lose? Will it be the incumbents—the big players with the market clout to dictate transformative changes in products, processes, supply chains, and markets? Or will it be the insurgents—the smaller upstarts, unencumbered with having to revamp legacy systems and relationships and unafraid to rethink mature markets and business models.

The modern history of innovation suggests that it will be a delicate dance between the two, with start-ups creating the breakthrough innovations that will be commercialized by their larger corporate brethren capable of deploying capital and market reach to create economies of scale. But that same history has shown us that there are risks for both large and smaller players. Consider that 6 of the 30 multinationals included in the Dow Jones Industrial Average in 1988 are gone today (i.e., Allied-Signal, American Can, Bethlehem Steel, Texaco, Union Carbide, and Woolworth), and a seventh, AT&T, exists in name only, the original entity having been scattered into multiple companies. Several others—Eastman Kodak, IBM, Sears, and Westinghouse—look radically different today than then. In many industries, the pioneers don't survive. Burroughs, Data General, Digital Equipment, NCR, Sperry, Univac, and Wang—all leading computer manufacturers of the 1970s and 1980s—are cases in point.

Of course, small start-ups are an even riskier bunch. And the successful ones often are gobbled up by bigger fish. Innovators in the early days of the green movement—say, the late 1970s to mid–1980s—seemed to thrive on equal parts idealism and iconoclasm. The pioneers of the day—ice cream makers Ben Cohen and Jerry Greenfield, Stonyfield Farm's Gary Hirshberg, The Body Shop's Anita Roddick, Aveda's Horst Rechelbacher, Patagonia's Yvon Chouinard, Odwalla's Greg Steltenpohl, Seventh Generation's Jeffrey Hollender, and Tom's of Maine's Tom Chappel—sought to integrate commerce and conscience, leading with the latter in order to accomplish the former. Wit and moxie often substituted for marketing plans and budgets, occasionally resulting in millions of free media impressions.

For example, Ben & Jerry's got started by projecting movies on the outside wall of the old gas station in Burlington, Vermont for the community's free enjoyment. Stonyfield Farm gained market share in Texas for its yogurt by promoting the idea that drivers should inflate their tires properly, thus boosting fuel efficiency. Company employees stood on the side of the road with signs saying, "We Support Inflation," and handed out Stonyfield-labeled tire gauges—along with a cup of yogurt, a spoon, and a coupon. Reporters and news producers found such entrepreneurial tactics refreshingly quirky and were all-too-willing coconspirators in getting the word out, helping them garner cultlike customer loyalty. Most of those early successes eventually were gobbled up by multinationals—companies such as Coca-Cola (Odwalla), Colgate-Palmolive (Tom's of Maine), Danone (Stonyfield Farm), Estée Lauder (Aveda), L'Oréal (The Body Shop), and Unliever (Ben & Jerry's). Patagonia and Seventh Generation remain two of the few independent, privately held firms of that era still controlled by their founders.

The question is: What happens to such companies, born of passion and politics, once they are mainstreamed? The aforementioned natural foods marketplace is a case in point. If you roam the cavernous halls of the Natural Products Expo, the industry's semiannual conclave, you'll be struck at how much the industry has grown—its principal retailer, Whole Foods Market, is now a Fortune 500 company—but also how much the industry has lost its passion and its politics.

This is no small matter. Eating, it's been said (by many, mostly attributed to California restaurateur Alice Waters, but also to others), "is a political act," although you wouldn't know it from visiting the expo, at least from my visit there in 2007. Where were the activists—those advocating family farms, animal welfare, local foods, farmers' markets, the integrity of the U.S. organic labeling law, slow food, GMO-free food, healthy produce for the underclass, genetic biodiversity, organic school lunches, and the connection between factory farming and climate change? If they were present, I couldn't find them.

It concerned me, both for the future of food and for the future of green. As environmentally minded companies grow and the markets mature, will the politics that underpin their products and services similarly get glossed over or ignored altogether in the name of revenue growth, mergers, and acquisitions? Will concerns over biodiversity, clearcutting, access to potable water, asthma epidemics, endangered species, loss of wetlands, nuclear waste, and smart growth be swept aside by green businesses' rush to claim market share?

Don't get me wrong: I'm not against seeing businesses prosper and flourish. I'm just hoping that companies don't lose their souls in the name of sales.

# Chapter 22

# Green Up or Green Out?

What's a better strategy—gradually greening up all your existing products or launching new ones that are unabashedly green? This is a fork in the road encountered by many companies, and there's no right answer. For example, automobile manufacturers are pulled between continually tweaking and improving their existing lines of vehicles—making all of them more efficient and less polluting but none of them dramatically improved—versus putting their technological and marketing muscle into an explicitly green vehicle, with all the incumbent PR potential. The first strategy—"greening up"—has typified General Motors' approach to its products; the latter—"greening out"—typifies Toyota and its iconic Prius. Of course, both companies are undertaking both strategies simultaneously, but each of them is better known for one strategy than for the other.

It's a quandary: Continual improvement makes good sense from a long-term business strategy point of view, as well as from the perspective of environmental protection, but it offers far less sex appeal from a marketing standpoint. It's hard to hype the fact that "This vehicle emits 12 percent fewer grams of smog-producing nitrous oxides per mile than last year's model," however impactful that may be to people and the planet. On the other hand, introducing a brand-spanking-new, greener product or brand allows you to beat the drum loudly despite the fact that the product may represent a tiny part of company sales and may belie the fact that the bulk of the company's products remain largely unchanged. This could lead to charges of "greenwashing" if activists seize on a seemingly hypocritical company stance.

Still, they're both valid approaches, each with its pluses and minuses. Consider, for example, the tale of two cleaners.

## GREENING UP

First up is SC Johnson, the Johnson's Wax people, founded in 1886 by Samuel Curtis Johnson, who purchased the parquet flooring business of Racine Hardware Company. Johnson's Prepared Paste Wax came along two years later to help care for those floors. Now run by the founders' great great grandson, H. Fisk Johnson, the company is a major producer of chemical consumer products, racking up more than $7 billion worth in 2006. In 2007, Forbes ranked it the twenty-ninth biggest privately held company. Among its iconic brands are Drano, Fantastik, Glade, Off!, Pledge, Raid, Saran Wrap, Windex, and Ziploc Bags.

In 2001, Fisk Johnson—who holds a bachelor's degree in chemistry and physics, a master's in engineering, a master's in physics, an MBA in marketing and finance, and a Ph.D. in physics, all from Cornell University—introduced Greenlist, a raw materials classification system designed to improve the environmental attributes of the company's products. It has since been called the "gold standard" of toxics reduction efforts by environmentalists.

Greenlist classifies the ingredients of all SC Johnson products into a simple scale: 3 for "best," 2 for "better," 1 for "acceptable," and 0 for "restricted-use material." Aggregate scores are derived based on the weight of the screened materials the company purchases. All the company's new or reformulated products must go through the Greenlist process. Greenlist's goal is to continually ratchet up products' overall scores by reducing or eliminating low-scoring materials. When the first assessments were conducted, the average product score was 1.2 out of a perfect score of 3.0. By early 2008, the average score had reached 1.53—on track, the company says, to reach its future goals. Making apples-to-apples comparisons challenging is the fact that when SC Johnson started the Greenlist process, it looked at 5 categories of raw materials. Today, it looks at 19 categories, covering four times the total volume of raw materials.

Why bother? "We do it because our base core brands are our bread and butter, and we feel it is imperative for us to continuously improve our core brands that are crucial to us," explains Johnson. "It has been a process that we've put a lot of time and attention and effort into. It takes time because you need to do it in a way that preserves or improves the efficacy of your product, and you need to do it in a way that, in most cases at least, doesn't add cost."

Johnson cites examples of both successes and failures. For example, in reformulating a concentrated floor cleaner sold in Chile, SC Johnson was able to replace seven restricted-use materials with ones that were biodegradable and free of volatile organic compounds (VOCs), which contribute to indoor air pollution and outdoor smog. The reformulated product cleaned better, was less expensive to manufacture, and—because SC Johnson has a rule that it won't export a formula with restricted-use materials beyond the country where it's manufactured—the new product could be rolled out to new markets. In another instance, though, removing chlorine from Saran Wrap produced an inferior product that resulted in a 50 percent hit in sales.

On balance, however, Greenlist has been a boon to SC Johnson, contributing to its strong brand image and reputation among thought leaders as an environmental leader, building strong relationships with federal and state regulators, reducing operating costs, and fomenting innovation. And it shows how a systematic approach to greening up products can yield a number of dividends.

But Greenlist doesn't necessarily translate at the supermarket shelf level. Few SC Johnson products make overt environmental claims. Most shoppers fail to appreciate greened-up versions of Drano or the other products as they cruise the aisles. They aren't likely to take note of the fact that SC Johnson has been doing such things longer than its competitors—that, for example, it removed ozone-depleting chlorofluorocarbons from its products in the early 1970s, years before it was required to do so. Or that in 1993 the company voluntarily eliminated paradichlorobenzene from toilet products because it is a water contaminant that can accumulate in the food chain. Or that in 2002 it eliminated chlorine-bleached paperboard packaging because the chlorine can contaminate air and water. Or that it reformulated Windex to replace a 0-rated solvent, removing almost 2 million pounds of VOCs while increasing the cleaning power by 30 percent.

In 2008, the company, eyeing a marketplace increasingly receptive to green messaging, began adding a Greenlist designation to products such as Windex indicating that they contain fewer VOCs. Granted, these aren't easy-to-tell stories. "Part of the challenge here is it's a very complex subject to talk about, and there's always tradeoffs, and there are differing views on what's good for the environment and what's not," says Johnson. "Take a natural ingredient, for example. We could have surfactants or we could have packaging materials that are naturally derived, like polylactic acid as a packaging material. It is biodegradable if you put it into a composting system. It's not biodegradable if you put it into a landfill. I'm just using that as an example—that it's a very complex subject to talk about. But I think there's going to be a growing need to be more transparent, to communicate with sound science, which a lot of people don't do, and do more from a labeling standpoint and other things."

## GREENING OUT

One of SC Johnson's biggest competitors is the Clorox Company, another venerable firm, dating to 1913, when five California entrepreneurs invested $100 apiece to set up America's first commercial-scale liquid bleach factory. In 1914, they named their product Clorox Bleach. Today, Clorox is a $5 billion company that, like SC Johnson, boasts a shelf full of blue-chip brands: Glad, Handi-Wipes, Liquid-Plumr, Pine-Sol, Formula 409, Kingsford charcoal, S.O.S. Pads, Brita water filters, Hidden Valley salad dressings, and Burt's Bees personal care products.

Until 2008, Clorox had a relatively blank slate from an environmental perspective. I spoke to a group of executives there in the early 1990s about the green marketplace, but whatever interest the company had at the time in greening its products didn't go anywhere. From an environmental perspective, it was neither a leader nor a laggard. It lacked any significant skeletons. It enjoyed a solid compliance record, joined several voluntary programs to reduce waste and emissions, and received modest recognition for its performance. Under CEO Don Knauss, who joined the company in 2006 from Coca-Cola, Clorox began to recognize that environmental and social sustainability are of growing importance for the company. Soon thereafter, Clorox began undertaking efforts to reduce its packaging and had begun to inventory its carbon footprint across its North America operations. But it didn't bother to disclose this on its Web site or on any other public materials.

The one environmental question mark the company had was its flagship product, household bleach, which is seen by some activists as a stain from an environmental perspective, although the company says that the product is misunderstood and safe. Household bleach, it explains, is a water-based solution containing 6 percent sodium hypochlorite, whose chemical symbol, $NaOCl$, is essentially table salt (sodium chloride, or $NaCl$) with a molecule of oxygen (O). That is, bleach comes from and degrades into salt. You wouldn't want to drink it, of course, but you wouldn't want to eat a cup of salt either. Moreover, the company points out that bleach's disinfectant properties are essential to public health—endorsed by the World Health Organization and others.

Some environmentalists disagree and warn against using bleach, pointing out that it is toxic and corrosive and can create suspected carcinogens in the water supply. Suffice to say that Clorox refutes this. "The bleach cycle—from production to use to environmental fate—is simple and sustainable," it states on its Web site.

In 2005, a small group of individuals within Clorox began investigating the green-cleaning market and conducted market research. Through a market-segmentation exercise, they identified a slice representing about 13 percent of the consumer market that they dubbed "chemical-avoiding naturalists," consumers who wanted greener cleaners but felt the incumbent products didn't work well, came from brands they didn't know or trust, were too expensive (some green cleaners were priced at twice the price of "regular" cleaners), and weren't always available where they shopped. These are the folks who want strong, effective cleaners but worry about their health effects— the ones who say, "Let's open the windows and send the kids outside—we're going to clean now!" They wanted greener cleaners but didn't believe that they would work. Beyond "chemical-avoiding naturalists" were other market segments that seemed open to and interested in green cleaners.

The Clorox team saw a big market opportunity. The existing green cleaner brands—Ecover, Method, Seventh Generation, and a handful of others—represented only about 1 percent of the cleaning market. And several of the other products on the market were considered green not for what they included but for what they took out, such as phosphates, ammonia, or other ingredients considered harmful to human or environmental health.

Clorox chemists started with a blank piece of paper, albeit skeptically, to see if they could create a cleaning product that was strong enough to wear the Clorox label but also passed their green screens. This went against the chemists' nature, given that they already had figured out the right combination of surfactant, water, preservative, fragrance, emulsion, and other components typically found in a cleaning product. But they soldiered on, eventually finding a formula made of 99 percent ingredients derived from coconut oil, corn oil, and lemon oil. (What about the other 1 percent? Ironically, the chemists couldn't find a suitable natural substitute for the color green. Two petrochemicals, Milliken

Liquitint Blue HP dye and Bright Yellow dye X, were blended to create the desired green hue.)

As the team tested the products with consumers, they recognized that they had a potential hit. "We were actually in a perfect position as a company," Jessica Buttimer, director of marketing for the new product line, Green Works, told me. "We have the Clorox brand. We have these distribution channels and great relationship with Wal-Mart. We have the science to make an efficacious product. And we have the scale to charge just a 20 percent premium, not a 100 percent premium." Moreover, Buttimer and her team found that the company's legacy worked in their favor: Consumers trusted the Clorox brand and the fact that a greener cleaner was coming from a company they'd known for years. (I had a small consulting assignment from Buttimer and her team in 2007, during the run-up to the Green Works launch.)

But the kicker was that the product actually did what it was supposed to do. "We did blind testing versus the market leaders," says Buttimer. "We were at parity or better in performance, which as a chemical company, you can imagine, was a huge surprise—that these things, with 99 percent or more natural ingredients, worked as well as Lysol, 409, and Pine-Sol."

The resulting product line, Green Works, emerged in early 2008 with modest fanfare, including an alliance with Sierra Club, a coup for the company. Sierra Club, hardly the most business-friendly environmental group, endorsed Green Works and created a partnership in which it would promote the cleaners—and allow Clorox to put the club's logo on its labels—in exchange for an undisclosed financial contribution. Previously, Sierra Club had endorsed only one other product from a large corporation—Ford's Mercury Mariner Hybrid SUV—back in 2005.

Green Works seems to have the potential to be a breakthrough brand—a line of cleaners competitive, environmentally speaking, with the leading green brands such as Seventh Generation and Method, effective enough to wear the Clorox label, priced less than other green cleaners, and enjoying widespread distribution; Wal-Mart, for one, immediately began featuring the products in its stores. If one of the goals of the green consumer revolution is to get brand leaders to create greener products at affordable prices, this seems a significant step in the right direction.

Time will tell whether Green Works will be a game-changer—whether it will make green cleaning more affordable and accessible to the masses. But all signs are promising: During the first six months of Green Works sales, Clorox revised upward its sales projections a half-dozen times. Clearly the potential is there. Clorox doesn't launch a new brand unless it sees a $100 million or greater market opportunity.

Clorox and SC Johnson are hardly the only companies targeting the green marketplace. Procter & Gamble (Cheer, Downy, Febreze, Ivory, Mr. Clean, Swiffer, and Tide), Reckitt Benckiser (Airwick, Calgon, Eletrasol, Lysol, Spray 'n Wash, and Woolite), Church & Dwight (Arm & Hammer, Brillo, Parsons, and Scrub Free), and other major consumer packaged goods companies are eyeing green consumers. Their interest is stoked in part by research reports, such as the 2008 finding by Information Resources, Inc., that "approximately 50 percent of U.S. consumers consider at least one sustainability factor in selecting consumer packaged goods items and choosing where to shop for those products." Even if this figure is off by a factor of two, it still represents a sizeable market. In 2007, for example, U.S. sales of all-purpose cleaners, one of the five initial Green Works offerings, totaled $432 million, according to Information Resources, Inc.

But there's a potentially bigger story here. Both SC Johnson—a privately held, multigenerational, family-owned company—and publicly traded Clorox—which ranked number 475 in the 2007 Fortune 500—are using their respective approaches to motivate their employees and invigorate them around green innovation. "I never ceased to be amazed at how people in our company really appreciate our environmental commitment, how it makes them feel proud to work for this company, and how it engenders their commitment to the company," Fisk Johnson told me. "I think a lot of companies out there would give their right arm to have the level of commitment that we have in our company of the people that work here. And I think doing the right thing, whether it's the environment, or doing the right thing from creating a great workplace here, or doing the right thing for our communities, they just make people proud to work here."

Meanwhile, at Clorox, CEO Knauss has identified sustainability as one of three core consumer trends with which he wants to align Clorox products. The combination of Green Works, Burt's Bees, and Brita gives it a toehold in that market space, a foundation on which it can build more offerings. All of this has energized the company, says Buttimer, a thirty-something mother of two who has become the corporate face of Green Works. "I can't keep my calendar clear of associate marketing managers, our entry-level positioning and marketing people, asking, 'How do I work on this project?' Or people coming to me and announcing, 'My parents are members of Sierra Club.' Everyone wants to be involved."

# Chapter 23

# The Green Retail Revolution

Retailers have been trying to insinuate themselves into the green marketing equation since the early 1990s, but with limited success. The failure of any major eco-label to catch on, the lack of consumer willingness to change their shopping habits, and the low quality and high price of many green products all conspired to frustrate major retailers' efforts to use green marketing as a differentiator, at least through the 1990s.

All this has changed now. A confluence of forces has pushed retailers into the green scene, largely whether they want to or not. Moreover, some big chains are leading the way, simultaneously pressing their upstream supply chains and their downstream customers to join in. Ironically, those very same "big box" retailers that environmental activists love to hate—because, they charge, the retailers contribute to suburban sprawl, lower labor standards to keep prices low, and promote the homogenization of society—could be a key driving force in creating robust markets for greener, cleaner products.

It's not that the activists have been ineffective. To the contrary: the relentless pressure put on Wal-Mart to change its environmental, labor, and community practices was directly responsible for that company having taken a lead role in transforming its operations and offerings. Until 2005, Wal-Mart was content to dabble with some green store concepts, starting in the early 1990s with some energy-saving building technologies at a store in Lawrence, Kansas, followed two years later with its first green supercenter, in a suburb of Oklahoma City. Among the innovations in those stores was virtually chlorofluorocarbon (CFC)–free cooling; a heating, ventilation and air-conditioning system that both cools and humidifies the store; a lighting system built around energy-efficient lights and placing skylights throughout the store; an "Eco Room" with interactive video displays, counters, benches, and tables made of recycled newspaper and soybean by-products; flooring throughout the lobby made of recycled tires; an in-store "green coordinator" and staff; a soft-drink dispensing system that offers a large discount to consumers refilling old bottles; and shopping cart corrals in the parking lot made of recycled plastic. The company has continued to experiment with green innovations as it designs new stores.

But this was tinkering at the margins compared with the environmental impacts of what Wal-Mart sells. Indeed, little changed until Coral Rose intervened.

Rose was the ladies apparel buyer for Sam's Club, a division of Wal-Mart. She had lived what she described as an "organic lifestyle" for about 15 years, born in part from having lost both her parents to cancer. In the spring of 2005, Rose placed an order for 190,000 organic cotton yoga outfits on behalf of her employer. To most people's surprise, the pastel-colored garments sold out in weeks. That success got the attention of Lee Scott, Wal-Mart's CEO, who saw an opportunity. "We gave our customers something they wanted, but something they might not have been able to afford at specialty stores," he later told *Fortune* magazine.

On the heels of that success, a corporate cross-functional sustainable fiber and organic cotton team was launched, says Rose. "Our goal was to further develop this new business model, a model that engages stakeholders in horizontal collaboration throughout the supply chain, beginning at the farm-gate." Partnering with the nonprofit Organic Exchange, Rose started visiting both conventional and organic cotton farms, seeking to understand how to bring more organic cotton to market. Today, Wal-Mart is the world's largest buyer of organic cotton and has made multiyear purchase commitments, thus helping to generate sustained, orderly growth for farmers willing to make the transition to organic.

Over time, Scott and his underlings have taken sizable steps into the organic world, causing both joy and consternation in the organics industry, the latter from activists who fear that the mass adoption of organics by Wal-Mart and other behemoth companies—including Kraft Foods, Dean Foods, and General Mills—will lead to organic factory farms, thereby lowering standards. (It's a classic challenge for activists, who need to be careful what they wish for.)

But it's not just organics. Starting in 2007, Wal-Mart began encouraging its 400 buyers to work with suppliers to create more energy-efficient, less-packaged, and less-toxic products and to obtain more ecologically sourced meat, fish, and produce—that is, choosing products not just because they are greener, but also because they meet all the company's other requirements. At an event that fall that I attended a few miles from Wal-Mart's Bentonville, Arkansas, headquarters, Scott set a goal for 2008 that 20 percent of items sold would be "influenced" by what he dubbed "live better innovations." To do that, buyers would ask suppliers to track those innovations so that suppliers could be rewarded for their efforts. In Wal-Mart's world, such rewards could mean millions of dollars of orders, featured positioning in stores, valuable promotional opportunities, and other incentives.

Many of the innovations are simultaneously meaningful and mundane. Consider liquid laundry detergent. For years, the technology existed to make detergent more concentrated and, therefore, the bottles more compact. In the early 1990s, Procter & Gamble (P&G) introduced "ultra" packaging, which reduced bottle sizes by 20 percent, but there was still more that could be done. However, consumers frustrated manufacturers' efforts to create ever-smaller bottles. The challenge was this: If a shopper saw two bottles on the shelf, one 64 ounces, the other 32 ounces, and the two bottles did the same number of loads and cost roughly the same amount, he or she inevitably would pick the larger version, which seemed a better buy. No matter that the smaller one was easier to carry home and did the same job. So innovators were penalized irrationally by shoppers, and the packages failed to catch on.

Then came Wal-Mart. In 2007, the retailer announced that it would stock *only* compacted versions of detergents; no more big bottles. That did the trick. Manufacturers had no choice but to heed Wal-Mart's mandate. Led by P&G, manufacturers created "2X" versions of their products, packing the same number of loads into a half-sized bottle. The smaller bottles reduced packaging, shipping costs, and warehousing and allowed more bottles to fit onto shelves, cutting retailers' restocking costs. Of course, the substantial development costs for the reformulated and repackaged products was borne by the manufacturers—to the tune of $200 million for P&G alone, according to one report—while most of the benefits inured to Wal-Mart. Still, P&G says that the 2X detergents require 35 percent less water, the equivalent of 230 million gallons a year, reduce greenhouse gases by the annual equivalent emissions of nearly 40,000 cars, and save enough plastic a year equivalent to 2 billion shopping bags. P&G, too, will prosper from the more efficient design.

Another example of Wal-Mart's influence is Hamburger Helper. Wal-Mart buyers convinced General Mills, which makes the product, to straighten the wavy noodles contained in its boxes. This allowed the noodles to fit in a smaller box, reducing packaging needs by 900,000 pounds of paper fiber annually and shipping needs by the equivalent of taking 500 trucks off the road. Such impressive savings have led Wal-Mart's buyers to noodle in other ways to convince suppliers to help align environmental and efficiency goals. As Scott told the *New York Times* in 2007, "The environment is begging for the Wal-Mart business model."

It's more than Wal-Mart, of course. Other big-box retailers and supermarket chains have started to push their suppliers to provide products that are greener, less packaged, less toxic, or otherwise more environmentally friendly. Reducing toxic ingredients has been one key area of focus. In 2007, for example, Target was among several large retailers to launch plans to reduce the toxic materials in its products. Following a campaign by health and environmental groups, Target said that it would eliminate or reduce polyvinyl chloride (PVC) from a range of products and packaging, including infant and children's products, shower curtains, and tableware. Sears Holdings, parent of Kmart and Sears & Roebuck, followed suit, phasing out PVC. That same year, the U.K.'s Marks & Spencer began screening products for toxicity, and Wal-Mart said that it would begin implementing "preferred chemical principles" to establish a clear set of characteristics for product ingredients. The French retail giant Carrefour has taken on a range of environmental supply-chain improvements, such as reducing the use of tropical woods and creating its own brand of organic products.

Greening up products is only part of the equation for retailers. Nearly all large chains are improving the energy efficiency of their lighting, heating, cooling, and refrigeration; improving the fuel efficiency of their vehicles; increasing recycling and composting; purchasing electricity from renewable resources; and taking other measures that, in most cases, save money and reduce waste.

It's in the United Kingdom that retailer activism has really kicked in. For example, supermarket leader Tesco committed in 2007 to ignite "a revolution in green consumerism," in the words of its CEO, Sir Terry Leahy. In a speech, Leahy announced that his company would reduce its energy use in half by 2010 and drastically limit the number of products it transports by air; items that were shipped by air would say so on their packaging—a kind of modern-day scarlet letter. And Leahy announced that Tesco would be the first supermarket chain in the world to assign a carbon label to every product on its shelves. The labels would record the amount of carbon dioxide emitted during the production, transport, and consumption of the 70,000 products the company sells.

Tesco is the largest U.K. supermarket but hardly the only one that has found its green gene. Britain's four top chains—Tesco, Asda (owned by Wal-Mart), Sainsbury, and Morrisons—are vying to outgreen one another in the public's eyes, variously improving their products and practices. It is "an out-and-out arms race," as one of my London friends told me during a visit there in 2007. Meanwhile, Marks & Spencer, which sells both groceries and apparel, announced plans about that time to go carbon-neutral by 2012 and put forth a 100-point action plan to get there. The program is called Plan A ("Because there is no Plan B") and is aggressively touted in its stores. Posters hanging on the wall during a one-floor escalator ride in Tesco's High Street Kensington store give a reasonable grounding in Plan A's goals.

Creating a labeling system related to a product's impact on climate change is no mean feat. Measuring and assessing the carbon footprint of even a simple product means drawing boundaries around the upstream and downstream materials and processes and then finding reliable data about the impact of those things.

Consider a pair of denim jeans—a fairly simple product with few moving parts and only a relative handful of ingredients. Jeans' main ingredient is cotton, of course, which requires copious water, pesticides, fertilizers, energy, and other inputs. To turn raw cotton into finished denim requires a dizzying series of ginning and milling processes. The other components typically found in a pair of jeans—zippers, rivets, buttons, and snaps—typically come from aluminum, copper, iron, and zinc, each of which requires mining and smelting into their respective metals and then electroplating and finishing. Each step of the process requires energy, water, and other ingredients and produces air and water emissions and solid waste, some of it hazardous (see Figure 23–1).

All these components meet at a manufacturing plant, where they are cut, sewn, laundered, and packaged, which can involve any number of chemicals, detergents, and other additives, as well as still more water and energy—and still more waste products. Finally, the jeans are shipped to market—typically, these days, from thousands of miles away from factories in Latin America, Asia, Africa, and elsewhere.

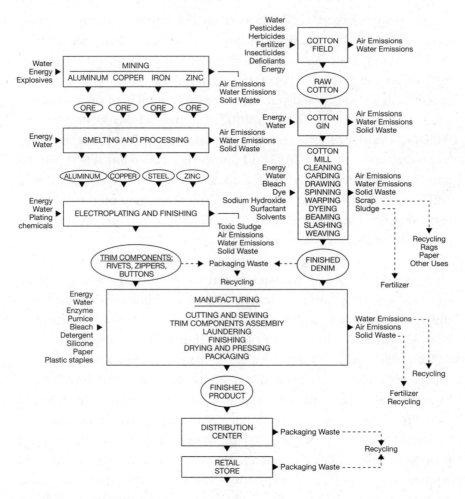

**Figure 23-1** Simplified life cycle of a pair of denim jeans.

So how do you measure the carbon footprint of all this? Where do you draw the boundaries? Do you include some portion of the pipeline that delivered the natural gas that went into manufacturing the fertilizer? Do you include the gasoline that went into the chain saw that cut down the tree that yielded the paper used for the label? Do you include some portion of the lighting and other energy impacts of the retailer? Or do you include some portion of the energy impacts of the consumer who drove to the store to buy the garment? Does it matter if he or she took the bus?

Finding answers isn't impossible. The British manufacturer of Walkers Crisps—a unit of Pepsico and the third most recognizable brand in Britain—managed to find its way through the thicket, becoming the first carbon-labeled product to reach U.K. stores. Walkers had to calculate the amount of energy required to plant seeds for the two principal ingredients in its crisps (known to Yanks as potato chips), sunflower oil and potatoes, and to make the fertilizers and pesticides used on the potatoes. The company also factored in the energy required for the farming equipment used to grow and harvest the potatoes and to process, package, store, and ship them. The impacts of the printing and packaging also were included, along with the energy used to bring the crisps to market and the impacts of tossing out the empty bags after the crisps were consumed. Working with the government-funded Climate Trust, Walkers' researchers crunched the numbers for a typical individual-sized (34.5-gram, or 1.2-ounce) bag. The raw materials—potatoes, sunflower oil, and seasoning—accounted for 44 percent of the impact, with manufacturing (30 percent) and packaging (15 percent) representing the next biggest chunks. Distribution (9 percent) and consumer packaging disposal (2 percent) represented the balance. The bottom line, Walkers found, was that there are 75 grams of carbon amid all those carbs.

It's not just carbon. As global water concerns rise, similar questions are being asked about products' *embedded water* (also referred to as *virtual* or *embodied water*), the amount of water required for the production and trade of food and consumer products. A cup of coffee, for instance, has 140 liters (about 37 gallons) of embedded water when you consider the amount of water used to grow, produce, package, and ship the beans. Similarly, a hamburger contains 2,400 liters (634 gallons) of embedded water, never mind the fries.

This is of more than academic interest. As water concerns flood a greater number of regions, the embedded water of common products provides a useful understanding of how water resources are affected by global trade. For example, it explains how and why nations such as the United States, Argentina, and Brazil "export" billions of gallons of water each year—in the form, say, of water-intensive grain or meat—whereas others, such as Japan, Egypt, and Italy, "import" billions of gallons.

All this may sound rather arcane, but answering such questions is necessary if you want to create an accurate labeling of a product's climate impacts. The energy or water impacts of a pair of pants or a potato chip are relatively simple. Imagine the complexity of a computer, whose scores of parts are manufactured by subcontractors in a dozen or more countries and then shipped to a facility where they are assembled and sold as a Dell, or whatever, machine. How do retailers accurately assess the impacts of such a product, let alone communicate those impacts to their customers?

Labeling is challenging even for a retailer that simply wants to steer its customers toward "better" products—ones that use less energy, are more recyclable, or contain fewer toxics, for example. Anyone trying to parse those claims can quickly find themselves traversing an informational morass. This was Home Depot's experience when it launched Eco Options, a labeling program in its stores to highlight green products. The retail goliath struggled to separate true-green products from poseurs.

The problem, says Ron Jarvis, Home Depot's senior vice president of environmental innovation, begins when "you sit down with a supplier who spent months and thousands or maybe millions of dollars coming up with a product that it thinks is environmentally friendly." He explained to me the tale of one product purveyor who approached Home Depot in 2007 to achieve Eco Options status—a manufacturer of organic gardening soil. "I started looking into the organic soil, and it kind of made sense. You would think organic is good. And as we looked at it, I said, 'Well, what are the marketing claims?' They said, 'Well, the marketing claims are that there were no chemicals used to manufacture this product.' I said, 'Okay, but there's no chemicals to use to manufacture any soil.' The second claim was, 'No trees have been cut to manufacture this product,' and I said, 'But there's usually not trees cut when you're bagging soil.' The company itself thought that they had a home run, that they would become Eco Options overnight, but they were denied."

Jarvis insists that any effort to help customers be greener must be based on competition, not favoritism. "When I think back to 2000, when we were occasionally pushing stuff out under environmental marketing claims that our supplier was bringing to us, they were typically, 'This makes the sky bluer and the grass greener, and it costs 15 percent more.' That was a no-sell. You cannot ask the consumer to completely change their lifestyle and to pay more for products than they normally would just to have less of an impact on the environment. When I sit down with suppliers, which I do every day, and they say, 'All right, here's a product that's going to replace Product X, but it doesn't perform quite as well and it's 25 percent more in cost,' we basically send them back to the drawing board and say, 'This isn't going to work. Come back to us with a product that performs as good as or better than the standard product, has less of an impact and is the same cost.'"

Will all this labeling and disclosure actually move consumers to make greener choices? Little real-world data exist to answer this. And it could be counterproductive if each retail chain imposes a different set of standards and disclosures on its suppliers, creating a confusing mass of inconsistent information. Some standards, voluntary or otherwise, may be in order.

To some extent, however, it doesn't matter. The mere act of large retailers asking their suppliers to examine and reduce their products' impacts, or highlighting environmentally improved products, or rating suppliers based on their environmental performance and their products' environmental attributes—these actions alone could be powerful market forces for change.

Of course, consumers need to do their part, lest these greener goods gather dust on store shelves. As Wal-Mart and others have learned, though, even if consumers remain clueless, innocent bystanders, there's motivation enough to foment these kinds of changes, including improved efficiency, increased productivity, reduced costs, and higher employee satisfaction and retention—and maybe, just maybe, increased sales.

# Chapter 24

# The Game-Changing Entrepreneurs

The advent of the green economy coincides with a new era for entrepreneurism. Unlike, say, Ben & Jerry's, today's promising young green companies are less likely to be influenced by the war than the Web. Today's entrepreneur has been chastened and emboldened by the successes—and excesses—of the Internet revolution. Indeed, many green-economy entrepreneurs are dot-com refugees, flush with cash, connections, and a can-do mind-set. They bring their innovations in business strategy, such as the notion of turning products into services, of customers as "members," of networks as marketplaces.

One of countless examples is SolarCity, founded by Lyndon and Peter Rive, two brothers who previously started a software company they sold to Dell. The Silicon Valley company became a fast-growing phenomenon by creating a residential solar purchasing program that encouraged neighbors to join together to receive special group pricing incentives on solar installations. It's a classic dot-com play: Break through the barriers of the incumbent business mind-set, in this case by using the power of human networks to do viral marketing on the company's behalf, thereby short-circuiting the marketing and sales cycles. SolarCity has attracted major investors, including Elon Musk, the brains behind PayPal.

And then there's Sungevity, another solar company, this one founded by two brothers-in-arms, Danny Kennedy and J.P. Ross, both ex-Greenpeace activists turned solar entrepreneurs. Their company similarly brings dot-com smarts to the relatively staid world of solar energy. It works like this: Simply enter your address on Sungevity's Web site. Within 24 hours (more or less), you'll get a complete analysis of your home's solar potential, including a proposal for three different types of solar systems and a picture of what your house will look like with each. You'll also get complete financial analyses of the three systems, a contract, and all the paperwork. All this used to take at least two site visits, usually over several weeks. Sungevity uses Web and mapping technology (similar to Google Earth) to calculate your home's solar profile—how much sunlight it gets, whether that sunlight is shaded in ways that negatively affect its exposure to the sun, and other factors—and automates a heretofore heavily manual, paper-based process. Such a smart, automated system seems like a no-brainer—but then again, no one has done it previously.

Another smart, automated player is mkDesigns, founded by Michelle Kaufman, an architect who previously worked with Frank Gehry and Michael Graves—renowned architects known for out-of-the-box thinking. The company has created affordable prefabricated green housing that breaks the mold for how people think about either. mkDesigns creates custom homes built in factories, which sounds like an oxymoron but actually makes a lot of sense. By building the core of each home in a controlled factory environment, the company is able to reduce costs, improve quality, and take advantage of economies of scale. On site, the homes are customized—they can be one story or many, small or large, even sizable multifamily structures. You'd never know their factory origins. However, Kaufman's process reduces waste by up to 75 percent and allows her to bake into her designs an ever-increasing number of green aspects, from materials and finishes to solar panels and energy-monitoring devices. Customers can design their homes online, even downloading software that allows them to "walk through" their designed homes and change specifications in real time. mkDesigns has attracted awards, venture capital funding, and some of the brightest minds in the building industry, all hoping to scale up the company to offer affordable green housing solutions globally.

The new business models don't always work. Consider Nau, Inc., a designer and marketer of outdoor clothing, based in Portland, Oregon. Comprised of refugees from Nike, Patagonia, and other companies, Nau was built from the ground up as a firm that would do things differently and sustainably. It began with the company's mission statement: "To combine the generosity of the human spirit and the power of technology with business innovation to increase shareholder equity, protect the environment, enhance social justice, and provide humanitarian relief worldwide." Its operation encompassed a range of innovations, including direct distribution, in which it would control its products from concept and design through marketing and sales; an online-offline "Webfront" sales model, in which customers could try on Nau products in stores and either buy them on the spot or, for a 10 percent discount, purchase them online; and customer-directed giving, in which every customer at the time of sale is offered the opportunity to select the nonprofit group of his or her choice to receive Nau's 5 percent contribution of sales.

Nau's vision and values were a great example for companies positioning themselves for the green economy. Notice that I said *were*. The company lasted only a year, the victim of a challenging financial climate in which to raise working capital. (The Nau brand was eventually acquired by another company.) Even in its demise, it was heralded as "the best kind of failure," in the words of Worldchanging.com's executive editor, Alex Steffen. He called it "a smart, creative, energized bunch of people who saw something wrong with the world, thought they saw how to do something better instead, and went for it with everything they had. In the process, Nau has prepared the ground for a whole crop of innovations and new thinking."

One of Nau's innovations was its messaging. "We are not just look-ing to make some new clothes," it stated. "We are aiming to redefine what it means to be successful." It communicated clearly, cleverly, and compellingly a deep sense of values without hitting you over the head with its progressiveness. (It evokes one of my favorite company taglines, that of Bronx-based Greystone Bakery, founded by astro-physicist turned Zen Buddhist priest, Bernard Glassman. Founded in the early 1980s, Greystone Bakery hires anyone, including former drug addicts and prisoners, providing training, child care, and coun-seling, as well as meaningful work. This profitable company, which sells baked goods to some of New York's finest restaurants, proclaims, "We don't hire people to bake brownies. We bake brownies to hire people." Clear, clever, compelling.)

Start-ups with baked-in environmental or socially responsible mis-sions aren't exactly new, but the newest breed is doing more than merely "greening up" a conventional product or service. In some cases, these companies are innovating on not just what they sell but also on the entire value chain.

Consider Shai Agassi. In 2007, the 40-year-old Israeli native left his job as the president of the Products and Technology Group at enter-prise software giant SAP to pursue a bold and audacious vision—to convert an entire country to electric cars powered by batteries that get their energy from renewable energy sources, employing a smart elec-tric recharge grid that covers the entire country. Dubbed Project Better Place, the company began its life with a business plan that called for deploying a vast system of recharging and battery-swapping stations so that they are nearly as ubiquitous as gas stations. By early 2008, Agassi not only had secured $200 million in venture capital but also had signed the government of Israel and the automaker Renault-Nissan as partners. At the launch event in January of that year, Agassi stood next to Israel Prime Minister Ehud Olmert and Renault-Nissan CEO Carlos Ghosn and explained his vision: "If we can provide the drivers an enjoyable car, that costs less but drives better, a country can build a virtual oil field—one that works forever, but leaves no foot-print on the environment. Such a virtual oil field is more natural than the holes we have been digging into the earth to fuel our addiction to oil." Since then, Nissan announced that it will build, in large volumes, the electric cars for Israel and then to go into other countries and cities that adopt Agassi's vision.

We'll see whether Agassi's vision gets traction, but it's hard to ignore the size and scope of the plan. And it shows how small players with big visions can be competitive in mature markets, such as automobiles, in part by changing the rules of the game, much as their dot-com forebears did a decade earlier.

Or consider the founder of SunEdison, Jigar Shah, yet another entrepreneur who has helped change the business model for solar energy. He started with a basic premise—the idea of turning free energy from the sun into electricity. This has long been simple and undeniably compelling, but the promise is clouded by a myriad of barriers. The technology is costly relative to conventional electricity and is complicated to install, especially in an existing home. The industry has yet to come up with a truly plug-and-play model roughly equivalent to buying satellite TV, in which a truck pulls up and installs a complete system in a few hours. Instead, solar energy is much more like home remodeling, requiring planning, drawings, and multiple players, often taking weeks.

Perhaps the biggest barrier is the fact that most people—whether homeowners or business owners—aren't accustomed to owning their means of electricity generation. That is, we're used to buying electricity as a service, not a product. We don't even want electricity per se so much as the services electricity provides—lights, television, cold beer, and warm showers. Most consumers and companies lack the capital budgets to pay solar energy's substantial installation costs. Government subsidies, where they're available, can help, but only somewhat. Buying even a small solar system can require outlays of thousands of dollars.

There's also the issue of reliability. Owning a solar energy system means that you're responsible for it. Warranties help, but they don't necessarily guarantee against the system malfunctioning or ceasing to work altogether. Again, this is not the case with conventional electricity, which is maintained by the local utility.

So how do you make solar affordable? One way is to transform it from a product into a service—selling solar *energy* instead of solar *systems*. Enter Shah, who left BP Solar in 2003 to start the company. Under his scheme, SunEdison finances, installs, owns, operates, and insures solar panels and systems on a customer's roof. In return, customers sign purchasing contracts that lock in the current price for as long as 20 years, creating a steady revenue stream for SunEdison. Customers get electricity at a fixed cost on a long-term basis, something few traditional energy utilities can offer. The company's focus began with commercial industrial rooftops—Wal-Mart hired the company to put solar panels on the roofs of several of its stores—but since has expanded into constructing utility-scale solar installations. The business model Shah pioneered is now being copied by other firms.

Of course, this isn't just an opportunity for little guys hoping to get big. Many of the world's biggest companies are innovating around green and clean technologies, sometimes investing significant sums with no immediate expectation of returns. They know that the markets for cleaner, greener products, processes, and services will come and that they will not necessarily be small, niche markets. They also understand the importance of having good stories to tell investors, employees, activists, the media, and others about the company's commitment to a better future and a cleaner world. A few of them will set the standard by which the rest of the business world—and all of us—will play. Many others will follow.

A growing number of green-economy entrepreneurs are to be found in China, India, and other developing markets. China's richest woman, Zhang Yin, owner of Nine Dragons Paper in south China's Guangdong Province, made her estimated $3 billion fortune recycling scrap paper imported from the United States. At the other end of the scale are countless entrepreneurs throughout India, Africa, and Latin America who are similarly turning waste into industrial feedstocks or deploying small-scale solar or other renewable-energy technologies at the village level to bring lighting, refrigeration, sanitation, and telecommunications to millions who lack them. The profits from such enterprises transcend financial remuneration.

So who will win in the green economy? Will large companies be the only ones with sufficient scale to move the needle on climate change and other problems or—as with computers and Web technologies—will audacious newcomers and small-scale social entrepreneurs trump experienced but stodgy incumbents? No one really knows, of course. Because the green economy includes the full spectrum of products and services—and the transformation of existing business processes and models as well as the creation of new, breakthrough ones—there likely will be room for everyone to play. But success will require innovative thinking, a firm understanding of the marketplace, a willingness to create new models, and more than a little patience.

# Chapter 25

# The New "Energy Companies"

T here's no better example than the energy business to demonstrate the breadth of opportunities emerging from the green economy and the way the lines are blurring across sectors, especially among the world's largest companies. Determining who was in the energy business used to be fairly simple, but no longer. Now it seems that just about everybody wants in on the quest for clean, renewable, and more efficient energy systems. It's no longer just oil, gas, coal, nuclear, and utility companies that qualify as being in the energy business. As the world's energy choices diversify, so too have the number and nature of companies jumping in. Now, "energy companies" are found in a wide range of decidedly nonenergy sectors, from electronics to chemicals to aerospace to agriculture.

Consider BASF, DuPont, Dow, 3M, and others that used to be called *chemical companies* (they now refer to themselves as *science and technology companies*). DuPont makes eight of the nine key materials used to manufacture conventional solar photovoltaic cells—everything but the silicon. This is hardly the first big energy bet for DuPont, the company who's tagline was, famously, "Better Things for Better Living... Through Chemistry." For example, it boasts an entire division making "more powerful, more durable, and more cost-efficient fuel cell materials and components," as the company puts it. German-based BASF views energy management as one of five "growth clusters," with a focus on energy storage, such as batteries and fuel cells. Dow is working to develop products and technologies that allow solar energy generation materials to be incorporated directly into the design of commercial and residential building materials, such as roofing systems and exterior sidings.

The agricultural sector is in the energy business, of course, making biofuels from corn and other crops. Cargill, the huge processor of food and beverage ingredients, helps farmers to source grain especially geared toward producing fuel and can help them to produce and sell the fuel their crops produce. It also operates its own biodiesel refineries. Its biggest competitor, Archer Daniels Midland, one of the world's largest processors of soybeans, corn, wheat, and cocoa, is also one of the world's largest manufacturers of ethanol and biodiesel for vehicles. It has a partnership with ConocoPhillips to develop fuels from crops, wood chips, and switchgrass. Its CEO, Patricia Woertz, was formerly a senior executive at Chevron.

It's not just the agricultural growers. John Deere, the tractor folks, has invested in several wind energy projects in the rural United States and has created a business unit to provide project development, debt financing, and other services to those interested in harvesting the wind. Another heavy-equipment manufacturer, Caterpillar, formed an alliance with FuelCell Energy involving the distribution and development of fuel cell power-generation products for industrial and commercial use.

The defense industry also is focusing on energy. Boeing supplies concentrator solar cell assemblies to an Australian solar company. (After all, it has been powering satellites by solar for decades.) Lockheed Martin, which gets almost $3 billion in annual revenue from managing military nuclear programs, provides engineering for solar power plants and has taken over administrative functions for utilities.

United Technologies makes fuel cells for buildings and vehicles and is part of a consortium of companies seeking to determine how buildings can be designed and constructed so that they use no energy from external power grids and be carbon-neutral. These are all "energy companies."

The electronics companies have long been in the energy biz. Fujitsu, Hitachi, Kyocera, Sanyo, Sharp, Siemens, and Toshiba are among the many firms in that sector making solar cells, fuel cells, components for wind turbines, and control technologies that make all these things work more efficiently. Sharp, for its part, is among the world's largest maker of solar cells and modules.

And then there are the information technology companies—the nice people who brought us the Internet and the personal computer, among other innovations. For several years they've been investing in ways to improve the electricity infrastructure to make it more efficient and reliable. Indeed, there's a lot that energy utilities can learn from computing and the Internet. Consider that the first computer systems consisted of a central computer hardwired to a lot of "dumb" terminals—so called because their principal purpose was to draw information from a big, smart mainframe. Then PCs came along and were able to do useful things themselves, as well as to talk to mainframes and to other PCs. Now, of course, everything talks to everything else—our computers with a billion other computers, as well as with our televisions, phones, and soon, our cars, refrigerators, and wristwatches—and can do so wirelessly.

Energy systems are developing along similar lines. Most of us still live in systems where a central "mainframe" electric utility feeds power to our "dumb" homes and businesses. Increasingly, some homes and businesses will become smarter as we install solar and other renewable systems to generate power, selling excess energy back to the grid. In the not-too-distant future, major appliances such as refrigerators and heating and air-conditioning systems will be "talking" to the electric grid, powering down for a few minutes here and there to help utilities, say, reduce their power load on hot days. Our plug-in electric vehicles and hybrids will store electricity in their increasingly better batteries and will sell extra power back to the grid when needed. Much of this will take place wirelessly. All these activities require switches, routers, microprocessors, and software—the essential ingredients of computing networks and the Internet—meaning that companies such as IBM, Intel, Cisco, and Microsoft increasingly will be in the energy business. (Mahvash Yazdi, the chief information officer at Southern California Edison, one of California's large electric utilities, once told me that when her company's service territory is fully retrofitted with "smart" meters that can be read wirelessly, her company will be able to collect data from 5 million meters *every 15 seconds*.)

There are still more companies in the energy business. General Electric, the largest U.S. wind turbine manufacturer, also is engaged in manufacturing solar panels, fuel cells, and other energy technologies. Google is making big investments to help make the price of renewable energy cheaper than that from coal. Owens Corning, best known for its pink building insulation, sells WindStrand, a "single-end roving and knitted fabric," to lower costs and higher performance for wind turbines. Tyson Foods, the world's largest processor and marketer of chicken, beef, and pork, created a renewable energy division to turn animal fat into biofuels. In 2007 it forged an alliance with ConocoPhillips aimed at leveraging Tyson's "advanced knowledge in protein chemistry and triglyceride production"—that is, roughly 2.3 billion pounds a year of chicken fat—with the oil company's processing and marketing expertise to launch "a next-generation renewable diesel fuel." Now, not only will the chicken be able to cross the road, but it also will burn rubber.

Of course, all this represents only large companies that traditionally have been in other sectors. There are thousands of smaller firms growing up around the demands for clean energy and increased energy efficiency—everything from local firms harvesting waste fry oil from fast-food joints and turning it into vehicle fuels, to chemists designing enzymes to more efficiently break down waste products into energy, to start-ups designing the next generation of everything from batteries to building automation networks. Each of these start-ups is, in effect, an energy company. In recent years, a vast sum of venture capital has been directed to these energy-tech entrepreneurs—$148.4 billion in 2007, according to U.K. research firm New Energy Finance. This encompasses all sectors of renewable energy and low-carbon technology, including wind, solar, biofuels, biomass, and energy efficiency, as well as the carbon markets.

Who else could become an "energy company"? Almost anyone who makes metals, plastics, advanced materials, or coatings. This includes big-box retailers, whose spacious flat roofs could collectively become solar farms for the surrounding community. And by extension, this also includes big real estate developers—of malls, warehouses, industrial parks, and other large complexes—creating microgrids of solar, wind, geothermal, fuel cell, and other energy technologies. Some of these players already are emerging, with many more still to come.

We may someday reach the point where it's easier to ask, "Who's *not* in the energy business?"

# Chapter 26

# Changing the Conversation at GM

The differences between the exhibits by the world's two largest automakers at the 2007 North American International Automobile Show in Detroit couldn't have been more stark. There they were: General Motors and Toyota. For one company, the focus was on an ingenious electric-powered vehicle. At a Hollywood-caliber unveiling held at the company's football-field-sized exhibition space, its chairman and other executives stood proudly by their slick, shiny eco-friendly prototype, reveling in the spotlight, no doubt hyped up by the adoring press. Meanwhile, at the other company's exhibit, it was all about big, muscular vehicles—trucks, sports-utility vehicles (SUVs), and the like, accentuated by a testosterone-pounding soundtrack. Off to the side, four hybrid-electric vehicles sat there looking forlorn, an afterthought, barely noticed amid the monster vehicles claiming the spotlight.

The first company was General Motors, the second was Toyota.

It may seem unlikely for General Motors to be poised for the green economy. After all, its legacy is one of big cars, trucks, and SUVs, most notoriously the Hummer. While Toyota has captured the attention—and the praise of environmentalists—thanks to its popular Prius gas-electric hybrid, GM seems to have been stuck in idle.

But don't count the Detroit company out. Over the past few years, GM has been working to change the conversation about the venerable U.S. automaker, finding small wins that enabled the company to dig itself out of the reputational hole as an environmentally unenlightened company. Little by little, GM has garnered respect, often begrudgingly, from some of its fiercest critics. (GM is a client of GreenOrder, the sustainability strategy firm with which I am affiliated.)

It's been a long and winding road. For years, GM was poorly regarded in the environmental community, which resented its seeming stubbornness to make cars that embraced an era of concern over gas prices and global warming. Moreover, along with Toyota and most other big car companies, GM spent millions of dollars fighting off efforts to raise U.S. fuel-economy standards and sued the state of California to block a law that would regulate greenhouse gas emissions from vehicles. A dozen other states also adopted California's "clean car standard" but were unable to implement it because of the carmakers' suit. By the middle of this decade, General Motors had become something of an environmental pariah. The 2006 documentary, *Who Killed the Electric Car?*, indicted, tried, and convicted GM of having willfully shuttered a promising gas-saving technology. It seemed there was little the company could do right, environmentally speaking.

It wasn't for lack of trying, though. For years, GM had been pushing several environmental story lines. It was making steady improvements in the emissions performance of its cars, it insisted. It was placing big bets in hydrogen and vowed to be the first company to profitably sell a million hydrogen-powered cars. The company was making impressive strides in reducing the environmental impacts of its manufacturing operations—for example, slashing packaging waste at its assembly plants from an average of more than 80 pounds per vehicle to less than 1 pound in some plants. It was America's largest user of energy derived from landfill gas.

But none of these things mattered in the court of public opinion. Customers, activists, the media, and others paid little heed to future vehicles or manufacturing efficiencies. For them, it was all about what they could buy in GM showrooms today. For GM, greener vehicles weren't to be found.

Then came ethanol, rising gas prices, and an opening. Starting in early 2005, U.S. retail gasoline prices began hiking upward, the average price of regular gas rising from $1.78 per gallon to over $3 per gallon on September 5 as the ruinous impacts of Hurricane Katrina further tightened gasoline supplies. Katrina was only one factor, albeit a dramatic one, that caused gasoline prices to spike in 2005. The price of West Texas intermediate crude oil, which started the year at about $42 per barrel, reached $70 per barrel in early September. Growing global oil demand already had stretched capacity along the entire oil value chain, from crude oil production to tankers and pipelines to refinery capacity, nearly to its limits. Then came Katrina, which had a devastating impact on U.S. gas markets, initially taking big chunks out of crude oil production and refinery capacity. With such a large drop in supply, prices spiked dramatically.

Enter GM flex-fuel vehicles and a loophole in the federal fuel economy law that automakers had been exploiting for years. In 1988, Congress passed the Alternative Motor Fuels Act, which included a "dual-fuel loophole" in its corporate average fuel economy (CAFE) requirements. CAFE required automakers to achieve a "fleet average" of 27.5 miles per gallon (mpg) for cars and 21.5 mpg for trucks or face so-called gas-guzzler taxes that would be passed on to the consumer, raising those vehicles' sticker prices. The dual-fuel loophole, which was renewed by Congress in 2005, gave higher mpg credit for cars that were capable, in theory at least, of running on E85 fuel, a mixture of 85 percent ethanol and 15 percent gasoline, regardless of whether the vehicles ever actually used that fuel. Ethanol was made primarily from corn, thus reducing petroleum consumption—again, in theory. Thus a full-size, V8-powered SUV such as the GMC Yukon was rated at 33 mpg for CAFE purposes when, in fact, it got only 15 mpg in city driving and 20 mpg on the highway, according to government tests. Making a car E85-capable boosted car makers' CAFE ratings and avoided gas-guzzler taxes, all for about $150 in additional cost per vehicle.

Over the years, GM, Ford, and other auto makers built millions of flex-fuel vehicles, although few owners of these cars were aware of this capability and, even if they knew, probably couldn't buy E85 fuel. It was offered in only a few hundred fueling stations, mostly in the Midwest.

In 2005, as U.S. gas prices became a political issue for the first time since the Arab oil embargo of the 1970s, GM saw an opportunity. It began to promote its cars' flex-fuel capability and made moves to increase the number of E85 fueling stations, no small matter because it cost stations tens of thousands of dollars to install E85 pumps. Suddenly, GM had a cause, or perhaps several—global warming, energy security, national security, and supporting Midwest farmers over Mideast sultans.

During the 2006 Super Bowl, GM unveiled an ad campaign, "Live Green, Go Yellow," designed to make consumers, energy producers, and policymakers aware of GM's E85 capability in current and future models. The color yellow referred to corn, as well as to the colored gas caps GM began putting on the more than 400,000 flex-fuel vehicles capable of running E85 that it would produce in 2006.

"Live Green, Go Yellow" was well received, albeit not without skeptics, both inside and outside the company. But for the first time, GM began getting positive press on an environmental issue. The company used the opening to begin a conversation with fuel suppliers to increase the number of fueling stations offering E85. It began talking with environmental groups again—and the activists, while skeptical, were listening for the first time in years. A small bandwagon developed. Within a few weeks of "Live Green, Go Yellow," New York Governor George Pataki promoted a plan to establish refineries "that make ethanol out of agricultural products from our farms and wood products from our northern forests" and to make such fuel "tax-free throughout the entire state." Suddenly, GM found itself at the front of a growing parade.

"We had the sense that people were really hungry for a choice," explains Elizabeth Lowery, GM's vice president, Environment, Energy, and Safety Policy. "Gasoline had become expensive, and people felt boxed in, and nobody likes to be in that position." GM saw that for perhaps the first time its products—millions of flex-fuel vehicles on the roads—were part of the solution.

Like many corporate cultures, GM's put a premium on the notion of "deeds, not words," says Lowery, "making sure we were doing what we had to do and that we were doing what we said we were going to do. So many times, we would keep our technology to ourselves, as far as working on it but not telling anybody about it. And I kept saying, 'No, I really think it's deeds *and* words, because if nobody knows what you're doing, then you're not going to get credit for it. It's not anybody's fault for not giving you credit if you haven't told them about it.'"

Lowery and her team recognized that promoting E85 couldn't be just a marketing campaign, however. "It had to be the products, which we had, and it had to be that we're doing real things." Moreover, the messaging couldn't sound arrogant. "We realized we needed a different tone. It was not dictating and forcing messages. It was more inviting, more educational." And it needed to come from the top. GM had been hearing from the activist groups about how important it was for the chairman to speak out on these topics.

All this came together in December 2006 at the Los Angeles Auto Show, where GM chairman and CEO Rick Wagoner delivered a keynote address, talking about "Live Green, Go Yellow" and telegraphing a significant announcement that GM would make the following month—of the Volt electric vehicle. It was a significant moment: the first time GM's top leader had been out front on environmental issues. It didn't hurt that his speech took place in car-conscious California, the state his company had been suing.

"Live Green, Go Yellow" gave GM new standing to have a conversation with stakeholders and the marketplace about greener cars. It was a small but meaningful opportunity to be relevant again in environmental circles. In January 2007, at the North American

International Auto Show in Detroit, Wagoner introduced GM's most ambitious contribution to the world of greener transport—E-Flex, a platform of plug-in electric vehicles that could recharge via a small, efficient engine that can burn anything from gasoline to bio-fuels to hydrogen. The first model in the E-Flex series, the Chevy Volt, would be capable of driving in pure gas-free electric mode for about 40 miles, after which the small supplementary engine would kick in to recharge the battery, extending the car's range to more than 600 miles, the equivalent of about 150 miles per gallon of gasoline.

Only one problem: It was just a concept car.

Still, even though the car was several years from hitting a Chevy showroom, GM knew it had a winner. The Volt provided a surge of energy to the company, its dealers, the automotive media, and even some activist groups. At the Volt launch in Detroit, I ran into Chris Paine, producer of the documentary *Who Killed the Electric Car?*. Throughout the event, I couldn't help but note his rapt attention and enthusiastic applause. I caught up with him afterwards to get his reaction, and he was positively ecstatic. "I think it's fantastic," he responded. "This is better than any award I could ever get as a film-maker." You can't buy that kind of buzz.

For GM, it was the combination of marketing, public policy, and communication that allowed the breakthrough moment. "That product broke through enough to allow us to talk about all the other things we've been doing," says Lowery. One year later, at the 2008 Chicago auto show, the buzz around GM was different from anything Lowery and her colleagues had experienced. "It was all about 'How soon are you going to get the plug-in here?' The negative and the cynical and the attack—I didn't have any of it. I didn't have one question about being late to the game, which we used to get. The time was right where people wanted to root for us." GM wasn't showing the Volt at the 2008 auto show, but after two days of being hounded by the press to see it, the company brought one in.

For GM, the medium was the messaging—finding the voice that allowed it to engage the marketplace in a manner it previously couldn't. The company had been seen as arrogant, uncaring, and not aligned with the market or with societal concerns. But GM was able to find a simple message, a hopeful and helpful message, in a time of public concern over gas prices—and back it up with a clever and compelling technology.

"People do want simple messages," says Lowery, "and I think there is such an opportunity for us and the environmental groups on the education side, because we share the idea that consumers have a role to play. And if we can figure out a way to say, 'Hey, you can do this, yes, there'll be some sacrifice, but it doesn't have to be painful sacrifice,' consumers will respond."

They're getting closer. Today, Lowery and her colleagues talk openly about GM's two-part strategy to reduce the use of petroleum through renewable fuels and vehicle electrification. This is a pretty compelling message—and a million miles from how the company positioned itself just a few years ago.

GM is hardly out of the woods, both environmentally and financially. It has legacy problems on both fronts—high pension and health care costs that add $2,000 to the price of every vehicle (much of this will be handed off to an independent trust fund starting in 2010. This is the same year that the Volt is expected to be in showrooms—along with plug-in electric vehicles from Toyota and others.) The age of persistently high gas prices—with the never-ending possibility that a border skirmish, petty dictator, or pipeline hiccup could further constrain supply and raise prices—makes GM's lineup of Hummers, Escalades, minivans, and full-size pick-ups vulnerable to the vagaries of the oil market. In 2008, the company announced it was closing some of its truck and SUV plants, and reevaluating its continued ownership of Hummer.

For the first time, there are scenarios in which GM—and, by extension, any of the other car makers—could shift gears, moving from laggards to leaders in an industry not known for turning on a dime. And this augurs well not just for automakers but also for heavy industry, for old-line companies' ability to adapt to the green economy's changing realities—and to bring their customers along for the ride.

# Chapter 27

# How Many Green Marketers Does It Take to Screw in a Light Bulb?

**A**s we've seen in previous chapters, one of the big challenges in the green economy is getting consumers to change old habits. Most people have proven pretty conclusively that they are unwilling, perhaps unable, to change habits, whether it be for their or their family's health, the well-being of their neighbors and community, or the future of the planet. Even when they know they must change, they often don't. So it's notable when a green product breaks through, especially one that all of us count on every day.

The marketing of the compact fluorescent light bulb is one such success. Consider that people are switching from an inexpensive, familiar, and reliable product—the incandescent light bulb—to a considerably more expensive, new-fangled bulb that works differently and can change the way familiar things look when it is lit. This shift is no small matter. Lighting consumes 22 percent of electricity produced in the United States, according to the Department of Energy, and most lighting is highly inefficient from an energy-use perspective. Light bulbs are everywhere—every home has one, and most have dozens—so there is high potential for a single product to transform our energy use.

How did the transformation to energy-efficient lighting take place? How did sales of compact fluorescent lights (CFLs) hit 290 million in the United States alone in 2007—about 20 percent of the light bulb market—and more than 2 billion worldwide compared with 70 million and 356 million, respectively, 10 years earlier? It took the combined effort of manufacturers, activist groups, utilities, government agencies, entertainers, Web sites, bloggers, retailers, and some creative marketers. The case of the CFL illuminates the need for both coordinated and individual efforts done over a sustained period to instigate fundamental changes in consumers' buying habits.

First, some background. The CFL was invented at General Electric in 1976, a response to the 1973 energy crisis, when engineer Edward E. Hammer developed a way to bend a standard-shaped 40-watt fluorescent tube lamp into a spiral shape able to produce a long electrical arc that simulated the optical properties of a frosted incandescent lamp. GE decided that the bulb was too expensive to manufacture and shelved it, but the design leaked out. Other bulb makers copied it before GE was able to start a licensing program, and by the early 1980s, the bulb had been introduced globally.

CFLs represent a major advancement over the conventional incandescent bulb, the technology of which hasn't changed appreciably since patented by Thomas Edison in 1880. A standard incandescent bulb produces light when electricity heats a small metal filament inside a sealed glass bulb to 2,300°C (about 4,100°F), causing the filament to glow. This produces light, but mostly heat. At best, only about 10 percent of the electricity used by incandescent bulbs becomes visible light.

In a fluorescent bulb, electrons are emitted by a ballast and strike the inside of the glass tube, exciting the bulb's phosphor coating and emitting visible light and far less heat. The process yields about four times more light per watt than an incandescent bulb. Moreover, because the bulbs operate at only about 300°C (about 570°F), they last longer because high heat produces wear and tear.

By the late 1980s, with the rise of concern about energy use and climate change, compact fluorescent bulbs were being touted by environmentalists as a key energy—and money-saving appliance. Stories abounded about the bulbs' potential, should they achieve widespread use. As the nonprofit Earth Day Network stated on its Web site, "If every household replaced its most commonly used incandescent light bulbs with CFLs, electricity use for lighting could be cut in half. Doing so would lower our annual carbon dioxide emissions by about 125 billion pounds. This action alone could halt the growth in carbon dioxide emissions from the United States, given recent growth rates."

We could save the Earth, we were told, one light bulb at a time. There was only one problem: CFLs were expensive, emitted odd hues, didn't work in all existing fixtures, and couldn't work with dimmers. The first bulbs cost upwards of $20 each. Did I mention that they were expensive?

The major CFL manufacturers—GE, Philips, and Sylvania—partnered with activist groups, government agencies, electric utilities, the media, and retailers to break through these barriers. It took a village to change a light bulb, it seemed.

Finding a sizable audience wasn't easy. Consider Netherlands-based Philips, one of Europe's leading proponents of green marketing and green design. It has a strong global eco-design program, supported by the Delft University of Technology. Philips believes that eco-design principles can be a strong basis to enhance business and that eco-design is not chiefly a technical activity but a concept to be embedded in the business value chain.

Philips' began manufacturing CFLs in 1978, marketing them in the United States as the Earth Light. For years, the bulbs languished in the U.S. market despite their success in Europe, which experiences much higher energy costs. Consumer resistance eased as the bulbs' prices dropped, the quality of their light got better, and their size decreased, making them suitable for more existing fixtures. Equally important to Philips' success in the United States, however, was a name change that illuminated a green-marketing reality: People want value first; saving the Earth comes second. So after CFL sales flattened, Philips took the bulbs off the market, reintroducing them with a new name. Overnight, the "Earth Light" had become the "Marathon Bulb."

In its consumer research, Philips had found a great deal of sympathy for green issues (50 percent positive, 25 percent neutral), combined with outright fear. And almost half of consumers wanted additional information about the environmental benefits of the products they buy. But a much lower percentage of consumers was willing to change their lifestyles (20 percent) or pay more (25 percent). Philips recognized that the environment was not the bulb's primary value proposition—in fact, it was fourth or fifth in priority. At the top of the list was that consumers wanted the bulbs to last.

Philips research also found that consumers were more willing to buy green products when their environmental attributes were bundled with other benefits. Therefore, linking environmental attributes—energy reduction, materials reduction, and toxic-substance reduction—with material (the bulbs' lower cost over their lifetime), immaterial (the convenience of not having to change bulbs as frequently), and emotional (the good feeling of doing the right thing) benefits raised consumer interest to 60 percent or above—including consumers who were negatively predisposed to the environment.

After the name change, U.S sales growth of Philips' CFLs went from essentially nil to 12 percent or more a year.

But times changed—again. At the end of 2006, the company changed the name once more, to "Energy Saver," reflecting consumers' growing interest in energy-saving products. Philips found that *energy savings* resonated more with consumers, who found it more appealing than the word *marathon*. At about the same time, GE rebranded its CFLs as "Energy Smart" bulbs, no doubt based on similar research findings.

Name changes aside, Philips and its competitors have used almost every marketing trick imaginable, and probably some new ones, to brighten markets for CFLs. Philips formed the Lighting Efficiency Coalition in 2007, aimed at garnering support from environmental groups, legislators, and even competitors to help market the bulbs. Philips also launched a global campaign, called a A Simple Switch. The name reflects the company's premise that "reducing energy consumption can be simple and actionable without compromising on quality of life." Philips partnered with the Alliance for Climate Protection and the global Live Earth musical events to promote energy-efficient lighting. At Live Earth, Philips passed out CFLs while educating concertgoers about the bulbs. Through the tours, Philips found that the younger generation, less rooted in old ways, was more receptive to CFLs. Tapping into celebrity support helped, too, particularly when media giants themselves made CFL pledges.

Philips also tapped into Web-based viral marketing. As part of A Simple Switch, the company launched a Web site allowing consumers to record a personal "simple switch" pledge. Philips used those pledges as a way to calculate energy and costs savings, feeding that data back to the audience. The site also featured an interactive map showing the number of people who made switches (including Philips employees). It also used the site to provide information on how people can take action and start a movement of their own, hoping to spark word-of-mouth marketing.

Sylvania, for its part, focused its marketing on partnerships with electric utilities and on the endorsement of its CFLs by the U.S. government's Energy Star program. Sylvania's marketing campaign involved a partnership with the U.S. Environmental Protection Agency (EPA) and included a 2007 bus tour from Disneyland in California to Faneuil Hall Marketplace in Boston. In Boston, during a celebration of American revolutionary history, Sylvania lit up an old church with 1,776 CFLs. The company also focused on package design. The company found that people wanted to see the product inside, something that wasn't true for incandescents. Sylvania originally designed its packaging with just a glimpse of the bulb but discovered that people wanted to see the entire product, so it redesigned its packaging accordingly.

All these measures were aided by a perfect storm, almost literally, for CFLs: Hurricane Katrina, Oprah, and Wal-Mart. On the heels of Katrina, which brought renewed focus on energy conservation and the perils of global warming, the prominence of CFLs grew. Oprah Winfrey flogged the bulbs on her show and in her eponymous magazine, with everyone from Al Gore to Leonardo DiCaprio touting the virtues of

CFLs. And then Wal-Mart chimed in following a face-to-face meeting in early 2006 between Wal-Mart chairman Lee Scott and his counterpart at General Electric, Jeffrey Immelt. The two agreed to collaborate in a full-court press to educate the public about CFLs, and GE agreed to help Wal-Mart sell 100 million of the bulbs by the end of 2007. In Wal-Mart's legendary, take-no-prisoners style, and with GE's help, it unleashed an arsenal of initiatives: interactive in-store displays to help customers choose the right CFL; educational displays to allow customers to compare qualities and styles and calculate the potential financial savings, increased shelf space in lighting aisles and displays in unexpected places in its stores, marketing promotions on the company's in-store TV and radio channels, and education and incentives to its employees to encourage them to generate sales.

Wal-Mart, too, worked the Web, partnering with Yahoo!, the EPA, Department of Energy, AC Nielsen, Environmental Defense Fund, and Lawrence Bender, producer of the movie *An Inconvenient Truth*, to produce the site 18seconds.org, the name describing the length of time it takes to install a CFL. The site—whose tagline reads, "Change a Bulb. Change Everything"—keeps a running tab on how many bulbs are sold; AC Nielsen collects purchase information for most grocery, drug, and mass-merchandise retailers and feeds it to the site. The idea, in part, is to stimulate competition and civic pride among cities and states to increase the market uptake of CFLs.

It all seems to be working. Wal-Mart reached its 100 million goal by September 2007 and closed the year with sales of about 146 million bulbs. Emboldened by its success, the company announced plans to launch its own house brand of bulbs.

Still, market penetration for CFLs has only scratched the surface. Some 95 percent of U.S. households lack a single compact fluorescent bulb. And while the technology is improving—dimmable bulbs are now being sold, and the bulbs' color range more closely mimics that of incandescents—getting the public to change from the affordable and time-tested incumbent bulbs remains an uphill battle. Policy changes around the world make the transition inevitable: Australia has already announced that it will phase out the sale of incandescent light bulbs by 2010, and Canada plans to meet that goal by 2012. The United States is taking a slightly longer view, phasing out the 125-year-old bulbs sometime between 2012 and 2020.

The fate of CFLs remains cloudy, however. For all the fuss—the Web sites, the marketing machinations, and the breathless environmental group incantations about the potential for the bulbs if everyone installed one—CFLs may be merely a transitional technology. New, improved bulbs—namely light-emitting diodes (LEDs)—are moving up the technology curve, improving in efficiency, efficacy, and economics. LEDs, which, like incandescent bulbs and CFLs, were invented at General Electric, are made from various concoctions of semiconductors, mainly gallium and indium. Unlike incandescent bulbs and CFLs, which produce light by heating something until it glows, LEDs are illuminated solely by the movement of electrons in a semiconductor material. In effect, they are more like little computers, using tiny transistors to produce light. Because they are tiny, groups of LEDs can be formed into almost any shape, including that of a conventional incandescent bulb, if that becomes a desirable and marketable form factor. And because they are, in effect, computer-controlled, a LED light source can change colors, intensity, or other characteristics to meet changing lighting conditions, enhancing both comfort and safety.

Like CFLs, LEDs represent a leapfrog technology, producing more light with less energy and lasting far longer than their predecessors—50,000 hours compared with 10,000 hours for a CFL and 1,000 hours for an Edison incandescent bulb. Their reliability already makes them affordable for applications where the hassle or labor costs of bulb replacement are relatively high—traffic signals, for example, or back-lighting mobile phones. LEDs also hold great promise for the roughly 2 billion Earth denizens who have neither modern lighting nor electricity. Efficient, cheap LEDs, combined with inexpensive solar panels and batteries for storage, could permit a leap past wired lights, much as cell phones permitted the developing world to leapfrog the need for a landline infrastructure. A solar-battery LED light already produces illumination at a fraction of the cost of a kerosene lamp, the incumbent technology in the developing world, and does so with far less pollution and harm to human health.

But LEDs have a way to go. In fact, the problems mirror perfectly those of CFLs. LEDs remain expensive—a lamp for household use can run $40 or more—and equally challenging, the quality of light leaves a lot to be desired, especially for indoor applications. They aren't yet available for most consumer lighting applications. Did I mention that they were expensive?

Here we glow again. The green economy—like all economies—will be a work in progress, a never-ending series of technological innovations, some incremental, some leapfrog. Today's green breakthrough inevitably will become tomorrow's Betamax—a relic of a time in which old models were shattered, illuminating a world of possibilities of how to do things cheaper, smarter, and cleaner.

# Chapter 28

# The "Greenmuting" Paradox

We've previously touched on the pejorative term "greenwashing," which was coined by Greenpeace in the early 1990s to describe "cynical, superficial, public relations marketing" aimed at projecting a falsely benign environmental corporate image. The nonprofit Web site SourceWatch defines it as "the unjustified appropriation of environmental virtue by a company, an industry, a government, a politician or even a non-government organization to create a pro-environmental image, sell a product or a policy, or to try and rehabilitate their standing with the public and decision makers after being embroiled in controversy."

However defined, charges of "greenwash" have been on the move lately, in lockstep with the rebirth of green marketing. Moreover, like so many other things green, "greenwash" is as vague a term as there is, existing largely in the minds of the beholders. Almost anything can be dismissed as "greenwash" these days, with the odds of garnering that moniker increasing proportionately with the size and stature of the company in question. For many activists, there is nothing that a big company—particularly a brand leader—can do, environmentally speaking, to curry favor. Whatever they do is "greenwash."

Through most of the 1990s and beyond, "greenwashing" was considered inside baseball, a conversation held largely among a scrum of environmental activists and corporate critics to describe offending companies. By the end of 2007, however, it began to break into the mainstream. There is now a Greenwashing Index, a Greenwashing Brigade, and other institutional efforts to illuminate perceived eco-marketing misdeeds. Most of all, though, there were the "Six Sins of Greenwashing." This 2007 study, by the Canadian firm TerraChoice Environmental Marketing, sent research teams into six category-leading big-box stores with orders "to record every product-based environmental claim they observed." TerraChoice instructed the teams that, for each environmental claim, they should "identify the product, the nature of the claim, any supporting information, and any references offered for further information."

The products studied included a wide range of offerings, from air fresheners to appliances, televisions to toothpaste. In total, the team identified 1,018 products making 1,753 claims. For each, TerraChoice sought to answer a basic question: What proof is there that a product actually meets this claim?

What the company found was that most of the products didn't have a good answer. In fact, all but one made claims that "are either demonstrably false or that risk misleading intended audiences," in the words of TerraChoice Vice President Scot Case, who headed the project. Case and his team identified six "sins" of the offending products:

1. *Sin of the hidden tradeoff*—claims that suggest that a product is green based on a single environmental attribute (the recycled content of paper, for example) or an unreasonably narrow set of attributes without attention to other important, or perhaps more important, environmental issues (such as the energy, climate, water, or forestry impacts of paper). Such claims aren't usually false but paint a misleading picture of the product than a more

complete environmental analysis would support. This was the most frequently committed "sin," made by 57 percent of all environmental claims examined.

2. *Sin of no proof* (26 percent of all claims examined)—any claim that couldn't be substantiated by easily accessible supporting information or by a reliable third-party certification. TerraChoice determined there to be "no proof" if supporting evidence was not accessible at either the point of purchase or at the product Web site.

3. *Sin of vagueness* (11 percent of all claims examined)—any claim that is so poorly defined or broad that its real meaning is likely to be misunderstood by the intended consumer, such as "chemical free" or "all natural."

4. *Sin of irrelevance* (4 percent of all claims examined)—claims that may be truthful but are unimportant and unhelpful for consumers, such as chlorofluorocarbon (CFC)–free products because ozone-depleting CFCs have been outlawed since the late 1970s.

5. *Sin of lesser of two evils* (1 percent of all claims examined)—environmental claims that may be true but that risk distracting the consumer from the greater environmental impacts of the category as a whole, such as organic tobacco or green insecticides.

6. *Sin of fibbing* (less than 1 percent of all claims examined)—claims that are simply false, typically by misusing or misrepresenting certification by an independent authority when no such certification had been made.

I'm not sure that all these "sins" qualify as "greenwashing," which I see as an intentional effort to misrepresent a product, service, or company as being environmentally responsible or improved. True, some of the claims that TerraChoice examined represent outright fabrications, but much of this seems less sin than sloppiness—marketers' efforts to place a green sheen on a product, perhaps rightfully so, but without offering some basic proof points. Either way, it's a poor showing for green marketers.

The TerraChoice study got the attention of, among others, McDonald's Bob Langert, who was moved to pen, in his corporate blog, an alternative view. "I agree there are dangers associated with environmental marketing," he wrote, "but I actually think many companies are reluctant to talk about their environmental efforts because they are concerned they will be met only with criticism. After all, true progress is so hard to define, and achieving perfection on the environmental front is impossible because there will always be ways to improve."

But not talking about environmental efforts—which Langert dubbed "greenmuting"—may be a sin as well, he said. Mirroring TerraChoice, he offered six (quoted here in Langer's voice):

1. Waiting for 100 percent understanding of the science behind the issues before taking action and making a claim. *The reality:* If you do, you'll wait forever. Don't get me wrong. Research is essential. But you can't let the "analysis cause paralysis" and prevent you from getting the public informed and involved.
2. Being cautious on environmental claims because nongovernment organizations (NGOs) will probably just rip into your organization. *The reality:* Solid NGO partnerships are essential, but if you think you can please all stakeholders, you're brainwashing yourself.
3. Not too many people choose products or services based on their environmental footprint. *The reality:* Conscious consumerism is on the rise, and I'm banking on consumers using their purchasing power to make a statement more and more in the years to come.
4. Green consumers are a small niche. *The reality:* Green is getting more mainstream than ever. There is enormous opportunity here to build the strength of a business, especially in terms of trust, brand, and reputation.
5. Communicating more on the environment will build pressure to take actions that are not practical or advantageous to the bottom line. *The reality:* Expectations are rising. Period. Why not get out ahead of the curve and develop the best solutions for your business?
6. When "greenwashing" is discussed, stay low and away from the conversation. *The reality:* Follow the advice on the "six sins" list. Let's get greener and talk about it in the right way.

"We need more public discourse on all things green," Langert concluded. "Greenmuting will only prevent the sea change in consumer awareness that is building toward real progress on the environment."

He's right. Activists need not let down their guard, but they do need to lighten up. It's not a binary world where everything *is* or *isn't* green. A lot of this is relative: A green product can be one that's improved, although far from perfect.

Or can it? As Langert says, we need less name calling and more actual conversation about what and how much it takes to be green.

# Chapter 29

# You Gotta Have CRED

How do you create a green strategy that is pitch perfect and tuned for long-term success? It's not easy, based on the efforts I've seen. Companies executives—and their advertising, marketing, and public relations partners—are prone to make broad, sweeping statements about their environmental commitment or the green attributes of their products or services, statements and claims that often pose more questions than answers. In other cases, companies simply seem uninspired. (How many more times can we stand yet another take-off on Kermit the Frog's plaintive proclamation, "It's not easy being green." Kermit first crooned that song lyric in—Would you believe?—1970, and nearly four decades later it still seems to be the best copywriters can come up with. (In mid–2008, I conducted a Google search of the phrase "easy being green," which yielded 1,570,000 returns. By contrast "til death do we part" yielded only 17,500 returns, while "check is in the mail" garnered 20,500 returns.) Moreover, each new slogan or press release quoting or paraphrasing Kermit seems to revel in its cleverness, as if its creators were the first to have thought it up.) Is it any wonder that the public is skeptical about companies' environmental commitments?

It's not just Kermit, of course. Too many green strategies, and the messages behind them, are variously vague, vapid, or vacuous.

How do you avoid this fate? To answer this, I turned to my colleague Andrew Shapiro, founder and CEO of GreenOrder, the sustainable business strategy firm with which I am affiliated. I've learned a lot hanging around Shapiro, managing principal Nicholas Eisenberger and their team for the better part of a decade, but what sticks most is GreenOrder's framework for crafting green strategies and messaging that work. It's called *CRED* (see Figure 29–1).

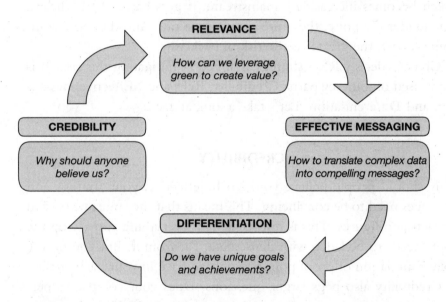

**Figure 29–1** GreenOrder's CRED strategy.

GreenOrder—whose blue-chip clients have included Allianz, BP, DuPont, General Electric, General Motors, Office Depot, and Pfizer—isn't the first consulting firm to come up with a multipart strategy acronym. Over the years, as I've encountered or worked with some of the leading consulting, PR, and marketing firms, I've seen my share. They all have value.

CRED evolved from GreenOrder's experience working on C-suite executive strategy and implementation, including creating the metrics companies must use to measure success and make their environmental initiatives thoughtful, effective, and believable. After all, it's no use having a green strategy and message if they don't work or if they don't drive value and fit with a larger vision—the story the company would like to tell about itself, both today and over the longer term. And telling a green story that isn't rooted in real-world accomplishments amounts to little more than arm waving.

This is only part of the problem. An equally vexing challenge is how to stand out in the crowd, to be heard amid the growing cacophony of green messages. Therein lies the green-strategy paradox: As green becomes increasingly mainstream, it gets harder to be heard. The louder the noise, the more people tune out. And the more companies boast, the greater is the risk of backlash.

GreenOrder's CRED strategy is aimed at mitigating this risk. It is comprised of four key parts: **C**redibility, **R**elevance, **E**ffective messaging, and **D**ifferentiation. Let's take a look at each.

## CREDIBILITY

Why should people believe you? To be effective, your strategy and messages need to be convincing. This means that they must be backed by facts and figures. This is not to say that everything you say on the topic needs to be laden with dense data. Far from it. But you need a solid foundation of proof points, if only to have in your back pocket.

Credibility also begs larger questions. Does your company's performance match its green rhetoric? Can you prove it? How does your company or its products compare, whether with competitors' best products, the installed product base, what the government requires, or even the historical performance of past generations of the same product? You'll be credible if you can show that you've done your homework. It needn't appear in ads, product labeling, or point-of-purchase information, but it should be available somewhere, whether on product fact sheets, Web sites, customer service lines, or some other place. "GE has done that well with ecomagination," says Shapiro. "They've had very detailed information about the environmental and operating performance of ecomagination products on a dedicated Web site, even though the advertisements on television, for example, haven't overwhelmed consumers with factoids."

The volume and nature of data may depend in part on your sector, as well as on how well your company is regarded from an environmental perspective. An eco-hip and well-regarded brand such as Patagonia, the maker of outdoor apparel, or Method, which makes cleaning products, may have a lower burden of proof than a company that lacks a green image or history. (Then again, maybe not. Informed, eco-conscious customers such as Patagonia's and Method's can be among the toughest audiences in the world in terms of questioning and challenging green claims.) Business and institutional buyers likely will have much deeper information needs and may not spend a lot of time hunting it down. Also, you may want to dial up or down the amount of information to reflect the importance you're placing on a product's green attributes and how aggressively you want to promote them. Sometimes, less is more.

The point is that it's important to assess what your customers and other audiences—activists, regulators, the media, etc.—know, need to know, and want to hear to ensure that you are meeting or exceeding their expectations. And then you must marry whatever environmental attributes you are promoting with all the other attributes customers expect for that product. "We call this 'twinning the benefits,'" explains Shapiro. "You're trying to talk about the environmental benefits while also emphasizing whatever else is appropriate—quality, durability, price, performance, style."

By the way, the principal reasons for doing this may not be your customers at all but rather your employees. They're the first group that needs assurance that any claims you make hold water and the first to become cynical if they find out otherwise. Thus, supporting data can be important to getting your number one constituency on board.

## RELEVANCE

This is using green to create value with key stakeholders. How do you craft a strategy that's not only going to meet your immediate business objectives—to move product, increase revenue, and be seen as a "good" company, for example—but also is going ensure that your efforts have staying power internally because they are generating business value for the firm? In other words, how do you ensure that they are sustainable from a business perspective?

Companies that don't leverage their environmental achievements and commitment in a way that produces business value often find that green is the first thing to go when times get tough—when there's a change in leadership, when shareholders raise questions, or when your company otherwise finds that being seen as an environmental leader is no longer convenient. On the other hand, if you can say, "Our sustainability initiatives have reduced costs and boosted revenue by creating new markets, adding new products, and deepening loyalty with customers," this creates a long-term justification for a sustainability strategy and for environmental issues broadly.

"It's critical that a company figure out the difficult task of aligning its sustainability initiatives with its core business objectives and its growth trajectory," says Shapiro. "If a company is in a product-introduction mode or a geographic-expansion mode or a cost-cutting mode—whatever mode the business cycle requires—it can leverage and use sustainability as a source of value creation, as opposed to simply something that is a marker of good corporate citizenship."

Companies run into trouble when they get too far ahead of themselves or too far away from their core business goals. Bill Ford, when he was president and CEO of the car company his great-grandfather, Henry Ford, built, took his eye off the prize partly in the name of building a greener image. Bill Ford was, arguably, one of the most committed environmentalists among CEOs of major companies and certainly within his sector. Under his leadership, he placed a major emphasis—and a lot of his political capital—on greening his company's historic manufacturing site, including increasing the building's energy efficiency, putting on a green (planted) roof, and transforming the surrounding site from an industrial eyesore to a community gem.

What about his company's cars? During this same period, Ford made and then retracted a commitment to achieve a 25 percent improvement in fuel efficiency in the company's light truck fleet, including sports-utility vehicles (SUVs); backed off from a pledge to build 250,000 hybrid vehicles a year by 2010; and terminated the company's ongoing electric vehicle program as impractical and unaffordable.

The obvious question: How relevant was the grass on the roof of the Rouge River manufacturing facility to the end customer compared with creating more fuel-efficient cars, producing more energy and environmental innovations, and marrying green attributes with high style, performance, and technology? Ford's financial woes aren't based entirely on the company's green focus, of course, but the timing suggests that the company's particular green focus and messaging weren't relevant to the marketplace.

Again, the relevance of your green strategy may not necessarily be to sell more stuff. It could be to attract and retain talent. "As companies start to think about their various constituencies, they may come to learn, 'We didn't realize that a huge number of our employees, as well as our recruits, are interested in working for a company that excels in green leadership,'" says Shapiro. "And they could actually reduce the cost of turnover and the cost associated with hiring and retraining people by demonstrating their green leadership. So the relevance factor could be, 'Is this something your customers want to buy?' But it could also be, 'Is this something you'll be rewarded ·for by your employees, or by investors, or by other actors in the marketplace?'"

## EFFECTIVE MESSAGING

How can you translate complex information into distinctive, compelling messages? Few companies do a good job at making sense of what often can be mystifying and mind-numbing facts and transforming them into a compelling story.

It's not that companies don't try. It seems like every other ener-gy- or climate-related advertisement or press release I've seen in recent years offers some comparison with taking cars off the road. "In 2005, HSBC purchased carbon offsets equivalent to 125,000 tons of carbon emissions—the same as taking 29,000 cars off the road," says the bank's Web site. Xerox prevented the emission of 87,000 metric tons of carbon dioxide in 2006, "the equivalent of taking more than 18,000 cars off the road," according to a compa-ny press release.

There's nothing wrong with either of these, of course. I'm assum-ing that the authors of each of these claims did the math correctly—that a typical late-model sedan emits about 5 tons of carbon dioxide gas in a year. The point is: Is an impressive number of eliminated cars—or planted trees, electrified homes, conserved Olympic-sized swimming pools of water, Eiffel Tower heights of reduced waste, trips to the Moon of saved driving, or other comparative metrics—even meaningful to consumers, especially after they've heard similar statis-tics from myriad other companies? (I sometimes wonder whether adding up all the cars-taken-off-the-road marketing claims would yield a number that exceeds the actual number of cars on the road. But I digress.)

So figuring out an effective way to translate environmental data is key.

It's also about figuring out the right channels. What are the appro-priate media? What are the best moments to reach people on these issues? Are advertising and PR the answer? Not always. "We're hear-ing more and more that consumers and activists are pointing out the irony that a company may spend twice as much promoting a green achievement as they did on the achievement itself," says Shapiro. "An effective message is not always one that's marketed with the most dollars." Rather, the effective message may be the one that's done cleverly, virally, or humorously. Or it may be one that's tied to a part-nership or delivered through nontraditional means.

In other words, it's the medium as well as the message.

## DIFFERENTIATION

Are you doing something that's unique and distinct? Does your strategy sound like you're truly committed or simply mimicking or mirroring what others have done?

Differentiation is difficult because the bar continues to rise. Just a few years ago, only a handful of companies had prominent green initiatives. Now you'd be hard pressed to find a major company that doesn't. So differentiating is getting harder than ever.

This is one place where smaller companies may hold an advantage. Small, local firms have been slower to the green scene because they lack both the human and financial capital needed to make changes and the prodding from activists, customers, employees, investors, and others. Because of this, it's easier for, say, a local printer, travel agent, or retailer to distinguish itself as an environmental leader. They don't have a lot of green competition, and environmental expectations of them typically are lower than for larger companies. A small company could distinguish itself simply through a single action—encouraging employee volunteerism with environmental groups, for example, or locating in a certified green building.

Even for larger companies, differentiation can have a lot to do with the competitive environment. For example, in the information technology arena, where Dell, Epson, Hewlett-Packard, IBM, Lexmar, and other hardware manufacturers have engaged in a race to see who can be greenest—with equipment that is energy-efficient and can be recycled easily, for example—it's harder to stand out.

"Differentiation doesn't necessarily mean that you're doing more than everybody else," says Shapiro. "It's doing something that is distinct in signature, so that people can identify you and what you do as green in a particular way."

Credibility. Relevance. Effective messaging. Differentiation. These are the components from which a successful green strategy are made.

The order of these four components may change for some companies. For example, it may be more appropriate to begin with relevance, identifying the value proposition that's appropriate for your customers and company culture, and then thinking about how to go about messaging it in a manner that's credible, differentiated, and effective.

"We've had this interesting debate internally about the right place to start—which of these four factors," says Shapiro. "I have come to the conclusion that it depends on where you are as a company. A company that is newer to sustainability may want to start with credibility, since that's most important for them. But if you're more evolved—say, Patagonia—you're going to be in a different place; you might start with differentiation."

Bottom line: You can start anywhere. The important thing is to cover all the bases.

# Chapter 30

# PR and the Many Shades of "Greenwash"

Y ou wouldn't think that the world of green business would need much more publicity, given the steady drumbeat of media stories, blogs, Web sites, TV shows, billboards, events, and other shout-outs plugging green companies, products, and services. But get ready for more. The world of public relations has discovered green with a vengeance, and the big global firms seem locked, loaded, and ready to intensify their drum beating. Nearly all the major PR firms have set up practices focusing on sustainability and corporate responsibility, including Burson-Marsteller, Edelman, Fleishman-Hillard GCI Group, GolinHarris, Hill & Knowlton, Ketchum, Manning Selvage & Lee, Ogilvy, and Weber Shandwick.

The greening of PR reflects a newfound reality: It's now safe, or at least safer, for companies to tell their green stories. Two companies helped break the ice. The first was General Electric (GE), whose "ecomagination" campaign launch in 2005 signaled to the world that a big company that hadn't previously been seen as a green leader could come out publicly with a bold plan—and not get viciously attacked. (Indeed, more than three years later, Jeff Immelt and other GE execs remain high on the list of desired speakers at environmental and green business conferences.) Then came Wal-Mart, with its dizzying array of environmental commitments and initiatives. The retailer, while hardly universally admired among environmentalists, has managed to transform itself from a laggard to a leader in the eyes of at least some thought leaders. Those two success stories made it comfortable for other companies to jump into the water—to be more public about their environmental goals and initiatives, even if they're less than perfect.

But the water may still be a tad icy. As the market research firm Ipsos Reid reported in 2007, "Consumers appear to be wary of companies who label their products as being 'green' or environmentally friendly." The study found that seven in ten Americans either "strongly" (12 percent) or "somewhat" (58 percent) agree that "when companies call a product 'green' (meaning better for the environment), it is usually just a marketing tactic."

The PR industry will have its work cut out for itself.

Of course, the bigger question is whether all this PR heat will shed any actual light. That is, will the growing number of press releases and increased media coverage reflect an increase in company efforts and environmental performance or just more attention to efforts that have been happening all along? Will increased coverage of green business issues lead to a virtuous cycle, in which heightened public attention and expectations of companies lead to even more, and more substantive, commitments and actions? Or will the public tire of a steady stream of me-too stories, thus feeding their existing skepticism and spurring them to get off the green bandwagon even before it reaches cruising speed? It could go either way.

All this leads me to challenge PR professionals: Will you steer your clients beyond short-term media hits to create longer-term value by counseling them to aim high, to make bold, even audacious commitments in order to stand out from the crowd? Or will you focus on next quarter's results, creating flash-in-the-pan media moments that celebrate incremental change in lieu of substantive progress?

When it comes to PR, how good is "good enough"?

Here's an example of one company that seems to get it—at least as evidenced from this one press release. My colleagues and I at GreenBiz.com get dozens of such releases every day and read only a small handful. (Do I really care that next Saturday is National Canvas Bag Day?) This one caught my eye. It came in spring 2008 from Bissell Homecare, Inc., the century-old maker of vacuum cleaners and sweepers (although in today's marketing parlance, it is a "floor-care innovator and international manufacturer of home-cleaning products"). "Bissell Is Getting a Little Greener" was the modest headline of the press release, which read in part:

> Bissell's goal is to reduce the impact it has on the global environment by identifying and implementing sustainability strategies consistent with overall key business objectives. "We know Bissell can't become green overnight, but the important thing is that we're making a serious effort to become a little greener and setting realistic, yet ambitious, goals to make that a reality," says Mark Bissell, Bissell's president and CEO.

It went on to introduce the company's new Little Green vacuum, which boasts polyvinyl chloride (PVC)–free tanks and hose and parts made from 100 percent postconsumer recycled plastic.

It was a clever tie-in—"a little greener" with "Little Green"—but it also felt authentic and honest, right down to the humble CEO.

This is exactly what's missing from most corporate missives. Too often there's a tendency to showcase only the good stuff. In traditional PR circles, this makes sense; indeed, it's the essence of the craft. In the green economy, though, where there's a general sense that no company is environmentally perfect (and most are far from it), putting on a green gloss can be counterproductive. A skeptical populace naturally will assume that a product or company that sounds too green to be true is probably hiding something. The challenge, then, is to find a way to accentuate the positive without claiming more credit than you deserve—and maybe even a little less.

For purposes of being seen as green, it might be helpful to think of a company much as you would an individual human being. You may choose to extol a particular person's virtues and accomplishments, but it's unlikely that you'd refer to him or her as an icon of perfection. Everyone knows that each of us has flaws, some serious, including even the most idolized individuals. To claim otherwise is seen as hyperbole or worse.

It's been said that the only "normal" people are those who you don't yet know very well. So, too, with green companies and products.

# Chapter 31

# Polar Bears, Tree Frogs, and Blueberries

I t's hard enough to get the words right. But the pictures, too?

Time was, a green-minded advertiser or marketer could include an image of a tree, the universal symbol for nature, or perhaps a child at the beach and be done with it. Images were intended to complement the words, helping to set a mood or communicate visually what the text was saying. It was fairly straightforward.

No longer. Every picture tells a story, of course, but in the age of broadband, where Internet and TV images fly by at lightning speed, those stories must be, by necessity, microscopically brief. Today, images, just like every other aspect of communications, aren't just art—they're science. Picking the right one isn't a job for merely the photo editor or art director. There are now social scientists, market researchers, and focus groups standing by to parse the visual subtleties—the right tree, critter, or evocative scene—that will most effectively convey the message.

Consider Getty Images, one of the leading suppliers of stock images for business and consumers, with an archive of 70 million still images. In 2008, it published a study looking at the images that most resonate with consumers on environmental topics. Getty assessed 2,500 advertising campaigns from the previous year and concluded, unsurprisingly, that many of the conventional images used to promote green campaigns were in danger of becoming visual clichés.

Getty also partnered with Yankelovich, Inc. to survey 3,000 consumers to elicit which shade of green most resonated as being associated with environmentalism. It showed consumers four different hues, which Getty dubbed "forest," "kelly," "olive," and "lime" green. (These were internal names only; it didn't reveal them to the consumers for fear of influencing them.) While a subset of mature women identified most with the kelly green, overall, forest green won overwhelmingly.

Getty also found that one particular amphibian—no, it's not Kermit—also found favor—the red-eyed tree frog (*Agalychnis calidryas*), which inhabits the rainforests of South and Central America. The small tree-dweller, about 2 to 3 inches long, is characterized by its huge red eyes, bright neon-green body, and red or orange feet. The frog seems to have become something of an ambassador for the campaign to save the rain forests. (Although the frog itself is not in danger, its habitat is.)

Denise Waggoner, vice president of creative research at Getty Images, couldn't explain exactly why the frog leapt out from all the other creatures as an eco-favorite. Perhaps, unlike other frogs, because it can breathe through its skin, absorbing all the impurities in the air and water, she suggested. Or maybe it's the connection to Kermit. More likely, she says, "We tend to anthropomorphize the red-eyed tree frog because he looks right at the camera"—and does so with those amazing eyes.

Picking animals can have a downside, especially if your chosen critter suddenly finds itself looking at the business end of extinction. This is what happened to Coca-Cola, which, since 1993, has employed, figuratively speaking, polar bears for its ads and commercials. But a not-so-funny thing happened to these white, fluffy mammals: They started becoming victims of climate change. Technically, polar bears are classified as a "vulnerable" species, but this sounds rather tame compared with the concern of some zoologists and climatologists, who believe that the projected decreases in the polar sea ice owing to global warming will reduce their population by two-thirds by 2050.

What's a feel-good beverage company to do?

The issue was handed to Coke by Greenpeace in 2005, when the activist group created an online video as part of its climate campaign. The ad, meant to echo Coke's own ads, shows a polar bear cub drinking from a Coke-shaped bottle as the ice around it breaks apart. Finally, the bear falls into the water, struggles, and eventually sinks. The ad borrowed from an old Coke slogan: "Global warming, it's the real thing."

Suffice to say that the dark parody caused heartburn among Coke's marketing executives. They wanted the company to take legal action for trademark infringement. Cooler heads prevailed, though, and the company eventually recognized that it had an opportunity to turn the issue in its favor. It sought out the World Wildlife Fund (whose own mascot is a panda) to launch a partnership to educate consumers about the polar bear's plight and to directly support polar bear conservation projects through the fund. The company created the Coca-Cola Company Polar Bear Support Fund and launched a small Web site "so you can learn about polar bears and what you can do to help the planet."

One small step for the polar bear, one giant leap for Coke's image.

It's not just images of cute and cuddly creatures that can be problematic. Picking images of humans can have unintended consequences, too. Consider the fate of a group of Oregon blueberry growers. Several years ago, they began doing what has become de rigueur in food marketing these days: They put pictures of the farmers on blueberry crates.

The reason, of course, is that food now needs a story. It's hard to walk the aisles of a Whole Food Market or practically any other store without seeing food stories everywhere you look. Buy a dozen eggs, and you can find out the names of the chicken and the farm where she lives, as well as the farmer, his wife, kids, and golden retriever—sometimes right on the package. Yogurt maker Stonyfield Farm will even send you a "moosletter," in which one of its dairy cows will give you an updates on her life and times. In an age of globalization and agribusiness, where a typical meal travels 1,500 miles from farm to fork, people want to know more about where their food comes from. Hence, stories.

So the Oregon blueberry growers, or their marketing mavens, decided to display the farmer's mugs on the boxes. This was all well and good, except for one small hiccup. It didn't go over well in Japan, one of the grower's biggest markets.

In Japan, blueberries are thought to contribute to good eyesight, owing to their high concentrations of anthocyanin, a natural compound linked with many health benefits, including reducing eyestrain, improving nighttime visual acuity, and promoting quicker adjustment after exposure to glare. Blueberries are so popular in Japan for such benefits that they have been nicknamed "the vision fruit."

All good, except for one thing: Some of the pictured Oregon blueberry farmers wore glasses. In order to save face, as it were, they had to reshoot the photos, sans specs.

Talk about 20/20 hindsight.

# Chapter 32

# The Power of Pooling and Collaboration

Nike, Harley Davidson, Herman Miller, Ford.

What on Earth is the connection? At first blush, there isn't one. A footwear and apparel company, a iconic motorcycle maker, a furniture manufacturer, and an automobile company—what could they possibly have in common?

They all buy leather. And they're all seeking to buy "green" leather.

A modest experiment has been taking place among these and other companies to explore how they can join forces to support their individual and collective goals of reducing or eliminating toxic or wasteful materials in leather and other industrial feedstocks. The idea is called *materials pooling*.

Inspiration for this comes from Michael Braungart, the visionary German chemist well known for his collaborative work with William McDonough in creating the cradle-to-cradle concept for product design. Simply put, materials pooling brings together several companies—often from different sectors to avoid competitiveness issues—to work with suppliers to find more eco-efficient alternatives to problematic materials.

Explains Braungart: "Partners in an intelligent materials pool agree to share access to a common supply of a particular high-technology, high-quality material, pooling information and purchasing power to generate a healthy system of closed-loop material flows."

A group of companies working under the auspices of the Society for Organizational Learning formed working groups around leather and three other materials. The companies' experiences suggest that while the concept remains nascent, it holds promise to become a potent means for them to collaboratively and cost-effectively break through seemingly impenetrable barriers in the way of reaching toxics- or waste-elimination goals.

Manufacturing leather, it turns out, is harmful to more than just cows. Hexavalent chromium is used for a wide range of plating applications. The compound is best known as the pollutant that led activist Erin Brockovich on her successful legal battle with Pacific Gas & Electric, made famous in a 2000 movie staring Julia Roberts. It is a known carcinogen and source of chronic respiratory illnesses. Several years ago, the materials pooling companies came together to find sources of leather tanned without hexavalent chromium.

It wasn't easy. Each company has its own needs, which aren't necessarily the same as the needs of the others. Ford wanted leather that was optimized for performance characteristics, whereas Harley Davidson wanted to optimize for appearance. The group created a Web site to allow information sharing but found that people weren't using it, nor was the group collaborating to leverage its collective purchasing power. A steady parade of vendors offered greener alternatives, and the group shared expertise and experience with these to determine which, if any, may be viable. Again, each company has different issues: Some leather needs to be waterproof, some needs to be durable, some has to be appropriate for a high-end motorcycle jacket, and so on. It's a slow process—far more so than anyone hoped—and some of the "wins" are relative baby steps compared with McDonough's and Braungart's guiding vision of "closed-loop material flows" creating "technical nutrients" that could be reused in industrial systems.

Materials pooling is one of several examples in which companies coming together from across industries are managing to solve problems collectively that none could solve individually. Another is the Clean Cargo Working Group assembled by Business for Social Responsibility (BSR), a membership group helping companies to integrate sustainability into business strategy and operations.

The environmental impacts of shipping goods from place to place only recently has moved onto the radar screens of companies. The impacts of shipping seemed relatively obscure, the true costs hidden amid complex tariffs, and there seemed little companies could do to change the performance of truck, rail, and marine cargo companies. Moreover, few, if any, activists or regulators were pressing for action on the issue.

All that's changed in recent years as climate change and air pollution concerns have brought shipping's environmental impact into the limelight. Activists are waging campaigns against dirty ocean-going shippers. And a handful of companies—including some of the world's largest shipping customers—are taking action.

The environmental cost of moving goods across oceans can be significant. The trillion-dollar shipping industry—the means by which more than 90 percent of the world's traded goods are transported—spews 14 percent of all nitrogen emissions from fossil fuels and 16 percent of sulfur emissions from petroleum, according to Carnegie Mellon University. In 2008, scientists commissioned by the United Nations International Maritime Organization found that ships account for 4.5 percent of global carbon dioxide emissions, double the latest estimates for aviation.

One reason is that cargo ships run on "bunker fuel," the dirtiest, cheapest product that remains after gasoline and other high-grade fuels are refined from crude oil. Bunker fuel contains up to 5,000 times more sulfur than diesel fuel. As a result, according to the activist group Bluewater Network, a single container ship emits more pollution than 2,000 diesel trucks. Ships also pollute when docked but idling. More than 400,000 residents within 45 square miles of the ports of Long Beach and Los Angeles in California have a cancer risk 200 times higher than the federal government deems acceptable. Emissions from ocean-going ships cause about 60,000 deaths a year from heart- and lung-related cancers, according to another study.

Ballast water is another key impact. Modern cargo ships hold millions of gallons of water within their hulls, which can be moved around to ensure that the ship is properly trimmed; this improves safety and speed. Ships routinely exchange ballast water while in port as cargo is loaded or unloaded. The water pumped out of the ship is alive with organisms from ports previously visited. An analysis of ballast water from foreign oceangoing ships entering Canada found nearly 13,000 marine creatures per cubic meter of water. Most don't survive in their new environment, but some do, successfully invading their adopted homes, sometimes wreaking havoc. The zebra mussel fouling the U.S. Great Lakes is just one example. That alone has cost communities surrounding the lakes millions of dollars a year to protect their water supplies, and the mussel continues to spread.

How to reduce such impacts? BSR established a working groups of its members to address shipping-related climate issues. Its Clean Cargo Group consists of nearly 20 percent of the top U.S. importers, including such companies as Chiquita Brands, Del Monte Foods, Hewlett-Packard, Home Depot, IKEA, Mattel, Nike, and Williams-Sonoma. BSR also assembled a group of vessel operators, including K Line, Maersk Sealand, NYK Line, and P&O Nedlloyd.

In creating the group, BSR and its company members recognized that shipping represents a gaping hole in supply-chain environmental management. While many of the leading cargo carriers have been addressing their environmental impacts, their shipping customers had no means to track their progress or hold the carriers accountable. Meanwhile, shippers were bombarding carriers with endless questionnaires, most of which asked different questions—sometimes the wrong ones. Even when carriers were complying with industry standards, shippers knew there was room for improvement. The industry's International Maritime Organization had rules that were pretty bare minimum.

One thing that was needed was a common language. The shipping companies and their customers had no shared vocabulary for talking about emissions, environmental management, or policies. Moreover, if a company had an environmental policy, there was no way to know who signed off on it—senior management or some guy in the shipping department.

The shippers began meeting under BSR's auspices to discuss pathways to greener, cleaner shipping. Eventually, the group invited the carriers to join them. Eventually, the shippers came up with a draft questionnaire and presented it to the vessel operators for comment. They didn't merely edit questions; they added some of their own. For example, shippers hadn't asked about safety—a prime concern for the carriers. And the questionnaire hadn't covered some things the carriers already were tracking in their environmental management systems. The two groups came together to review the questionnaire line by line, ironing out details, until both sides were satisfied. It took a few years overall, but the questionnaire is now the de facto standard.

The Clean Cargo and materials pooling experiences are notable beyond their value to the companies directly involved, although that may well be significant. They show what can happen when companies share buying power, resources, information, and knowledge. And they demonstrate the powerful impacts when trading partners commit to finding a common language, understanding each other's needs and concerns, working to find tools and solutions that reflect their common business interests—and sticking with it, no matter how long it takes.

They also show the power of collaboration and the need to share solutions. As companies seek out ever-increasing ways to reduce their impacts and increase the business value of going green, many are finding that they are reinventing the wheel—that is, addressing a challenge that other companies, perhaps dozens of companies, already have addressed, sometimes with great ingenuity. Over the years, I've been struck by companies' willingness to share what they've learned, even among competitors.

In some cases, the wisdom bubbles upward from small firms to bigger ones. Case in point: I once met an executive from New Belgium

Brewery, brewer of Fat Tire beer, among other well-regarded micro-brews, and a company that has received acclaim for its progressive environmental and workplace practices. I asked if her company's awards and recognition in the green arena had led to other breweries making the pilgrimage to New Belgium's Fort Collins, Colorado, brewery for advice.

"Absolutely," she responded. "We get calls all the time from local breweries, and we love to show them what we've done."

"Like who?" I asked, expecting her to name other small, local microbreweries.

"Well, like Coors and Anheuser-Busch," she replied.

That's telling. In the green economy, companies are finding that they need to tap the experience, ideas, passion, and wisdom of players large and small to quench their thirst for progress.

# PART 5

# HOW GOOD IS "SUFFICIENT"?

There's another aspect of the question, How good is "good enough"?—one that transcends all the relatively trivial questions about standards, messaging, and public perception. It's a question that cuts to the heart of green business thinking and strategy: How good is "sufficient"? That is, how good must a company be not just to be seen as an authentic and effective environmental leader but also to actually effect authentic change in our environment? And how good must all companies be to collectively have a salutary effect on global climate change and other societal and environmental challenges?

The truth is that many of the environmental achievements being celebrated are relatively trivial in the scope of things. They are necessary but not sufficient. After all, does a cosmetic with a few grams of rainforest-derived botanicals really make a difference when it comes to drastically reducing, if not stopping, tropical deforestation? Can a lighter-weight aluminum can reduce resource and energy use sufficiently to slash greenhouse gases to an acceptable level? Is a brand of bottled water that uses less plastic per bottle sufficient to mitigate concerns about plastic waste and the energy associated with the shipping of water? Is it progress if a cannibal eats with a fork?

There's a tendency to respond, "Well, it's all good," and to leave it at that. And it *is* all good—that is, we don't want to discourage any company from thinking and acting in a more environmentally responsible manner. At some point, however, it's critical that we step back, take stock, and ask, "Is this enough to move the needle?"

# Chapter 33

# The BHAGs of Climate Change

There's a good case to make that all the great progress and promise of the green economy may be far from what's needed to address our environmental challenges adequately. To make that case, I'll proffer Exhibits A, B, and C.

Exhibit A is work done by Robert H. Socolow, an engineering professor, and Stephen W. Pacala, an ecology professor, who together lead the Carbon Mitigation Initiative at Princeton University. In 2004, in a paper published in the journal *Science,* the two took a 50-year view of climate change and described two pathways: a business-as-usual scenario that could lead to catastrophic devastation—droughts, floods, massive storms, starvation, resource wars, massive migration, and all the rest—and another path, in which societal and technological innovations could avoid those calamities. Those two paths—one unimaginable, the other not yet imagined—are largely our choice, they maintain.

Socolow and Pacala argue that stabilizing greenhouse gas concentrations will require reducing emissions by 7 billion tons a year by 2054. To make this number more understandable, they identified 15 potential "wedges," each of which could handle 1 billion tons of the total, as examples of what Herculean efforts will be required. Thus it would take seven such wedges to accomplish their goal. The idea was that looking at seven big goals might be easier than looking at hundreds or thousands of smaller ones, allowing us to focus on solutions that give us the biggest bang for our buck.

These so-called stabilization wedges are sobering in their scale and scope. They are the quintessential BHAGs—big, hairy, audacious goals. Here are just seven examples of things Socolow and Pacala say we must do worldwide, each of which, when phased in over the next 50 years, will result in the 1-billion-ton goal:

- Double the fuel economy of 2 billion cars worldwide from 30 to 60 miles per gallon (mpg).
- Decrease car travel for 2 billion 30-mpg cars from 10,000 to 5,000 miles per year.
- Cut carbon emissions by 25 percent in buildings and appliances.
- Cut electricity use in all homes, offices, and stores by 25 percent.
- Replace 1,400 large coal-fired power plants with gas-fired plants.
- Increase solar power 700-fold from current levels to displace coal-fired power plants.
- Increase wind power 80-fold from current levels to produce hydrogen for cars.

Keep in mind that this isn't an either/or proposition. We'd have to do all seven of these things or their equivalent to keep greenhouse gas levels stable and in check at below 550 parts per million (ppm), double preindustrial levels. And even this may not be enough: Some experts believe that 550 ppm is too high of a ceiling, that it should be 450 ppm, or even less, meaning that we'd need even more, or more ambitious, "wedges." (Dr. James Hansen, director of NASA's Goddard Institute for Space Studies and one of the world's eminent climatologists, stated in 2007 that 300 to 350 ppm is the safe, sustainable level for the biosphere and human survival. At the time, the planet's climate concentration stood at 383 ppm now and was increasing by about 2.5 ppm annually.)

Moreover, some of the wedges make assumptions about the future that are merely educated guesses. For example, the notion of doubling the fuel economy of 2 billion cars by 2054 should be put into context. Currently, there are only about 850 million cars on the planet.

Arguing over the numbers isn't the point. The point is the scale of the solutions we'll need. And therein lies the potential danger: As interest in green business continues to heat up, and media lavish growing attention on companies that are being environmentally proactive, it's easy to be lulled into thinking that we've reached some inflection point, that there's an inexorable wave of activity taking place. This may be true—to a point. But as Socolow and Pacala point out, we've barely begun to solve the problems.

## THE STATE OF GREEN BUSINESS

Exhibit B is "State of Green Business 2008," a report prepared by my editorial team at GreenBiz.com. In mid–2007, we set out to measure a representative basket of indicators that would tell us, in aggregate, the progress companies are, or aren't, making in 20 measures of environmental performance. Among the trends we measured were macro indicators—the amount of energy required to produce a unit of gross domestic product (GDP) over the past few decades, as well as the emissions of toxic chemicals and carbon dioxide per unit of GDP. We also looked at trends in employee carpooling and telecommuting, the rise of certified green buildings, paper use and recycling, disposal and recycling of electronic waste, packaging material use, carbon trading, clean-technology investments, and more. We'll be updating these annually. (You can download the latest edition of the free report at *www.stateofgreenbusiness.com.*)

What we found was mildly encouraging but also sobering. As much activity as is taking place in the green business scene, it's not having much of a positive impact, environmentally speaking. In several instances, the progress being made is offset by growth of the economy. In other instances, the progress is dwarfed by the magnitude of the problems.

A few examples:

- The carbon intensity of the U.S. economy has begun to show steady declines on a normalized basis—that is, greenhouse gas emissions per unit of GDP. This speaks to the steady improvement in energy efficiency that's been taking place for more than 50 years. (Since 1950, U.S. energy use—measured per dollar of GDP—has declined more than 75 percent, from 9.4 British thermal units per dollar of GDP to just 2.5 British thermal units.) Overall, however, carbon emissions have been steady or dropping only slightly; in 2006, the latest data available, U.S. emissions of greenhouse gases dipped for the first time since 2001, a 1.5 percent decline over a year earlier. This is encouraging, to be sure, but anemic progress, considering the task at hand—and certainly compared with the dramatic reductions Socolow and Pacala are calling for.

- The growth in the collection and recycling of electronic waste, or e-waste, is gaining slowly, barely outpacing the growth in output of used computers, printers, monitors, servers, and assorted other digital detritus—but in absolute terms, we're getting buried. While the number of recycling programs grows, the percentage of equipment captured for recycling remains small. In 2006, for example, the amount of e-waste collected for recycling was relatively unchanged from a year earlier, whereas the growth of consumer electronics—stuff that will need to be recycled in just a few short years—climbed by more than 400,000 tons over the previous year.

- On the positive side of the ledger, demand and planning for green buildings is rising like a skyscraper on steroids, the product of everything from high energy prices to corporate vanity to a better understanding of the dividends paid by environmentally sensitive facilities in the form of reduced costs and enhanced worker productivity. Investments in clean technology also are on a steady upward trajectory; so, too; with clean-tech patent filings, a leading indicator of new technologies and business opportunities. There was a small but steady growth in companies publicly reporting their climate impacts. Paper use per dollar of GDP is on the decline, whereas paper recycling is on a sharp increase, both positive trends.

In an attempt to create some order out of this informational chaos, we assigned each of the 20 trends one of three icons, indicating whether companies are making steady progress ("swimming"), losing ground ("sinking"), or holding their own ("treading water"). Eight of the 20 were deemed to be "swimming," with 2 "sinking" and 10 "treading water." It was a mixed report, at best, because even most trends that were "swimming" weren't doing so at Olympic speed.

## THE FOURTH QUADRANT

Exhibit C is courtesy of Van Jones, an articulate and inspiring voice for environmental and social equity. Jones, cofounder and executive director of the Oakland, California–based nonprofit Green for All, manages in a few sentences to link seemingly disparate worlds: *environmental justice,* how poor people even in industrialized countries tend to suffer disproportionately the ills caused by environmental problems; *economic justice,* the gaping and widening inequity between the "haves" and "have nots"; the *incarceration economy,* in which the police car that brings a troubled young man to prison boasts a newer, more sophisticated computer than the one in the classroom where the young man was arrested; the *clean-tech revolution,* and all its potential to create entry-level green-collar jobs; *environmental problems,* from climate change to childhood asthma; and the *role and responsibility of corporations* in creating a just and equitable society.

Within a few minutes, Jones manages to weave these things together in a coherent and compelling way. His message: Let's make sure that the clean and green economy benefits everyone, not just the privileged few. It's a message that applies not just to communities within wealthy countries such as the United States but also to the entire global community, in which some countries and some segments of those countries stand to gain mightily from the rapid growth of the green economy, and others could be left behind.

In his presentations, Jones describes what he calls the "fourth quadrant." It starts with a standard two-by-two diagram, where the horizontal *x*-axis represents the old, "gray" economy on the left and the emerging green economy on the right. The vertical *y*-axis represents rich at the top and poor on the bottom. The four quadrants that result represent the impacts of the gray economy on the rich and on the poor and the potential impacts of the green economy on both those groups (see Figure 33–1).

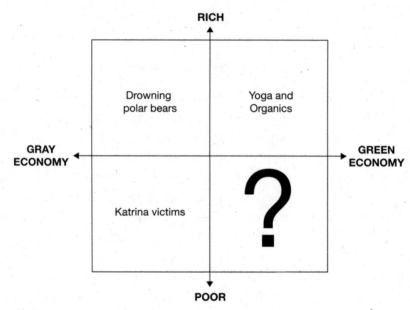

**Figure 33-1** The fourth quadrant.

The upper-left quadrant represents mainstream environmentalism, at least as we've seen it evolve over the past several decades. It shows an image of a drowning polar bear, which Jones describes as a symbol of society's concerns in the wake of climate change, at least in the eyes of the economically secure. "The first quadrant represents what affluent people think about environmental problems. They tend to focus on polar bears, on charismatic megafauna, rainforests, whales, all that stuff. And it's a damn good thing that people are focused on that, because those species can't defend themselves; they can't speak for themselves. So it's good to have people who are in that first quadrant,

who are concerned about environmental harms, so they have a particular kind of conversation."

In the lower-left quadrant is a visually eerie analogue to the swimming polar bear—an image of an African-American woman wading
through flood waters in the aftermath of Hurricane Katrina. It symbol-
izes the effects of environmental excesses on the less well off. "These
people aren't talking about polar bears or the rain forest," says Jones.
"They're talking about cancer, toxic waste, lead paint—all of the environmental health injustice that befalls low-income people. When poor
people talk about 'the environment is bad,' they're not talking about
polar bears. They're talking about the fact that their kid has asthma."

Jones is quick to point out that this isn't about values judgments—
about right, wrong, good, and bad. It's just about trying to understand distinctions. "Both of the left quadrants—the upper left and the
lower left—are really important conversations, valid, incredibly necessary. Unfortunately, in the past, there's been a real division, between
the mainstream environmentalists and the environmental justice community." They're each having different conversations, he says.

Jones then takes us to the right side of the chart—"the solutions
space," as he calls it. In the upper-right quadrant is the cornucopia of
solutions that are increasingly available to those with the means to
afford them: organic foods, green fashion, eco-friendly cosmetics,
socially responsible investing, yoga and other wellness practices,
hybrid cars, solar energy, and all the rest. "It's really important stuff,"
says Jones. "We want wealthy people to be investing in companies and
products and processes that are going to help the planet. And we
want consumers who have disposable income to spend it on those
products. So, that's all good stuff."

It's the fourth quadrant—the lower-right one—that Jones wants us
to focus on. It represents the intersection of the green economy and
the have-nots, and it is symbolized by a large question mark. The
message is obvious: What are the opportunities in the green economy
for those at the lower end of the economic ladder? Where are the jobs,
the access to renewable energy, the affordable organic produce, the
availability of wellness programs? And what are the opportunities—

and the responsibility—of the private sector to ensure, as Jones poignantly puts it, that "the clean-tech wave lifts all boats"?

Jones makes an important point. The promise of the green economy and the clean-tech revolution is that they will bring a new wave of job opportunities—productive and respectable jobs at every part of the economic spectrum, from line workers to senior executives. Nonprofit groups such as the Apollo Alliance have made this their raison d'etre. A steady drumbeat of studies since the late 1990s has told us that burgeoning markets for solar and wind energy, clean transportation, and other technologies represent the next big wave of job creation. Cities and states have been positioning to become clean-tech hubs, eyeing the workforce development potential. Organizations representing low-income populations have been viewing the green economy as an entry point for those near the bottom of the economic ladder.

So now that clean technology and the greening of business seem to be in full swing, where are all the jobs? So far, they haven't yet emerged—at least not in any appreciable numbers.

The reasons are many and varied. Most of the big companies in the clean-energy business—the BPs, General Electrics, and Kyoceras of the world—don't seem to be going on hiring sprees, typically creating clean-tech business units from within. So, too, with much of the greening of companies—it has to do with efficiency, with doing more with the same or fewer resources, and that includes human resources. Few of the clean-tech start-ups are yet doing massive hiring, and when they do, they are more often in the market for engineers and other skilled professionals. And the jobs being created are disperse, geographically, meaning that there are few robust Silicon Valley–like clean-tech clusters, where companies congregate and jobs proliferate. Thus, while green jobs are available—there were about 8 million green jobs in the United States alone in 2007, according to Piper Jaffray—the huge wave of opportunity has not yet arrived.

The greening of the lower class seems to be falling through the cracks, between the opportunities available to the well-to-do and the increasing attention being given to those at the base of the pyramid

(BOP)—the 4 billion people on the planet with disposable incomes of $5 a day or less. The BOP, as it has come to be known, is the focus of a growing corps of academic, business, and multisectoral organizations and efforts. The topic has been covered in *Harvard Business Journal*, *Strategic Management Review*, and other thought-leader publications, and there are institutes on the topic at business schools at Cornell, Harvard, the University of Michigan, and the University of Navarra in Spain. Companies such as CEMEX, Danone, Hindustan Lever, and SC Johnson have engaged in BOP initiatives. Microsoft's Bill Gates has sung its praises at the annual Davos World Economic Forum. Mohammad Yunus won the 2006 Nobel Peace Prize for his groundbreaking work on the topic.

But what about the next layer up, the underclass—not the poorest of the poor, but the low-income wage earners in the developed world? Where is the analogous activity on the fourth quadrant, helping to create, as Van Jones calls it, "green for all"? Where are the jobs, the product innovations, the new business models, and the business engagement? Where are the corps of entry-level workers helping to, say, weatherize and solarize homes and small businesses? Where are the job-training programs aimed at green-economy jobs? Who is nurturing inner-city eco-entrepreneurs? What companies are taking the lead—not out of charity, but out of opportunity to design and deliver innovative new products and services that drive down the cost of green technologies for those in underserved markets while providing environmental and health benefits for everyone? Companies are doing this in the third world. Why not the fourth quadrant?

Says Jones:

In that fourth quadrant, the focus has to be more on collective solutions, much more focused on what we call work, wealth, and health for low-income people. If the green economy doesn't target and include these folks, the gray economy will. And, similarly, if the green political movement doesn't target and include folks, the polluters will. It's not like you can just leave out whole demographic categories. You may not necessarily see these people, but they exist, and they eat, they consume, and they have their eco-logical, economic, and political impacts.

Jones doesn't explicitly say this, but it's clear: We need all four quadrants to make a green economy.

The stabilization wedges, the "State of Green Business," and Jones' fourth quadrant represent sobering reality checks on all the cheery news about the greening of business. Increasingly, companies are not merely going to be asked what they're doing to combat climate change and other environmental challenges or to simply disclose the full complement of their environmental impacts and actions. They'll be asked, in effect: "Are you doing enough? If all companies did what you are doing, would it change things?"

And increasingly, companies will find that they'd better have an answer and that it better be good.

# Chapter 34

# The Selling of Climate Change

There's no better place to explore the questions of "How good is 'good enough'?" and "How good is 'sufficient'?" than when it comes to a company's response to climate change. As the stabilization wedges mentioned in Chapter 33 suggest, addressing climate change is not simply a matter of making a few small changes. Our attempts to thwart climate change's worst impacts may well be disruptive to companies and the rest of society, requiring any number of changes in how we live, work, shop, and play. Inevitably, some of these actions will be effective, others will have unintended consequences, and still others may prove to be anything from ineffective to counterproductive.

The idea of companies becoming *carbon-neutral* could end up in any one of those categories.

The idea of being a carbon-neutral company is compelling. In an age in which greenhouse gas emissions are the twenty-first-century equivalent of spewing smokestacks and drainpipes, the notion of *neutralizing* seems a worthy goal. And a vast number of products and services have emerged to help companies and individuals achieve that goal, some of which involve merely writing a check. And therein lies the problem: Few companies or individuals, however well intentioned, will address their climate impacts effectively without making changes, sometimes significant ones. Of course, some of the folks in the carbon-neutral business see it differently. And therein lies another problem.

First, a brief digression. Pretty much everyone from preschool on up these days can recite the "three R's" of solid waste: reduce, reuse, and recycle. There are countless Web sites on the topic and more than one song.

What many people don't seem to know (or have forgotten) is that the "three R's" represent more than just a clever alliteration; they are a hierarchy of priorities. That is, in addressing one's solid waste— whether a household, a business, or a society—the most important thing to do is *reduce* the amount of stuff that ultimately will need to be disposed of (by buying things in bulk, for example, or things with less packaging, or simply buying less). Next most important is to *reuse* things as much as possible to maximize their value (by repairing, refurbishing, or refilling them, for example). Finally, after you've used the least amount of stuff and reused as much of it as possible, you should *recycle* what's left.

This is simple stuff, although most people, it seems, focus on recycling as their sole goal, despite the fact that it's a decidedly third choice.

So, too, when it comes to climate change.

While there's no clever alliterative equivalent of solid waste's "three R's" (believe me, I've tried), there is a hierarchy. To wit:

- When addressing your energy use and climate impacts, the single most important thing to do is to reduce the overall amount of energy you use—by purchasing energy-efficient appliances, light bulbs, cars, computers, etc. and by running them as little as necessary. This is as true for individuals as it is for businesses.

- Of the energy you do use, next best is to purchase as much of it as possible from renewable sources such as solar and wind, whether from a local utility program, by generating your own (say, by installing solar panels), or by using biofuels for your transportation needs.

- Finally, after you've used the least amount of energy and the highest possible percentage of renewable energy, you should remedy the climate impacts of the nonrenewable energy you use by purchasing carbon offsets.

What's the point? The point is that, much as they do with recycling, a great many smart people and companies focus on offsets as their principal strategy for addressing their climate-change impacts, despite the fact that it's the third choice. This is apparent from the seeming gold rush of offset providers of late. You can now offset almost everything: your home, business, driving, vacations, and other purchases and activities. You can buy carbon-neutral plane flights, go to carbon-neutral rock concerts and conferences, purchase carbon-neutral gasoline, and in general, have a carbon-neutral life—all by writing a check.

Not that there's anything wrong with this—assuming you've already maximized your energy efficiency and renewables purchases. But buying offsets for an energy-wasteful business and calling it a responsible approach is akin to buying a diet cola to go with your double bacon cheeseburger—and calling it a weight-loss program. (Except that in this case, you're having someone drink the diet cola for you.) Efficiency—and calorie reduction!—come first. (There is a marvelous Web site, www.cheatneutral.com, that nicely skewers the hypocrisy of all this. I won't spoil its delicious premise. Check it out for yourself.)

Signs of a backlash already are coming to the nascent carbon market. One big problem is that there are no common standards or certification or monitoring systems in place and no easy way to know whether offsetting companies are even doing what they promise. Several organizations are scrambling to fill that void, hoping to bring consistency and certainty to a confused and fragmented market. Meanwhile, activists (and their media allies) are gearing up to bring to task companies that appear to be wielding a checkbook as the principal means of absolving their climate sins.

Of course, the opining over offsets is really a sideshow compared with the more substantive conversation taking place in this arena about risks and opportunities companies are facing in a carbon-constrained economy. There are at least six types of risk: *regulatory risk* (the impact of emissions caps or carbon taxes on a company's bottom line), *supply-chain risk* (disruptions or price hikes in materials or energy, in many cases because of the huge distances such supplies are shipped), *product and technology risk* (companies' ability to identify ways to exploit new market opportunities for climate-friendly products and services), *litigation risk* (the threat of lawsuits for significant carbon generators, similar to the suits faced in the tobacco, pharmaceutical, and asbestos industries), *reputation risk* (companies found guilty in the court of public opinion for selling or using products, processes, or practices that have a negative impact on the climate), and *physical risk* (the direct impacts of droughts, floods, storms, rising sea levels, etc.).

The financial services industry—banks, investment firms, and insurance companies—view these risks with rising concern. A 2007 report from Lehman Brothers warned that companies that do not respond quickly and effectively to changes in the physical and economic environments could face extinction. "The pace of a firm's adaptation to climate change is likely to prove to be another of the forces that will influence whether, over the next several years, any given firm survives and prospers; or withers and, quite possibly, dies," the report says. It called climate change a "tectonic force," similar to globalization and aging populations, that leads to gradual economic change and "causes periodic sharp movements in asset prices."

Of course, there will be climate winners as well as losers. A 2007 report from Citigroup offers up dozens of companies that are well positioned to do business in a climate-constrained world. "Someone must sell the products and services that will help companies meet, say, emissions targets should they become law; and companies are clearly responding to perceived public demand that they address environmental issues." Whose fortunes will rise? The report names 12 companies as examples, from Caterpillar (which produces low-emission diesel engines for trucks, clean gas turbines for power generations, and has a substantial parts recycling and remanufacturing business) to Johnson Controls (the largest provider of facilities management services to the Fortune 500, focusing on services for comfort and energy efficiency) to Magna International (which makes lightweight, high-strength auto body parts that can help to improve vehicle fuel efficiency). It's far from a complete list. Almost any renewable-energy company could have been included on the list, not to mention dozens of companies focusing on energy efficiency, grid optimization, waste management, and other resource-efficient businesses.

Increasingly, the conversation among leadership companies is about "carbon management," in which companies more strategically manage the risks and realize the opportunities associated with a changing business landscape in response to climate change. For example, carbon management allows companies to view carbon as a business variable that needs to be managed just like any other variable, taking into account such things as the fluctuating price of energy and carbon and, therefore, the risks and rewards for being proactive. Under a comprehensive carbon management program, a company develops an overall understanding of its carbon profile and evaluates the risks and opportunities. It then creates a detailed picture of companywide greenhouse gas emissions with a focus on opportunities for reducing them in the most cost-effective manner. This leads to prioritization, an action plan, and implementation. Rinse and repeat.

These issues aren't going away any time soon, and companies and others seeking to be seen as climate leaders would do well to examine the bigger picture: What, besides "going carbon-neutral," are you doing to address your climate footprint? Lacking a carbon management strategy—and hence a good answer to this question—could undermine any carbon-neutral claims, perhaps even garner publicity you weren't seeking.

The grilling you get may not be as easy-going as the one received in 2006 by Jeffrey Swartz, CEO of Timberland, when he was interviewed by Stephen Colbert on the satirical U.S. TV show *The Colbert Report*. Swartz, for years a progressive business leader concerned about a range of environmental and social issues, explained to Colbert about his company's carbon-neutral initiative. "Carbon-neutral sounds wishy-washy," Colbert responded. "You should be pro-carbon or anti-carbon. Carbon-neutral sounds like Switzerland. Take a stand!"

Take a stand, indeed. And make sure it's on solid ground.

# Chapter 35

# The "Small-Mart" Economy

For many, the idea of a green economy run by big, global corporations is anathema. To be truly sustainable—in the true sense of environmental, social, and economic well-being—requires a return to localization, to smaller, more personal systems of commerce that connect each of us to the origins of the things we buy, as well as to the people who make and sell them.

Michael Schuman refers to this as the *Small-Mart Revolution*, which is the title of his 2006 book on the topic. "Small-Mart" refers to locally owned businesses that are, in aggregate, more reliable generators of good jobs, economic growth, tax dollars, community wealth, charitable contributions, social stability, and political participation, according to Shuman.

In his book, Shuman makes clear that this "revolution" is about "far more than fighting chain stores." In fact, he says, it is notable as much for what it stands for as for what it is against. Shuman is for profit-making businesses, even big ones (under certain circumstances). He is for jobs and, presumably, some reasonable level of consumption. In fact, the only thing for which he is demonstrably against is "the vast web of laws and public policies that directly disadvantage small and local businesses" in favor of large, global ones. Oh, and the global financiers that facilitate this: It's the capital markets, stupid.

Shuman isn't the first to pitch the notion that local is beautiful. Around the industrialized world, communities have been exploring alternatives to global mass marketers for, well, as long as there have been global mass marketers. In the United States, groups such as the Business Alliance for Local Living Economies, Global Exchange, the Institute for Local Self-Reliance, and Co-op America have been actively promoting the notion of "local living economies" for years. There's the international "slow food" movement, founded in Italy in 1989 by activist Carlo Petrini as a resistance movement to combat fast food. It aims to combat the disappearance of local food traditions and "people's dwindling interest in the food they eat, where it comes from, how it tastes and how our food choices affect the rest of the world," according to its Web site. The movement claims 80,000 members from Taiwan to Turkmenistan. Slow food has given rise to the notion of "locavores," coined in 2005 by a group of self-described "concerned culinary adventurers" in San Francisco who proposed that local residents should try to eat only food grown or produced within a 100-mile radius. The idea of the "100-mile diet" has whetted the appetite of a growing corps of eco-connoisseurs, the twenty-first-century equivalent of the back-to-the-earth crowd of the 1960s and 1970s, albeit with a bit of flair not just for the simple life but also for the good life.

In his book, Shuman paints a compelling portrait of how small, local business networks can work and succeed. In the "Small-Mart Nation," many of your neighbors run their own businesses, consumers spend more of their money on locally produced, high-quality goods and services, some of their savings sit in a local bank or credit union, and communities don't bend over backwards—financially or otherwise—to lure global companies to set up shop nearby. It's not that they don't want automobile factories, big-box stores, and other manifestations of globalization in the 'hood. It's just that these entities will have to compete on a level playing field when it comes to zoning, taxes, schools, policing, and other government services. If they succeed on that basis, they're welcome.

Sometimes, "Small-Marts" can be not so small. Shuman tells the story of the Hershey Chocolate Company. The $4.6 billion candy company is publicly traded, which normally makes local ownership impossible, but a local charity, the Hershey Trust, keeps ownership local by controlling 77 percent of all voting shares. The trust "is effectively the heart that pumps monetary blood" throughout the region surrounding Hershey, Pennsylvannia, writes Shuman.

So, can "Small-Mart" replace Wal-Mart? Probably not for a while, if ever, concedes Shuman. "I believe that over time Small-Mart will reduce the size and the influence of Wal-Mart with a bunch of local alternatives," he told me. "It will never get rid of it, and we may never want to get rid of it. At the end of the day there are some economies of scale that some global companies have that are superior to local companies."

This, of course, is the key to Wal-Mart's success—its laser-perfect attention to sourcing, pricing, and distribution, allowing it to leverage its size—and clout—as no company has ever done to keep prices dirt cheap. However, those economies of scale, deployed effectively, could create positive impacts. If each customer who visited Wal-Mart in a week bought one long-lasting compact fluorescent light bulb, the company estimates, that would reduce electric bills by $3 billion, conserve 50 billion tons of coal, and keep 1 billion incandescent light bulbs out of landfills over the life of the bulb.

Of course, thousands of small, local merchants could have a similar impact, should they decide to coordinate, cooperate, or simply get into the same marketing groove. And "Small-Mart" even offers a model. Shuman described how True Value and Ace, two U.S.-based hardware chains, are comprised of individual, locally owned hardware stores banded together into marketing and buying cooperatives. They allow local hardware stores to buy collectively and engage in the kind of global bargaining that only giants such as Wal-Mart can do.

Local isn't always better, at least from an environmental perspective. Consider *food miles*, a metric that has gained currency in recent years among sustainability advocates. The term is shorthand for the distance food travels from farm to fork, with greater distances suggesting that the food has a larger environmental footprint. This makes intuitive sense. Transporting great distances requires energy and fuel and release of concomitant emissions. But food miles turns out to be short-sighted. Transport, it seems, can represent a relatively small portion of environmental impacts. So, in New Zealand, where farmers tend to apply fewer fertilizers (which require large amounts of energy to produce and cause significant greenhouse gas emissions) and animals are able to graze year round on grass, reducing the need for indoor animal feeding, livestock and dairy products use a fraction of the resources as the same products produced in other countries. A 2006 study found that dairy products shipped from New Zealand to the United Kingdom required half the energy and produced half the greenhouse gas emissions as dairy products produced in the United Kingdom, even after considering transportation. Similarly, the *New York Times* reported in 2008 that wine shipped to New York City from the Loire Valley in France had a lower carbon footprint than comparable product shipped from the Napa Valley in California. The reason: The Napa wine is trucked to New York—a more energy-intensive mode of transport—whereas the French wine travels mostly by ship, then is trucked the final distance.

Such findings are significant, but so too are the questions being asked: What is the optimal role for "local" in a globalized world? How do companies balance the growing desire for locally based commerce—whether born of patriotism, planetary concern, personal security, or other things—against the economies of scale that are possible through globalized systems of commerce? How much should your company—to borrow the famous environmental credo—think globally and act locally?

What's the "local" story your company can tell? Is that the story your customers, employees, and other stakeholders need and want to hear?

# Chapter 36

# The Elephant in the (Well-Appointed) Living Room

Talking to consumers about buying less stuff just might be the third rail of green marketing. Reducing or limiting consumption is antithetical to marketing, or at least it has been so far. Practically no one seems to want to go there.

I'll accept my portion of responsibility. In the late 1980s, when I penned *The Green Consumer*, I helped advance the notion of solving our planet's environmental ills by making good purchasing choices—that we could, in other words, shop our way to environmental health. "By choosing carefully, you can have a positive impact on the environment without significantly compromising your way of life," I wrote. "That's what being a green consumer is all about." I didn't stop there:

> It wasn't very long ago that being a green consumer was a contradiction in terms. To truly care for the environment, it was said, you had to drastically reduce your purchases of everything—food, clothing, appliances, and other "lifestyle" items—to a bare minimum. That

approach simply doesn't work in our increasingly convenience- and consumption-oriented society. No one wants to go back to a less-comfortable, less-convenient way of life.

This is still true, of course—no one wants to be less well off. And, for the large part, few people seem willing to change or be inconvenienced in the name of Mother Earth. Sure, people are making small changes—turning off computers, swapping out light bulbs, using cloth bags instead of disposable ones, buying hybrid cars, and recycling stuff. All necessary, but hardly sufficient.

Sustainable consumption is decidedly more complex and more global than just environmental concerns. It has to do with satisfying basic human needs and with spiritual, moral, and ethical matters. It has to do with the growing appetite in China, India, and other developing countries for cars, appliances, fashions, fast food, and many of the other things accessible to the consumption class. According to Norman Myers, a professor of environmental science at Oxford University, more than a billion people in 20 developing and transitional nations have recently become wealthy enough to begin consuming like Americans. Sustainable consumption also has to do with the *under*consumption that characterizes roughly a third of the world's populace.

So how on Earth do companies acknowledge the elephant in the living room—sustainable levels of consumption? Should they?

It won't be easy. For better or worse, we live in a commercial world and consumer society. You can see it at work in the cacophony of advertisements and commercial messages that intrude on our daily lives, in the companies and webs of commerce whose existence depends on consumers' endless appetite for more, and in the political leaders who work to promote unsustainable levels of economic growth, often at the expense of ecological and human needs. You can see it at work in our culture of debt and our need for keeping up with the Joneses.

Yet the environmental impacts of our consumption are virtually hidden. Most of us don't see firsthand the roughly 120 pounds of natural resources extracted from farms, forests, rangelands, oceans, rivers, and mines that go into the products that are consumed each day. For example, experts have estimated that the sum of all substances required to support one American for a year, including water used that is no longer available for reuse, totals nearly 1 million pounds—or roughly 109 truckloads for a family of four. And do we recycle those 1 million pounds of resources? Not likely—in the United States alone, individuals discard nearly three million plastic bottles every hour and enough steel and iron to continuously supply all the country's automakers.

A study published in the *Proceedings of the National Academy of Sciences* reports that average human consumption of water, forests, land, energy, and other natural resources exceeds the capacity of the biologic systems that support our planet by 20 percent. This means that we must change the way we produce goods and services lest we risk "overdrafting" our "ecological account," as ecologists put it, with devastating effects on economies and the environment.

Of course, we suffer in other ways from this buying binge. For several decades now, psychologists, sociologists, and other observers of the human condition have discussed and deconstructed the disparity—or perhaps it's a gulf—between consumption and happiness. More, it seems, is not necessarily better in terms of engendering security, self-esteem, meaning, personal fulfillment, or any of the other Maslowian traits that make for individuals, communities, and societies that are healthy, in every sense of the word. Americans, for one, consume more per capita than anyone else, yet we're chronically unhappy.

It would be one thing if all the stuff we buy somehow made us better people, but this doesn't seem to be the case. There is an extensive literature on materialism demonstrating a negative relationship between materialism and well-being. For example, in a 1985 study by Russell Belk, now a marketing professor at the Schulich School of Business at York University, materialistic people were found to be possessive, in that they preferred to own and keep things rather than borrow, rent, or throw things out. They were seen as nongenerous, or unwilling to share their possessions with others. And they tended to covet their neighbors' stuff, feeling displeasure when others had things they themselves desired. This is no victimless crime. Materialistic lifestyles can infect marriages (by devaluing nonmaterialistic bonds that keep relationships together during tough times) and parenting (since our children's value systems tend to imitate our own).

The reason we often seem powerless to resist this maelstrom of marketing messages is that we've been conditioned to buy, buy, buy from nearly the moment we emerge from the womb. Journalist Thomas Hine, in his fine book, *I Want That*, explores the history of acquisition—finding, choosing, spending—from our amber-coveting Neolithic forebears to twenty-first-century bargain hunters on eBay. Three of four American babies visit a store, usually a supermarket, by the age of six months, although some start "virtually at birth," he says. "They soon begin to realize that the store is the source of some of the good things that they had previously associated solely with their parents." It's not long before they're pointing at and choosing, often insistently, their breakfast cereals, toys, entertainment, and fashions.

For toddlers, teens, and grown-ups alike, exercising the power of choice in the marketplace is exactly that—a form of power. Shopping enables us to take control and wield authority in our often-powerless lives. Indeed, as Hine deftly points out, the mere act of going shopping itself can be more important than anything that ends up in one's shopping cart as a result. Shopping, Hine argues, "is an exercise of both profound responsibility and profound freedom."

Not that we manage to exercise the former or achieve the latter. When it comes to navigating the marketplace, rational thinking often gets short shrift. Hine cites a study in which 36 percent of women and 18 percent of men admitted buying things they didn't need. Roughly one woman in four says she "can't resist a sale," and one in three says she shops to celebrate. Hine notes that shoppers "conspire in their own seduction," allowing themselves to be manipulated by marketers.

Given all this, the idea of consuming less rings hollow. We are looking to be seduced, it seems, and the marketing world is ready, willing, and able to beguile us with its respective psychological pheromones.

What is the business opportunity in confronting consumption? Few companies have likely asked this question, and fewer still have made it part of their strategy. Patagonia, for one, raised the issue with an essay in its fall 1993 catalog. After the company had undergone an environmental product audit, the company's founder, Yvon Chouinard, came to the conclusion that "Everything we make pollutes." As a result, the company "decided to make a radical change: We are limiting Patagonia's growth in the United States with the eventual goal of halting growth altogether." The company dropped 30 percent of its clothing line in its most recent catalog. "What does this mean to you?" Chouinard asked his customers. "Well, last fall you had a choice of five ski pants, now you may choose between two. This is, of course, un-American, but two styles of ski pants are all that anyone needs. They contain all that we have learned about design and the best available coatings for weather protection."

Kia, the Korean car maker, promoting its Sedona model in the United Kingdom, attempted to differentiate itself from competitors by encouraging walking instead of driving for short trips, not your typical car company tactic. Kia promoted the notion of a "Walking Bus," in which "a group, or 'bus,' of children walks from home to school each morning quickly and safely under the guidance of trained adult supervisors."

There *are* opportunities here. "We've all talked about sustainability, but suddenly having to sell less product is what frightens most companies," says Sarah Severn, director of corporate responsibility horizons at Nike. "Selling less isn't necessarily what's called for. Consumption is not the problem. It's the nature of consumption." The problem with most products—Nike's and others'—is that their materials have a relatively short life span before becoming unusable waste. Severn believes that companies able to improve on this model may be well positioned to succeed in a society geared toward sustainable consumption. So, for example, if Nike or anyone else could make shoes from materials that can be taken back and remanufactured into new shoes, all done with renewable energy and closed-loop manufacturing systems, "You have a regenerative model," says Severn. "The key is to maximize the use of resources that are already in play, radically reducing virgin materials input, but still meeting the consumer's requirement for innovation and freshness."

As Severn makes clear, this is no bah-humbug movement. The idea of sustainable consumption increasingly is being discussed well beyond the back-to-nature crowd. The Geneva-based World Business Council on Sustainable Development, a global alliance of mostly large companies, convened a summit several years ago to talk about how to respond to a world in which the notion of sustainable consumption gains currency. The meeting—attended by 3M, British Telecom, Coors, Dow, DuPont, Fiat, General Motors, Johnson & Johnson, and others—was designed to stimulate corporations into considering the subject.

The public already is starting to think about sustainable consumption. For instance, there's the voluntary simplicity movement, which in recent years has grown beyond the Birkenstock crowd to include burned-out yuppies and others wishing to escape the fast-track treadmill. Voluntary simplicity courses now are being taught in schools, even inside companies. And there's the growing attention paid each year to "Buy Nothing Day" (or, in some countries, "No Shop Day"), a small but increasingly global annual Earth Day–like event aimed at promoting reduced consumption, celebrated on the last Friday of November. Few companies' bottom lines have suffered from this day-long rash of anticonsumerism, but that's not necessarily the point. It's all about education, raising consciousness, and a metaphysical smack upside the head just as the holiday shopping season commences. It's an all-too-brief reminder: *Think before you shop.*

How will your company fare should sustainable consumption, by whatever name, become part of the public conversation? What is the story you will be able to tell? Will anyone believe it?

To a large extent, this is the ultimate green-economy strategy— enabling customers to reduce their impacts by doing business with your company. What is the opportunity to create products or services that become the green default—the no-brainer option that is better *and* greener? What is the opportunity to be disruptive—changing the economics, the business model, the market perception in a way that renders such barriers as the unaffordability and inconvenience of "going green" moot? What is the opportunity to create products that solve customers' problems—enabling them to fulfill their needs in a way that makes them genuinely part of the solution?

# Chapter 37

# Patagonia versus the Laws of Nature

If it hasn't by now become clear, addressing the realities of the green marketplace isn't easy. (I'm trying hard here not to quote Kermit.) For one thing, you never know what's going to undermine even the best-intentioned, well-thought-out strategy. Sometimes, it's Mother Nature herself.

Several years ago, Patagonia, the progressive and thought-provoking purveyor of clothing and gear for what it calls "human-powered sports," designed a shirt whose buttons were made from the tagua nut. The tagua nut—also referred to as "vegetable ivory"—grows in the South American rain forest. It has a very hard shell, which, when sliced, drilled, and buffed, yields a very attractive button, especially when compared with the plastic buttons found on most clothing. Environmentalists have long appreciated the tagua nut because its use stimulates economies in South America, provides an alternative to cutting down rain forests for farming, and prevents elephants from being killed for their ivory tusks.

Patagonia appreciated it, too, for the statement it made: The rain forest can have economic viability indefinitely as a living entity, as opposed to being razed for timber, grazing, or agriculture.

This synched well with Patagonia's environmental ethic. The privately held company has a long history of green innovation, even provocation. It was the first company to go to organic cotton for 100 percent of its cotton products. It invented "synchilla," a fleece material made from recycled soda bottles, now commonly used for outdoor wear. The company was named one of 10 "green giants" by *Fortune* magazine. It's founder, Yvon Chouinard, is famous for saying, "There is no business to be done on a dead planet."

It's a company known for radical moves. The tagua nut button shirts were just another one of those moves.

Before launching the tagua nut button shirts, Patagonia put them through a research and development exercise that it dubbed a "killer wash"—from washer to dryer to washer to dryer and so on, a total of 50 wash cycles—to make sure the buttons held up to the most punishing customer care. The shirts survived handily, so with much fanfare, Patagonia ramped up and rolled out the line of shirts. They sold well, not surprising for a company that had garnered rabid loyalty among its customers. The shirts were a runaway success.

A few weeks later, however, something happened: The shirts started coming back—with broken buttons. Hundreds of shirts. Thousands. Tens of thousands. All with broken buttons.

What happened? It turned out that Patagonia's "killer wash" hadn't unearthed one of Mother Nature's dirty secrets. In the rain forest, the tagua nut is genetically programmed so that after a hard rain at night, followed by the hot sun the next morning, it breaks open and spills its seed. This is how the trees reproduce. And in the day-to-day world of doing laundry, it turns out that not every piece of clothing goes directly from washer to dryer. Some families do the wash at night, then get caught up with TV or the Internet or the kids, and dry laundry in the morning.

For the tagua nuts, it was all very logical—a "hard rain" from the washing machine at night, followed by the "hot sun" from the dryer the next day. They were simply doing what comes naturally.

In the end, things turned out okay for Patagonia. The company sent out replacement button kits to customers with a note of explanation. For the company's eco-minded customers, the whole episode probably added to the company's cred—and the shirts' eco-mystique.

But the tale of the tagua nut button shirts offers a moral for companies seeking to sell green products and services. In striving to be a green company, you must obey the laws of the government—pollution laws, fair marketing practices, antitrust, and so on. And you must obey the laws of the marketplace—supply and demand, price elasticity, and all the rest.

But you also must obey the laws of nature.

And that includes what may be the hardest nut to crack—*human* nature.

# Hockey Sticks and Tipping Points

**A**mong the questions I hear most often—from reporters, corporate executives, business students, market researchers, audiences, and others—is some version of these: Is green business a fad or a trend? And have we reached a tipping point?

The answer to both is emphatically, "No."

Such questions are understandable, albeit misguided. The world of green business appears to have come out of nowhere to grace the cover of most major magazines, business and otherwise, not to mention scads of other articles on inside pages. Where stories about business and environmental issues used to appear sporadically in the *New York Times, Wall Street Journal, Financial Times,* and other major publications, they are now daily fare, with sometimes as many as a half dozen news stories, feature articles, and opinion pieces in a single daily edition. In 2008, the publishers of the *Wall Street Journal* and *Fortune* both convened major conferences featuring presentations from the chief executives of companies such as Dell, Dow Chemical, Duke Energy, General Electric, and Wal-Mart. Clearly, this is not business as usual.

For those of us who have been toiling in these fields for a decade or two, this has been a slow, steady evolution. For those who are more recently discovering the greening of mainstream business, it all seems so sudden. And with that suddenness comes tenuousness: Will all this disappear just as quickly as it came?

Hardly.

The quality movement of yore represents a good analogy. During the late 1980s and early 1990s, *total quality management* (TQM), popularized by American statistician W. Edwards Deming, was the rage. There were books, magazines, conferences, and untold experts making the rounds, preaching the gospel of *kaizen,* quality circles, and other business practices. Inevitably, it ran its course.

When TQM faded from the limelight and the business world turned its collective gaze elsewhere, quality didn't go away; companies didn't revert to their old, inefficient ways. Quality became part of the fabric, eventually showing up in the form of Six Sigma, lean manufacturing, just-in-time inventory, and other business processes and strategies.

So, too, with the greening of business. Yes, some green products and companies will, inevitably, fail or lose favor. But the hardcore (and largely unsexy) stuff—energy efficiency, waste reduction, pollution prevention, supply-chain management, environmental reporting, etc.—will be around in one form or another for decades. So will the innovations that are increasingly streaming into the marketplace: green chemistry, bio-based materials, nature-inspired design, cradle-to-cradle products, and many others. They're not going away once the green fever cools.

Given our society's microscopic attention span and the apparent need of the media to deflate trends they've helped pump up, coverage of green business likely would seem headed for a fall. And this might indeed happen for any number of reasons. From the public's perspective, this would make it seem like the greening of business was yet another cynical fad that's now past its prime. It might even "prove" to some that this was all just hype. But the "bubble," to the extent that there is one, is in media reporting. And there are many days that I wish it would finally burst.

Media perceptions aside, the greening of business isn't going away anytime soon. Here, in no particular order, are 10 reasons why I think this will be an enduring issue for businesses for years to come, regardless of the media's attention span:

1. *The problems aren't getting any better.* This is fairly obvious, if you've been paying attention at all. The environmental movement, it's been said, is rapidly morphing into the climate movement, and there's a parallel shift taking place on the business side. The motivations may be different—for activists, climate has become a rallying cry that gives disparate groups a singular focus; for companies, it's about the need to squeeze efficiency out of every operational nook and cranny while reducing risk and enhancing image—but the upshot is the same: Until the climate problem is under control, it will be Job One, environmentally speaking, inside companies. And as concern, regulation, and market-based mechanisms to address climate change ramp up, this will be a key business focus for a long time. Of course, it's not just climate. A host of other issues—the availability of water, toxic ingredients in consumer products, and the rampant growth of electronic waste, to name just three—will continue to plague companies and society for decades.

2. *The political will is finally emerging.* Again, climate is the reason. Around the world, political leaders are realizing that this isn't a topic that will go away; indeed, it is gaining steam. Heightened political attention could increase public scrutiny of how company lobbyists are pressing for favorable treatment, and some of the attention could focus on the perceived hypocrisy of companies otherwise seen as leaders in corporate climate action, leading to activist charges of "greenwashing" or worse. If there's evidence of a parade of public concern over climate change, politicians certainly will want to get in front of it, and companies may end up finding that there's simply no longer enough lobbying money to buy their way out of the problem—or, better still, not enough politicians willing to be bought.

3. *Consumers are waking up.* This remains to be seen, of course, but there are encouraging signs that the consuming public is finally ready to vote with their pocketbooks, choosing greener products or products from companies perceived to be green leaders. One thing is certain: The pipeline of greener products from major consumer brands is filling up. We'll be seeing a steady stream of green product introductions in the coming years, including some from well-known companies that haven't previously been associated with the green marketplace. If these companies' products catch on, that stream could become a gusher.

4. *The supply chain is gaining power.* Wal-Mart, which is pushing its 60,000 suppliers to perform all sorts of sustainability somersaults, is one big reason, but they're hardly alone. Corporate and institutional buyers of a wide range of products are looking upstream for solutions, asking suppliers to, variously, reduce packaging, eliminate hazardous materials, use more organic or bio-based ingredients, and take other measures to green up their products and operations. This is moving some markets toward cleaner production methods far faster than any mass consumer or activist movement could.

5. *The environment has become a fiduciary issue.* We've begun to see a growing number of stories and reports from large financial institutions—banks, insurance companies, reinsurers, and investment houses—talking about the risks of climate change, toxics, water scarcity, and other environmental issues to stock prices. And shareholders, especially pension funds and large faith-based institutional investors, are starting to hammer hard on companies to acknowledge, reduce, and report on their risk profiles in these areas.

6. *The bar keeps moving.* The lack of standards that answer the question of "How good is 'good enough'?" will become increasingly problematic. But there may be an upside to the dearth of definitions. With no standards, the bar is free to drift continually higher. And this seems to be what is happening. For example, as more companies claim some form of carbon neutrality, the value of carbon-neutral as a marketing claim becomes increasingly devalued. And as the bar rises, laggard companies, even if fully compliant on

the regulatory front, may find themselves further and further behind from a reputational perspective.

7. *Companies are moving beyond "sustainability."* Given the rising bar, it would follow that companies are continually innovating and that the leading edge is moving increasingly further out. Within the next few years, it would not surprise me if being a "sustainable" company is no longer seen as a leadership goal. The real leaders will have focused their sights on being *restorative*—for example, not being merely carbon-*neutral*, but being carbon-*negative*, taking more carbon out of the atmosphere than they put in.

8. *More companies are telling their stories.* As I've said, being humble is no longer an asset. This doesn't necessarily mean that companies should be needlessly boastful, especially if it's not in their nature to do so. But doing the right thing and keeping it quiet is less of an option these days. Customers—both consumers and business customers—want green heroes, companies they believe are setting the pace. Companies holding onto the notion that walking more than talking can insulate them from criticism may find that the risks of being overly exposed are outweighed by the risks of being seen as disengaged. Expect green advertising and marketing campaigns to mushroom in the coming months and years.

9. *Clean technology is changing the game.* The clean-tech boom is making it easier and cheaper for companies to transform their products, processes, and performance to use more renewable energy, bio-based or lightweight materials, and fewer toxic ingredients. Given that some of the most promising game-changing technologies are only just now reaching their intended markets, we are on the cusp of a new generation of clean-tech products and services. As they roll out, whether from start-ups or from megaconglomerates, they'll enable a wide range of new green business opportunities.

10. *There's money to be made.* This is the real bottom line: Addressing environmental concerns is now being seen increasingly as a potential value-add, not merely a cost to be minimized. Hence green leaders are emerging throughout companies, not just in the environmental

departments, as forward-thinking entrepreneurs (and intrapreneurs) identify and exploit new ways to leverage green thinking into new products and markets. As the number of success stories moves beyond hybrid automobiles and organic foods to include other categories of products and services, green will be seen as a more "normal" part of the marketplace.

There's more. I managed to get through all this without once mentioning China or India. They, of course, are game changers as they move forward—slowly at times, leapfrogging the industrialized world at others—in building their fast-growing economies.

And then there's the specter of surprises: a cataclysmic hurricane or tsunami, a terrorist attack, an oil refinery explosion, an unstable dictator, a nuclear meltdown, a deadly heat wave, an infectious pandemic, a discombobulating iceberg, or other catastrophe. Each of these could help to move the role and responsibility of the private sector to be green leaders back into the limelight.

And once again, the media—and everyone else—likely will "discover" the greening of business.

What about the question of a tipping point? Has all this green business activity signaled that we have reached one?

Not even close.

First, a refresher: Malcolm Gladwell popularized "tipping point" in his 2000 best-selling book of that title. "Ideas and behavior and messages and products sometimes behave just like outbreaks of infectious disease," explained Gladwell. "They are social epidemics."

He continued: "As human beings, we always expect everyday change to happen slowly and steadily, and for there to be some relationship between cause and effect. And when there isn't—when crime drops dramatically in New York for no apparent reason, or when a movie made on a shoestring budget ends up making hundreds of millions of dollars—we're surprised. I'm saying, don't be surprised. This is the way social epidemics work."

The tipping point, Gladwell told us, is "the name given to that moment in an epidemic when a virus reaches critical mass."

The virus called the green economy has not hit critical mass. The number of large companies that have embraced sustainability as a core business strategy remains small—no more than a score of the Global 500. True, more companies are paying attention, asking some form of the question, "What's our green strategy?" And that's a sea change.

For the most part, the answers companies are coming up with are more programmatic than strategic—a few noteworthy changes here and there, some random acts of greenness, but mostly business as usual.

And small and midsized companies—the roughly 98 percent of all firms around the world that have fewer than 100 employees—remain largely uninvolved. Look around your community and you'll find that most local business haven't changed much: Dry cleaners, auto mechanics, small parts manufacturers, metal finishers, printers, butchers, bakers, and candlestick makers have largely been AWOL from this conversation, except in rare instances. They represent a large chunk of the economy that hasn't yet discovered "green."

This is not to say that the conversation about green business remains unchanged. As I've said, the amount of interest and inquiry has grown immeasurably in recent years. But a high level of interest and inquiry does not a tipping point make.

Entrepreneurs and venture capitalists often use a hockey-stick metaphor to describe the meteoric growth that successful companies enjoy. The blade of a hockey stick is flat, sloping gradually upward away from the tip. At some point, the blade curves steeply upward and turns into a long, straight shaft. This is the growth curve that entrepreneurs and their investors expect: slow, gradual growth in the early years and then suddenly skyrocketing into strong, exponential growth, often the point at which companies go public or get acquired.

So where on the hockey stick is the green economy? It is just beginning to round the curve from the blade to the shaft. We've still got a long, straight pathway to traverse—lots and lots of room for growth.

# The Ecological Roadmap—Earthjustice Findings on Environmental Values

## *Cara Pike*

**M**ost people in the United States say that they care about the environment. Yet whether shopping, driving, voting, or investing, they often don't walk their talk.

To understand this disconnect between ecological concern and action, it's important to consider the social values that shape opinions and behavior. Developed early in life—by our families, social networks, and institutions such as church and school—social values go beyond moral and religious values. They express our ideals of how we think the world should be and influence everything from political opinions to consumer behaviors.

To identify the social values that shape Americans' environmental attitudes, Earthjustice, the largest public-interest environmental law firm in the United States, created the Ecological

Roadmap. The Ecological Roadmap is one of the largest segmentation studies that has ever been done and shows how Americans can be grouped into 10 distinct environmental worldviews. These worldviews have more of an influence on whether someone is already or willing to go green than demographic factors such as race, gender, or age. A 25-year-old Latino, for example, will see the world much more similarly to a 55-year-old white female in the same segment than a 25-year-old Latino in another group.

The Ecological Roadmap is based on the data gathered in the American Values Survey, conducted by American Environics, an Oakland-based subsidiary of Environics, the Canadian-based public opinion research firm that developed the methodology in the 1980s. Through a series of 900 questions, this national survey, with a sample size of 1,900 respondents, tracks 130 values such as *ecological concern, civic engagement,* and *everyday rage.* Responses are analyzed to determine how these social values cluster and relate to each other and how they shift over time. Geographic and demographic information is incorporated as well, making it easy to identify and locate people who have specific worldviews.

Nationality, geography and culture help to shape values, and as a result, social value trends are unique in each of the 20 countries where these surveys have been done. American culture has been moving from fulfillment to survival since Environics started tracking U.S. social values in 1992. This is the reverse of what typically happens in industrialized nations. In Canada, for example, the culture is moving toward fulfillment values, with greater tolerance and flexibility. For the majority of Americans, though, growing insecurities around the economy, health care, and terrorism have put them in survival mode, leaving ecological concerns low on their list of priorities.

There is a core group of Americans—23 percent—who hold the value *ecological concern* strongly. And they are getting more engaged than ever. But they're not all the same; one of the key roadmap findings is that there is more than one way to be green.

Take, for example, the three most environmentally friendly segments of the American public. The *Greenest Americans* want protections for wild places and biodiversity and are the most politically active. To the

*Postmodern Idealists,* environmental protection tends to be about living green and creating car-free, low-energy cities. And the *Compassionate Caretakers,* the largest segment, mainly focus on local community issues because they want clean outdoor places for family and community recreation.

The three groups in the middle of the environmental spectrum don't spend a lot of time worrying about the environment, but they aren't necessarily opposed to environmental protection either. The *Proud Traditionalists* believe in responsibility and duty, but their view that humans are dominant over nature often puts them at odds with the notion that all species are important and worth protecting. *Driven Independents* are mostly concerned with themselves and care about the environment only if it contributes to their prosperity. The *Murky Middles* don't hold any values strongly and just follow along.

Day-to-day realities and priorities tend to trump any environmental leanings for the remaining four groups. *Ungreens,* who view environmentalists as extremists, see environmental degradation as inevitable if we want to maintain the American lifestyle. The youngest group of all, the *Antiauthoritarian Materialists,* feel that life has little meaning and are out for themselves, whereas the almost-as-young *Borderline Fatalists* may care about the environment but don't see how they can make a difference. And finally, the *Cruel Worlders,* who have been left out of the American dream and are resentful about it, just don't care about the environment.

Earthjustice has been using the Ecological Roadmap in strategic planning and is developing new litigation campaigns aimed at expanding the base of public support for environmental protection. For for-profit strategists and marketers, the roadmap is a targeting tool; by focusing on common values, it is possible to create strategies that resonate with the majority of Americans.

In addition to profiles of the 10 environmental worldviews, what follows features analysis and answers to several key questions, including: How do you convert the converted? How can America's youth be the next big green market? How widespread and lasting will the impact of climate change be on what it means to be green?

Motivating the public to act on their ecological values is a big part of what needs to happen to address increasingly complex challenges. In sharing this information, it is my hope that business leaders will use it with success in helping to create a new green economy.

## THE 10 ENVIRONMENTAL WORLDVIEWS

See Table A–1 for the 10 environmental worldviews.

**Table A–1** The 10 Environmental Worldviews

| Segment | Percent of U.S. Population | Worldview in Brief |
|---|---|---|
| Greenest Americans | 9 | Everything is connected, and our daily actions have an impact on the environment. |
| Ungreens | 3 | Environmental degradation and pollution are inevitable in maintaining America's prosperity. |
| Compassionate Caretakers | 24 | Healthy families need a healthy environment. |
| Proud Traditionalists | 20 | Religion and morality dictate actions in a world where humans are superior to nature. |
| Murky Middles | 17 | Indifferent to most everything, including the environment. |
| Antiauthoritarian Materialists | 7 | Little can be done to protect the environment, so why not get a piece of the pie. |
| Driven Independents | 7 | Protecting the earth is fine as long as it doesn't get in the way of success. |
| Cruel Worlders | 6 | Resentment and isolation leave no room for environmental concerns. |
| Borderline Fatalists | 5 | Getting material and status needs met on a daily basis trumps worries about the planet. |
| Postmodern Idealists | 3 | Green lifestyles are part of a new way of being. |

*Source:* The Ecological Roadmap.

## The Greenest Americans

If you can prove it, they will come.

For 9 percent of Americans, *ecological concern* influences their worldview more than any other social value. This group of largely older, highly educated, white Americans represents the best market for the best green products.

The Greenest Americans vote at extremely high levels, read newspapers, and pay fairly close attention to politics. However, this doesn't mean that all of them are politically active when it comes to their environmental concerns. For the Greenest Americans, environmental values are primarily acted on through daily lifestyle and purchasing choices. This isn't great news for environmental advocacy organizations, but it presents a business opportunity for companies providing green products and services.

The Greenest Americans believe in taking the steps they can to reduce their impact on the environment. They buy environmentally friendly cleaning materials, recycle avidly, and look for environmental options when making large purchases, such as cars or home renovations. These daily acts have become part of their morality—taking environmental actions is just the right thing to do. This morality is connected to the Greenest Americans' concern for their own health and well-being, which results in an active lifestyle and pursuit of alternative and holistic health treatments.

This group has the money to support their environmental lifestyles. A third of them have household incomes of more than $100,000. Furthermore, the Greenest Americans are the only group to highly value *ethical consumerism,* which is a focus on the ethical and social responsibilities policies and practices they buy from. Going green is the way members of this affluent segment of the public can expresses their status rather than by consuming just because they can.

The Greenest Americans may be dedicated, but they are not naive. Green product choices are not viewed as the whole solution to environmental protection. While cynical about politicians and bureaucracy, these progressive Americans still believe that government needs to drive large-scale political change to deal with climate change and other issues. Members of this segment see their green purchasing habits as the most direct way to send a message to government and corporate leaders about their environmental beliefs and what they hope for in terms of alternatives.

But beyond having the sense that they are voting with their pocketbooks, the Greenest Americans have little way to tell if their green purchases make a difference (unless those differences can be experienced directly, such as nontoxic cleaners not burning your eyes or organic produce tasting better than conventionally grown food).

When trying to reach the Greenest Americans, keep in mind that they do their homework and research their green choices. They are four times more skeptical of advertising than the average American and care little about brands. As a result, they are unlikely to take marketing claims at face value. This is a group that looks at environmental issues intellectually and understands their complexity and their ties to other issues. They want to know not only a product's organic content but also how far it was shipped, how much energy was used to create it, and the labor conditions under which it was produced. Health claims need to be researched and documented.

They want proof for themselves—and for others. While the Greenest Americans aren't likely to buy a product plastered with a giant corporate logo, they do want products that help them to stand out by making the green attributes obvious—such as hybrid labels or biodiesel stickers on cars.

One final caution: Despite being eco-minded, even the Greenest Americans don't strongly self-identify as environmentalists. Marketing that is shrill or conveys that the sky is falling might turn them off. If your product works as well as its traditional counterpart, just make your environmental case, provide tangible proof, and the Greenest Americans likely will give it a try.

## The Ungreens—Reaching Environmental Cynics

The Ungreens are those who hold a worldview most different from that of the Greenest Americans. These mainly rural, politically conservative Americans feel that environmental degradation is an inevitable part of our prosperous economy. They have the weakest level of *ecological concern* of any of the segments and are 13 times more likely than the general public to put themselves at the bottom of the scale for identifying as environmentalists.

The good news is that only 3 percent of Americans are Ungreens, and pretty much everyone else cares to some degree about protecting the environment. Yet while members of this group are not a large segment of the public, they wield considerable political and economic clout. Ninety-six percent of Ungreens consider themselves conservatives—more than twice the level of any other group. The majority of this segment has moderate to high incomes, are likely voters, and report paying a great deal of attention to news on politics and government.

Although they are in many ways the polar opposite of the Greenest Americans (on racism, religion, pride in America, etc.), Ungreens express interest in a number of activities that relate to environmental concerns. Their interest in hunting is greater than any other group of Americans, and they are into outdoor recreation such as hiking, biking, and surfing. As a result, The Ungreens actually have some green market potential, particularly for outdoor products.

The key is that it just can't be done the same way as when targeting more eco-minded recreationalists. One of the lowest values for the Ungreens is *ethical consumption;* their motivation when making purchases is primarily to advance their sense of material success and status. This, in combination with their fatalism and conservative political orientation, means that making-the-world-a-better-place messaging won't go very far. However, speaking to the Ungreens' sense of duty, tradition, and pride in America when marketing outdoor products can.

Another opportunity for green marketers is to tap into this group's perhaps surprisingly strong interest in *holistic health*. In fact, like the

Greenest Americans, they hold this as one of their top values. Ungreens put time and effort into taking care of their health and feel better about themselves when they are confident about their appearance. This provides an opportunity to market natural health products as long as health remains the focus, and political and environmental issues are downplayed.

For a large company, all the better. The Ungreens hold the values *importance of brand* and *confidence in big business* twice as much as the average American, meaning that they give weight to brand names, have favorite products, and associate good quality and service with big companies. They believe more in the private sector's ability to act on social and economic problems than they do in government action. Messages that focus on what is great about America, such as America's ingenuity and ability to innovate to solve our problems, might work with Ungreens.

Just don't do anything that will make this group think that it's turning green.

## Postmodern Idealists—Connecting with the Next Generation

A committed consumer base for green products and services is the Postmodern Idealists. Making up 3 percent of the U.S. population, these young—79 percent are under 44 years of age—independent thinkers with moderate to high incomes hold ecological values twice as strongly as the average person.

While their environmental interest is significant, it is only half of what it is for the Greenest Americans. This speaks to the need to distinguish this group. For Postmodern Idealists, environmental concerns represent only a part of their worldview. They enjoy outdoor activities such as hiking and biking more than any other group, but when it comes to environmental issues, they take a personal approach, caring as much about switching to alternative energy solutions as they do about protecting nature.

Although not as diverse as the other young segments, Postmodern Idealists hold the value *racial fusion* more strongly than other groups.

They believe that ethnic diversity enriches people's lives. As a result, they want to know not just the environmental impact of products and services but also companies' labor and personnel practices, such as being a family- or gay-friendly workplace.

Unlike the Greenest Americans, Postmodern Idealists are low on the value *liberal communitarianism,* the belief that it is important to think about life in the context of others rather than focusing on themselves. Instead, they are driven by values such as *unfettered individualism,* which is the sense that individuals should have the right to make decisions about their own lives. These are do-it-yourself environmentalists; they prefer to engage directly in the issues they care about, such as renovating their houses with environmentally friendly materials and running their cars on biodiesel.

This segment is low on the value *trust,* which indicates that while they are passionate about environmental issues and making green choices, Postmodern Idealists are cynical about government and business. They want to know whether or not green product claims are valid but don't trust that they will find the answers in the mainstream media. Instead, members of this group spend a lot of time online reading blogs and exchanging information with friends. To them, small social groups and organizations are better than large ones, and trusting peers is the way to go.

Postmodern Idealists are searching for meaning and want to define that meaning for themselves. They are higher on the values *culture sampling* and *religion a la carte* than any other segment, reflecting an openness to other cultures and religions as well as a tendency to incorporate a range of cultural influences and spiritual practices into their lives.

Among the top values for this group are *enthusiasm for new technology* and *pursuit of intensity.* This reflects their youth. Unlike the Greenest Americans, they are fascinated by technology and the possibilities it offers and enjoy seeking out the latest products and innovations. This makes them a natural market for alternative and energy-efficient products. Postmodern Idealists are also guided more by their emotions than by reason and ideology. They strongly hold the value *interest in the unexplained,* which is a rejection that all knowledge must be rational or scientific. While they accept the argument for green alternatives, they are less intellectual about the environment than the Greenest Americans and more emotional.

Don't be put off by the relatively small size of this segment. Despite being cynical—and in some cases because of it—Postmodern Idealists are trying to make a difference. More than one-quarter of them are students, so it's quite likely that their incomes will increase over time. Thus it's good to try to get these folks now because if you do, you'll probably have them for life.

### Compassionate Caretakers—The Next Green Market

This segment represents a significant opportunity for green-minded companies. Compassionate Caretakers are concerned about the environment, and there are a lot of them—a quarter of all Americans. But life is busy for these family-focused individuals with many demands on their money and their time.

The Compassionate Caretakers are three-fifths women, one-quarter African American, and largely middle income. They have strong feelings about *social connectedness* and are actively involved in their communities, as Boy Scout leaders, church volunteers, and PTA moms. These are nurturing, open-minded people who believe that everyone deserves a chance. Their top value is *flexible families,* the acceptance of alternative forms of families from common-law to single-parent homes, and is followed by such values as *no group inherently superior* and *group egalitarianism,* the belief that society shouldn't have groups of people with more rights than others.

*Ecological concern* and *ethical consumerism* are also top values. Yet Compassionate Caretakers do not strongly identify as environmentalists and are not as political and engaged as the Greenest Americans and Postmodern Idealists. To them, protecting the environment means ensuring that there are safe and healthy places for their families to be together, such as clean city parks and easily accessible outdoor recreation. The members of this group, strong on the value *intellectual and open,* have abandoned the notion that protecting the environment equals job loss. Instead, they think that there is a good chance that going green can lead to job creation as well as improved quality of life in their communities.

While they want to be doing more in their daily lives, Compassionate Caretakers don't believe that they can afford to choose more environmentally friendly options. Despite being extremely concerned about climate change, these Americans worry even more about the rising costs of energy and consider it a more pressing national priority.

And they don't necessarily have the time to act on their values either. Compassionate Caretakers feel torn between the convenience of many everyday products they buy and the amount of energy required and waste generated to produce them. They wish that green alternatives were widely available and integrated into daily life so that they wouldn't have to go out of their way to find them.

If you can catch their attention, green messages tied to children, family, and health issues will resonate with Compassionate Caretakers. Given the involvement of members of this segment in their communities, companies may want to tie their products to local events through cause-related promotions. These partnerships need to be genuine commitments of time and resources because these political moderates tend to follow the news and pay attention to what is making a difference.

Even with their hectic schedules, if green products are affordable, of good quality, and available where they already shop, the Compassionate Caretakers represent one of the next green markets and a big one at that.

### Antiauthoritarian Materialists—Apathy and American Youth Culture

Far younger than any other group, Antiauthoritarian Materialists see the world as a harsh place, with everyone out for themselves. Making up 7 percent of the population, these low-wage workers will do whatever it takes to get ahead.

The self-indulgent attitude of the Antiauthoritarian Materialists extends to political and civic life as well. They are less likely to vote than any other group, don't concern themselves with environmental issues, and are apathetic about civic life altogether. In fact, they hold the value *ecological fatalism*, the belief that some amount of pollution is unavoidable, at more than three times the average. *Social isolation* is another value they hold highly, an indication of how they don't feel connected to other people and often don't want to be.

What they seem to care most about is stuff. *Crude materialism*, placing great importance on accumulating material possessions, is one of their top values. And not only do they want to get stuff, but they also want to show it off. Antiauthoritarian Materialists hold the value *ostentatious consumption*, the desire to impress others with objects that symbolize affluence, more strongly than most.

This is their materialistic side. This puts them at odds with the more environmentally friendly segments of the population. But values such as *rejection of authority* indicate that there is a small amount of common ground with the Greenest Americans and Postmodern Idealists, even if this rejection has a harshness to it and results in checking out rather than engaging in change. Green products, services, and campaigns that have an edge to them and question authority have a chance of appealing to Antiauthoritarian Materialists.

This group also shares with the greener segments the value *largesse oblige*, the belief that society's "haves" have a duty to help or share with those less fortunate. This belief can be tapped into by associating green products and services with eco-minded young celebrities who share some of their antiauthoritarian values.

If you are going to reach them, it will be online because the Antiauthoritarian Materialists are a group of which 71 percent watch videos on YouTube and 57 percent have their own blog. Moreover, given their strong interest in new technologies, green products with high-tech appeal could catch on.

Almost a quarter of Antiauthoritarian Materialists are students. For one thing, this means that the group's low to moderate incomes might increase over time. More important, it might mean that they won't always be part of this group. While most values are set by the time people reach the age of 18, experiences, such as education, can influence worldviews. It's conceivable that some members of this segment could evolve into Postmodern Idealists and become steady consumers of environmentally friendly products and services.

## Borderline Fatalists—A Green Potential?

It's perhaps telling that the segment of the population most interested in buying organic products is the least able to afford them. Borderline Fatalists represent 5 percent of the public and are so intense that they rank either very high or very low on all the social values. Whether they are a good potential market for green products and services remains to be seen.

Life isn't easy for the Borderline Fatalists, who tend to be young, of low income, nonwhite, and urban. More than a third are unemployed. This group generally is pessimistic and tends not to see a lot of meaning in their lives. They want things to be better but don't feel that they are in a position to make much of a difference. This explains why they are high on the value *active government,* the desire to have government resolve social issues, but don't see the point of getting involved in civic life. Borderline Fatalists have the highest level of identification with the Democratic Party but largely don't vote.

Despite the challenges life is dishing out, Borderline Fatalists have not given up. They still hang onto some hope amid their hopelessness, even if they don't turn to themselves for solutions. What distinguishes them from Cruel Worlders, the other group of society's "have nots," is that they are not socially isolated. Instead, they have a sense of connection to their community and a pride in their cultural background. The Borderline Fatalists are high on values such as *search for roots* and *community involvement,* which is a measure of interest and engagement in what is going on in one's community.

When asked, Borderline Fatalists express a strong interest in camping, fishing, and hunting. They also self-identify as environmentalists more than most Americans. Yet their values tell a different story. In addition to *ecological concern* being one of their weakest values, they place great importance on being able to buy things that reflect status, and they take pleasure in shopping on a regular basis. They score way above the norm in values such as *confidence in big business, joy of consumption, importance of brand,* and *need for status recognition*. Even though they express environmental interest, Borderline Fatalists are more concerned with making it than they are with going green.

To reach Borderline Fatalists, green companies need to prove how their product makes a tangible difference, and they need to do it in a straightforward way given this group's *discomfort with ambiguity*. Going local and creating partnerships with trusted community organizations are other ways to build credibility.

Perhaps most important is that the image of green being mostly white needs to change as well. Continuing to position health and sustainability products around images of older, affluent, educated Caucasians has its limits when trying to reach such a young and diverse segment of the public. Until the image of environmentalism has evolved to reflect the broader cross section of who Americans have become, the full potential of this market will not be realized.

### Driven Independents—Green Is the New American Dream

For 7 percent of Americans, being driven to succeed defines them. Driven Independents are young, professional, predominantly male, and politically independent. Their strongest values are those that relate to making it and not being obliged to share.

While they could care less about civic life in America, Driven Independents are open to change as long as they don't risk losing what they have gained. Making moderate to high incomes, this group prizes financial security. Yet they do not consume to impress others. They already see themselves as winners and care little about what people—outside their immediate peer groups—think of them.

Driven Independents don't worry too much about the environment. Only 29 percent, when surveyed in 2007, think that global warming is an important problem. They score very low on *ecological concern,* as well as on *ecological fatalism*. Thus, while they don't necessarily think that environmental degradation is unacceptable, they also don't believe that our economic progress has to come at a cost to the environment either.

This group is independent not just politically but also socially. Members score very low on *social intimacy* and *introspection and empathy* and very high on *just deserts,* a measure of confidence that people get what they deserve. This attitude does not bode well for marketing green products with "together, we can make a difference" language.

While not a top target for green strategists, Driven Independents do hold some values that can be tapped into for promoting environmental products or services. For example, this segment rates high on the value *saving on principle,* believing that it is important to save money for the future and to help prepare for the unexpected. This doesn't make them big consumers overall, but green products that promote energy efficiency or other ways to save money through green actions could appeal to this group. Rating very high on *status via home,* Driven Independents value their homes as a personal marker of success. Green building and home products could appeal to this group as long as these products have an upscale, rather than a folksy or earthy, image.

Driven Independents are high on *adaptive navigation,* which means that they have the flexibility to respond to events that threaten their plans. In addition, they are excited about technology and are willing to try the latest high-tech products. These traits might be good news for companies marketing new or unusual green products, as well as goods and services focused on providing technical solutions to environmental challenges.

Driven Independents rank very low on *spiritual quest,* so it's best to avoid marketing efforts that rely on new age spiritualism. The same goes for advocacy or political approaches. However, if being green becomes equated with being successful, this group just might make the switch.

### The Murky Middles—The Ecologically Indifferent

It may be hard to believe, but 17 percent of Americans do not hold any social values strongly. The Murky Middles are average in every way, from demographic measures such as age, income, race, and education levels to their moderate interest in politics, the outdoors, and green products. Their potential as an audience for green-minded business is, well, average.

Neither pessimistic nor optimistic about their future, Murky Middles do not believe that they can improve their situation in life, let alone influence broader social issues. They are even indifferent about taking care of themselves, with low values around *effort toward health* and *holistic health*. Likewise, they are low on *work ethic* and *personal challenge,* which is about setting difficult personal goals and rejecting failure. Not surprisingly, members of this group hold both *ecological concern* and *ecological fatalism* at average levels, reflecting an overall indifference to environmental matters.

At least, this group is not uncomfortable with environmental values. Although members have little in common with the Greenest Americans, the Murky Middles do share some values with the younger but also environmentally minded Postmodern Idealists. This is not surprising given their tendency to go along with the mainstream, which today is dominated by youth culture, even though they themselves are not particularly young. Although they are not relatively strong values, *equal relationship with youth,* the belief that youth deserve to experience freedom and individualism as adults do, *penchant for risk,* and *unfettered individualism* are toward the top of their values list. Environmental products and messages aimed at youth that have more of an edge than the typical green options just might resonate with the Murky Middles if they become popular enough.

Values around consumption and status, such as *joy of consumption, importance of brand,* and *need for status recognition,* which is the desire to be held in esteem and respect by others and to express social standing, are in the top third of values for the Murky Middles. Again, though, these values are not held very strongly compared with other segments of the public. As with other parts of their lives, they go along with the materialism in American culture without feeling strongly about it.

On the other hand, one of the most important values to the Murky Middles is *openness to change,* which indicates an acceptance of spontaneity and flexibility when organizing their lives. If green indeed does become the new black, it's conceivable that Murky Middles, without either realizing or intending it, could end up giving green products a try.

## The Proud Traditionalists

One of every five Americans is a Proud Traditionalist. This older, rural, moderate to conservative group is highly religious. Although not an obvious target for green marketers, there are reasons to believe that it may be possible to convert members of this segment into environmentally responsible consumers.

Clear hierarchies play a fundamental role in the worldview of Proud Traditionalists. They value *traditional family* at four times the national average, believing that the traditional concept of family should not be changed. They have a strong sense of duty, and *obedience to authority* is more important to them than it is to any other group.

On environmental values, opinions, and activities, Proud Traditionalists are moderate. *Ecological concern* is low on their list of values, yet so is *ecological fatalism*. Other than a strong interest in fishing, this group has an average level of interest in the outdoors. Health values are not held strongly either.

More promising are a number of values that relate to environmental concerns. Like the Greenest Americans, Proud Traditionalists are strong on *social responsibility,* the belief that things can improve when people work together, *liberal communitarianism,* the principle of considering others when making decisions, and *altruism.*

One major obstacle to members of this segment going green is their negative perception of environmentalists. To Proud Traditionalists, environmentalists are too liberal and too challenging of authority. Another barrier is their strong belief in *humans superior to animals.* This clear sense of humans being dominant over nature is at odds with the environmental view that we are all part of an interconnected web of life. Lately, however, the huge gap between worldviews is beginning to close as many religious organizations are starting to engage more in environmental protection. Recent campaigns on endangered species and habitat protection, as well as on climate change, are promising because they connect ecological values to a morality around stewardship and legacy.

Owing to its size, this segment collectively consumes a lot, but individually, members are not high on consumption values. Proud Traditionalists don't have the need to display material wealth, don't have particular brands they care about, and don't shop just for the fun of it. They are not interested in *ethical consumerism* either and, as a result, do not place great importance on the social or environmental record of the companies from which they buy products.

To market green products and services to Proud Traditionalists, avoid politically progressive messages and earthy images. Rather, the focus should be on the responsibility to future generations. Spokespersons with credibility within the religious community will be more effective in reaching this group than those without a strong religious and traditional orientation. A sense of moral obligation to be responsible stewards of the earth could make members of this segment go greener than one might think.

### Cruel Worlders—Why Some Americans May Never Go Green

Six percent of Americans have a pretty bleak outlook on life. More than any other group, Cruel Worlders feel left out of the American Dream and are resentful of others who have been more successful. Along with their low socioeconomic status, this makes the prospects of Cruel Worlders turning green any time soon as grim as their view of the world.

Cruel Worlders are at the bottom of the nation's economic ladder, with 26 percent making under $30,000. They also have some of the lowest education levels and typically work as part of the unskilled labor force. It is the second oldest segment, after the Greenest Americans. However, other than also being predominantly white, the two groups have few similarities.

The Cruel Worlders are near or at the bottom of the scale on a range of environmental factors, from self-identification as environmentalists to interest in the outdoors and buying organic food. The same is true for the values *ethical consumption* and *social responsibility*. Instead, *meaningless life and future* is one of the most important values for Cruel Worlders, which they hold at a level more than two times the average. Given that they lack a sense of purpose in their own lives and don't believe that the future will be better, it is not surprising that they pay no attention to broader social or environmental issues.

The top value for Cruel Worlders is *modern racism,* a belief that racism is a thing of the past and that minorities have gained more than they deserve. This group also ranks highly on *xenophobia, parochialism,* and *social isolation,* the feeling of not wanting to be connected to other people. To them, the world has become a confusing place, and they don't feel a part of it. They experience a lot of *technology anxiety* and *aversion to complexity* because they are threatened by changes in society and the complexities of modern life. Despite the fact that most members of this segment work hard at full-time jobs, they know that the information-based economy is leaving them behind.

From a business strategy standpoint, it makes the least sense to go after the Cruel Worlders. Understanding the values behind this group does, however, provide insight into why some Americans may never go green. It is hard to act on environmental values when meeting basic needs is a challenge. But even more of a barrier than their socioeconomic status is the Cruel Worlders' negative view of the world and their social isolation. It is hard to imagine that they will ever care about the environment or believe environmental progress is possible. And given their age, their values are unlikely to change.

## CONVERTING THE CONVERTED

Getting the greenest of green consumers to buy your product is far from a slam dunk. This is so because even many of the most environmentally minded Americans report that they are skeptical and/or confused about their choices.

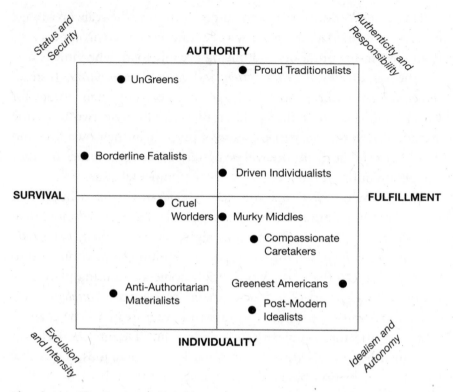

**Figure A-1** The Segment Graphic

No wonder. With a range of green certification programs and labels, none of them consistent or connected, it is hard to know what's what. Green marketing terms such as *natural* and *organic* have been misused over the years, and the public is understandably confused.

In focus groups conducted in California and New York in 2007 with the Greenest Americans and Postmodern Idealists—the 12 percent of the public that have the strongest environmental values—people reported that going green can be a chore. They don't know how to identify the impact products have on the environment, and they don't know whether standards or guidelines exist, let alone who is responsible for setting and enforcing them. This holds true for organic food and energy-efficient appliances—two of the more mainstream green product categories—even though both are regulated by the federal government and have robust certification and labeling programs.

It's not for lack of intention. The daily acts these eco-minded Americans engage in, such as recycling, are part of their morality. However, except for perhaps when they're making large purchases, people don't have the time or the tools to research environmental claims to determine what's real and what's hype. They make their choices using instinct and the limited information they have and hope for the best—while wishing someone would make it easier.

Without the existence or availability of clear standards, the Greenest Americans and Postmodern Idealists place great importance on two factors: the source of product information and the credibility of where they shop. If environmental organizations make claims for or against a product or company, they are taken seriously because these groups are seen as watchdogs of corporate America and politicians. In addition, environmental consumers are more likely to believe green retailers with reputations for being socially responsible, whereas they may have their doubts about a big box store.

To reach the greenest consumers, simply saying that a product is green is not enough. Environmentally motivated consumers want to know not just a list of ingredients but also the environmental impact of the materials used and the waste generated. They want to make sure that a green product is produced in a facility where workers are paid a living wage and isn't shipped halfway across the world to get to their local store. Details and facts need to be provided, ideally in a simple and compelling story.

In the focus groups, the most information-hungry green consumers say that they want the particulars behind any marketing claims. This doesn't mean that they want to spend a lot of time reading it, though. A concise Web site that offers information about such things as the amount of energy used, recycled or natural material content, and reuse or recycling potential in a product should be referenced in marketing materials and kept current.

Given consumer confusion and skepticism about green claims, it is worth pushing for industry-wide standards. In the meantime, companies may want to create rating systems with simple accounting that compares the impacts of their products with those of the competition and with those of nongreen products. Basing this on third-party information is critical, as well as partnering with organizations that green consumers already trust.

The Greenest Americans and the Postmodern Idealists spend a lot of time online. Take advantage of technology by asking consumers to rate the greenness of products and share this information with others. This assumes that the green claims are top-notch and can be backed by credible third parties.

Whatever the standard or rating system, the important thing is to clearly let consumers know how your product will make a positive difference and their role in creating that change.

## ENVIRONMENTAL SAINTHOOD—THE DISCONNECT BETWEEN CONCERN AND ACTION

Most surveys, including the American Values Survey, show that the majority of the public cares to some extent about environmental issues or at least enjoys the outdoors and doing things in nature. Yet this interest doesn't always result in buying green products, joining environmental organizations, or changing behaviors.

Earthjustice commissioned American Environics to conduct 12 focus groups with members of several segments from the American Values Survey to explore the disconnect between concern and action. Held in 2006–2007 in San Jose, New York, Portland, and Spokane, these groups provided a great opportunity to further understand the environmental worldviews revealed in the quantitative data. In addition to talking to the most environmentally minded groups—the Greenest Americans, the Postmodern Idealists, and the Compassionate Caretakers—we included one of the most fatalistic groups—the Antiauthoritarian Materialists.

As with the survey, the focus groups confirmed that most people have some level of concern for the environment and interest in the outdoors. More important, they revealed that getting in the way of action is a view that environmentalists are not like regular people. Instead, they are seen as being willing to sacrifice all self-interest and do whatever it takes to protect the environment 100 percent of the time. Like saints, they are either revered or thought of as crazy extremists for taking their passion and commitment to an unattainable level. As a result, even the Greenest Americans don't strongly identify as environmentalists.

It is true that some of the most eco-minded Americans go out of their way to make green purchasing decisions—spending sometimes hours doing research online for big-ticket items or going to four different stores to find organic groceries at a decent price. Most people, though, even if they care, don't know how to evaluate what is green and don't feel that they have the time or the money it takes to act on their environmental concerns. They feel guilty for not doing more. In the focus groups, even the few people who did call themselves environmentalists added the disclaimer that they are not very good environmentalists because they could be doing more.

As long as being an environmentalist is equated with saintly dedication, it will be out of reach for most Americans, particularly given that green products are still hard to find and often cost more. Environmental purchasing behavior will continue to be sporadic because, as we heard in the focus groups, people aren't willing to be environmental purists.

Companies have an opportunity to motivate people to act on their environmental values and move toward greener purchasing decisions by creating new ways for people to identify themselves as environmentalists where perfection is not required. Rather than always be so earnest, green marketing should be fun and willing to play with some of the inherent contradictions environmental consumerism entails. Being green shouldn't have to mean being a fanatic.

## YOUNG AND GREEN—ARE AMERICA'S YOUTH THE NEXT GREEN MARKET?

As people age, their values tend to become more traditional and authoritarian. However, typically this is relative to where they start. What is unique in our culture right now is the extent to which there is a gap between the values of young people and those of their elders.

Although younger Americans can be found in all 10 of the environmental worldview segments, they are more fatalistic about life, less engaged civically, and have weaker environmental values. This has implications for a range of behaviors, including the purchase of green products.

Michael Adams, founder and CEO of Environics in Canada, has been tracking social values for more than 35 years. He shows that while youth in Canada and the United States are moving in opposite directions, the distance they have each moved from the older segments of the public is beyond any typical values migration. In both countries, youth have become hyperindividualistic and materialistic and have moved away from most traditional forms of authority or rules for how to live.

In Canada, that is perhaps not a bad thing because at least young people there hold strong environmental values. In the United States, however, the majority of youth have values that reflect a lack of concern for their own lives, let alone others or the planet.

This is not to say that there aren't engaged, motivated, progressive youth in America who care about the environment. There are. Three percent of the population are Postmodern Idealists, and many of them are quite young. Yet even they don't connect with the issue in the same way that older Americans do. While Postmodern Idealists care about wildlife and wilderness, they are more human-focused and more materialistic, and they want to know how environmental degradation affects them personally. In many ways, this makes them the ideal green consumers.

Unfortunately, they do not represent the majority of young Americans. The Antiauthoritarian Materialists and the Borderline Fatalists do. *Ecological fatalism* is a top value for both groups. Unless their attitudes shift, the environment is not likely to be a priority. The low socioeconomic status of both groups certainly shapes their worldviews, but it cannot account for all of it.

What does? Most social values are set by the time people have reached the age of 18. On an individual level, values can shift as a result of life-changing personal experiences and major societal events.

Young Americans have come of age in the time of September 11th, Hurricane Katrina, and the wars in Iraq and Afghanistan, so it's not surprising that many of them feel helpless and hopeless about the future. And now they're facing climate change.

Fatalistic youth are needed as the green consumers of tomorrow. The question is how to reach and engage young Americans.

Start with the Postmodern Idealists, the most eco-minded youth-oriented segment. They are high on the value *importance of brand,* so make them loyal customers by creating a sense of community and finding ways to engage them in developing your brand. *Social intimacy* is also a top value for this group, which is the desire to connect with smaller, close-knit groups of people and organizations. Partnerships and promotions with venues and groups that are small scale and off-beat are a good way to go.

Young Americans are more likely to listen to their peers online than pay attention to environmental messages they associate with older generations. Provide the Postmodern Idealists with incentives to reach out to their more fatalistic peers in the Antiauthoritarian Materialist and Borderline Fatalist segments to share issue and product information. The message cannot be too earnest or they will tune you out.

## CONNECTING SOCIAL RESPONSIBILITY AND ENVIRONMENTAL VALUES

Americans who care about the environment also tend to care about the ethical and social responsibility policies and practices of companies from which they buy. For those whom the environment is not a top priority, the reverse is true as well.

Forty-one percent of Americans hold the value *ethical consumerism* and consider the ethical and social responsibility practices of companies when making purchasing decisions. Most of these are concentrated in four segments of the population: the Greenest Americans, Postmodern Idealists, Compassionate Caretakers, and the Borderline Fatalists. What drives this concern, however, is unique for each group.

For the Greenest Americans, paying attention to how business behaves is part of an overall worldview that prioritizes responsibility and engagement over pleasure or status. *Ethical consumerism* goes hand in hand with their views on *ecological concern* and *deconsumption,* which is the desire to limit consumption of goods. They are higher on *brand apathy* than any other group and have low *confidence in big business,* which means that they don't believe that large companies balance profits with the public interest. As a result, they are informed consumers and don't hesitate to switch brands if a new company is offering better environmental or social performance. Of course, since their incomes are among the highest, they have the luxury to be picky.

Like the Greenest Americans, the Postmodern Idealists care about *ecological concern* and *ethical consumerism* and are low on the value of *confidence in big business.* They tend to be more materialistic than there older green counterparts, with strong values around *importance of brand* and *joy of consumption.* The Postmodern Idealists are happy to have environmentally friendly options because they want to be fashionable and hip without feeling guilty about their impact.

The Compassionate Caretakers care as much about *ethical consumerism* as the Postmodern Idealists and don't have as many values that they put ahead of it. Less ideological about their views—among their top values are *flexible families* and *intellectual and open*—this group's interest in supporting socially responsible businesses is more about being a good person than about politics or individual expression. Like the Greenest Americans, the Compassionate Caretakers don't place much importance on consumption and are equally skeptical of big business. They want to do more, but with middle incomes, they are concerned that they can't afford to be green. If they felt that environmentally and socially responsible business options were within their reach, the Compassionate Caretakers would be in a position to act more on their values.

The Borderline Fatalists are the only segment of the public where *ecological concern* does go not hand in hand with *ethical consumerism.* While the latter is high on their list of values, *ecological fatalism* is even more dominant, as well as *confidence in big business, ostentatious consumption,* and *crude materialism,* placing great importance on accumulating material possessions and the need to constantly buy. This group probably needs to achieve the status they associate with material success before they will consider *deconsumption,* even though this is an idea they are open to as well.

With the strong connection between *ethical consumerism* and *ecological concern* and the low values held around *confidence in big business,* it is clear that the most environmentally minded consumers are also the consumers who care the most about social issues, such as fair trade, health, and labor. Some may never trust large companies to deliver truly alternative goods, creating an opportunity for locally based, small-scale businesses to meet the needs of these most particular of consumers.

All companies, no matter what their scale, that offer green products need to pay attention to both their environmental and social records because much of their target audience will be watching to ensure that the corporate values of the companies they support are in keeping with their own.

## HEALTH AND THE ENVIRONMENT

The environment is a health issue. Whether it's air quality, drinking water, or food safety, the state of the environment affects us. But a lot of people who care about their health—and most people care a lot about their health—don't express concern for the environment.

As you might expect, Americans with the strongest environmental values hold the strongest health values. *Holistic health, effort toward health,* and *vitality* cluster together and help drive the worldviews of both the Greenest Americans and the Postmodern Idealists. These groups make the connection between physical, mental, and spiritual health and believe that taking care of themselves now will pay off later. And since these two groups want to take care of the environment as well, they prize products that offer both health benefits and a reduced impact on the earth.

On the other end of the environmental spectrum, there are two groups that prioritize health. Ungreens and Borderline Fatalists are strong on *holistic health, vitality,* and *effort toward health.* They are even higher on *look good feel good,* the belief that by taking care of how you look, you feel confident and are more likely to succeed. Their primary concern for good health is externally driven given that they care most about their appearance and what other people think of them. Even so, the fact that they are also interested in preventative health as well as the mind-body-spirit connection is a promising trend.

Another group with higher-than-average health values is the Driven Independents. This ambitious, confident group is indifferent to green issues (low on both *ecological concern* and *ecological fatalism*), yet *holistic health* is their top health value and one of the strongest they hold. This is not surprising because in addition to an interest in holistic approaches, this value reflects a feeling of being in charge of one's health.

Health is a good pathway into green. The Ungreens and the Driven Independents, for example, may not make the connection between personal and planetary health, but products that emphasize direct personal benefits and avoid political or shrill messages might appeal.

Another example is that 68 percent of the public say that buying food grown without the use of pesticides or chemicals is important to them. Whether their interest is motivated by health or environmental protection depends on their worldview. The hope is that once people get used to buying green for their health, they will start going green in the rest of their lives.

## ENVIRONMENTAL COGNITION

Forty-nine percent of the Greenest Americans have postgraduate degrees, more than three times as many as any other group. The next highest are the Postmodern Idealists, with 16 percent (with more to come because 29 percent of this group are currently students). The Compassionate Caretakers follow with 14 percent. These are the three groups with the highest level of *ecological concern.*

They are also the only segments of the public who hold high values relating to how people process their experiences and make decisions in the world. All three groups hold *introspection and empathy,* the tendency to examine their actions and others without judgment, at high levels. For the Greenest Americans and Compassionate Caretakers, *intellectual and open* is one of their top values and reflects a wide range of interests and a natural curiosity about the world. The Postmodern Idealists differ in that they prioritize *interest in the unexplained*—the rejection that all valid knowledge must be logical and scientific—over the two previous values. And unlike the older eco-minded segments, they strongly hold the value *intuition and impulse,* the tendency to be guided by emotions rather than by rational thought.

In focus groups with the most eco-minded segments of the public, we could see these values at play. The Greenest Americans approached environmental issues from a very intellectual place. This group, which relies on information and logic to form their opinions and tends to pay close attention to politics, was the most informed. The Compassionate Caretakers were not as informed but were still rational about environmental issues and straightforward about their view of protecting nature. The Postmodern Idealists, on the other hand, were much more emotional. They were comfortable imagining an elaborate eco-world of the future and saw environmentalism being integrated with quality-of-life issues such as having access to good food, the arts, public transit, and green space.

But even these highly educated, engaged groups find it daunting to track environmental problems. With so many environmental challenges facing us, people can't sort out what issues they should be paying attention to. The fundamental interconnectedness of environmental issues makes direct cause and effect difficult to determine and, with something such as climate change, impossible to see. Our brains are wired to process information that conveys a simple cause and effect, which is why people have so much trouble with interconnectedness and systems thinking.

Americans, even the greenest and most highly educated, want simple answers to the challenges we face. Education may lead to strong ecological values, but it doesn't necessarily lead to being an expert on the issues. Companies need to provide the big picture, making the connections for people between environmental challenges and solutions and how their products and services fit in. Don't dumb it down, but hook people in first and then provide the details.

The more people can see the direct cause and effect of environmental issues, the more likely they will engage, whether or not they have a Ph.D.

## THE EMERGING ENVIRONMENTALISTS—DIVERSITY AND THE ENVIRONMENT

A person's race does not determine whether or not he or she cares about the environment. Views on racism, however, can.

For four segments of the American public, *modern racism* is one of the top two values. This is out of 130 values tracked in the American Values Survey. These people firmly believe that racism is largely a thing of the past and that minorities have gained more than they deserve. This is the new racism.

*Modern racism* contributes to how Antiauthoritarian Materialists, Driven Independents, Cruel Worlders, and Borderline Fatalists see the world as a place where it's necessary to do whatever you can to get what you need because there's only so much to go around. This dog-eat-dog view doesn't translate into concern for the earth—*ecological concern* is one of the lowest values for all four groups.

Some of these segments are racially diverse, and others are not. For many in these groups, low incomes have played a role in shaping their outlook. Others, including the majority of the Driven Independents, are comfortable with their financial and social status yet still have this drive to get ahead of others. Clearly, it's possible to have feelings of insecurity and scarcity even if all your material needs are met.

The opposite of *modern racism* is *racial fusion*. The 36 percent of Americans who are high on this value—acceptance of ethnic diversity and belief that it enriches people's lives—tend also to be quite strong on the value *ecological concern*. The worldviews of the Greenest Americans, Postmodern Idealists, and Compassionate Caretakers reflect a movement away from more survival-driven values to ones that relate to fulfillment and seeking out a higher purpose in life. Those who value *racial fusion* run the gamut from the most homogeneous (i.e., Greenest Americans)—the stereotypical environmentalists—to one of the most diverse (i.e., Compassionate Caretakers).

All this points to the need to diversify the marketing of green products. For the segments that value *modern racism,* whatever you do will turn some off. They're not your core audience. The people who value *racial fusion* are, and even though a fair number of them fit the image of the white environmentalist, they want to see more diversity as well. And not just on the package. The greenest consumers all hold the value *ethical consumerism* at high levels and judge a company's diversity from the inside out.

## CLIMATE CHANGE AND INCREASING ENVIRONMENTAL VALUES

The growing awareness and concern about climate change represent an obvious opportunity for companies, as long as the price tag for energy efficiency is not too high. Only two segments of the public rank climate change as one of the most important problems we face—the Greenest Americans (68 percent) and the Postmodern Idealists (51 percent). For the other eight segments of the population, rising energy costs are a bigger concern than the impacts of a warming climate.

Why is this? Most Americans are aware of climate change and accept that it's a problem. Except for the Ungreens, the majority of the public, when asked, say that they believe that it is possible to reduce the impacts of climate change. Moreover, two-thirds of Americans agree that it's necessary to spend whatever we can to get off oil and start using alternative energy sources.

While they think something must be done, though, even the most environmentally minded Americans don't want to be the ones to foot the bill.

We heard the tension between cost and concern in the focus groups that Earthjustice conducted with the most ecologically minded segments—the Greenest Americans, Postmodern Idealists, and Compassionate Caretakers. At a good price or with the right incentives, people said that they would be willing to try efficient appliances and other energy-saving products. Ultimately, though, they want the government to step in and take charge.

Focus groups participants said that they believe that it's possible to generate economic growth from increases in energy efficiency and investments in a new alternative-energy economy. They were cynical, however, about the number of businesses they saw now claiming to be green. Given that the segments we interviewed are low on the value *confidence in big business,* such skepticism of green claims is not surprising.

The greenest consumers don't believe that just greening their purchases is going to solve climate change. Companies need to explain how their green alternatives are part of a larger set of solutions and what role their customers are playing by buying their products. Be sure to tout any consumer cost savings that can be quantified. And don't wait for government to create new reporting and certification programs around carbon emissions and energy use. Get ahead of compliance issues by looking at all aspects of your operation to develop a plan for how to transform your business.

Climate change is not just the environmental challenge of our time—it is the biggest issue of our time. Nearly everything needs to be redesigned to use less energy and emit less carbon, from how our toothbrushes are made to the ways we get around. Companies offering products or services that tangibly limit or reverse the impacts of a warming climate are in a good position to make money while at the same time doing something important for the planet. Just don't leave green consumers with the feeling they are stuck with the tab.

## THE EVOLUTION OF SOCIAL VALUES AND GREEN BUSINESS OPPORTUNITIES

Since 1992, when the American Values Survey was first conducted, Americans' social values have shifted dramatically toward survival and disengagement. Values such as *modern racism, acceptance of violence,* and *just desserts* are driving the worldviews of almost half the public, including the majority of the country's youth. Such views get in the way of people caring about, let alone acting on, anything except self-interest.

At the same time, other Americans are more engaged than ever. From 2004 to 2007, segments of the public with the strongest environmental values reported paying more attention to politics and giving more to environmental organizations. With climate change as a primary motivating factor, such concern and the number of people willing to take action about it are expected to continue to grow.

Whether this trend toward engagement can outpace—and hopefully reverse—the increasing numbers checking out is critical for the growth of green business (and, of course, for the planet). Will the Greenest Americans, Postmodern Idealists, and Compassionate Caretakers get so engaged in trying to reduce their ecological footprint that they pave the way to a more sustainable economy? And if this happens, will segments such as the Murky Middles, the 17 percent of Americans who don't hold any social value strongly, jump on the green bandwagon?

Right now it looks like it could go either way. In the meantime, what today's Ecological Roadmap tells us is that a one-size-fits-all approach doesn't work. Different strategies for different segments of the public clearly are required.

For one, tactics that appeal to the greenest consumers are turnoffs to other segments. But beyond this, green business needs to be more than a market niche. It can't be something off to the side, just for the elite.

Most people will never be a Greenest American, whose social values are influenced by their high income and education levels. But there's really no reason why most Americans shouldn't be able to regularly buy green products and services. Cost and access are obvious barriers, but there's no inherent reason that costs will remain high and access so low.

What green businesses can do to most effectively address the green economy is to create new stories and images of what it means to be green that avoid the other obstacles: environmental sainthood, negative stereotypes, and inconsistent and overly complex messages.

By understanding the social values that motivate different segments of the public to action, companies can play an integral role in shaping what it means to care about the environment. In so doing, more Americans will be able to see themselves participating in the green economy every day.

# Index

# About the Author

For 20 years, **Joel Makower** (www.makower.com) has been a well-respected voice on business, the environment, and the bottom line. He is executive editor of the acclaimed Web site GreenBiz.com® and its affiliated Web sites, reports, and events, and principal author of the annual "State of Green Business" report—all produced by Greener World Media, Inc., of which he is cofounder and chairman. Makower also is senior strategist at GreenOrder, a sustainable business consultancy, and cofounder of Clean Edge, a clean-tech research and publishing firm. He writes "Two Steps Forward" (www.readjoel.com), a popular blog on green business topics.

The Associated Press has called him "The guru of green business practices."

A former nationally syndicated columnist, Makower is author of more than a dozen books, including *Beyond the Bottom Line: Putting Social Responsibility to Work for Your Business and the World* (Simon & Schuster); *The E-Factor: The Bottom-Line Approach to Environmentally Responsible Business* (Random House); and *The Green Consumer* (Penguin Books).

Makower is a frequent keynote speaker at business conferences and events, and at business schools around the world. He serves as an advisor to VantagePoint Venture Partner's clean-tech venture capital fund and in a board or advisory capacity for more than a dozen other for-profit and nonprofit organizations.

He lives in Oakland, California.